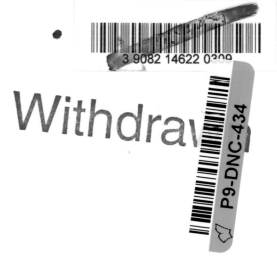

3 9082 14622 0309

Withdrawn

P9-DNC-434

MAY 2 5 2022
Northville District Library
212 W. Cady St.
Northville, MI 48167

"This book provides the tools that every business leader (and every team member, board member, and investor) will need to win in this increasingly customer-centered world. I consider *Winning on Purpose* to be Fred's most important work to date. It proves that the primary purpose guiding all great organizations is to enrich the lives of customers."

—**JOHN DONAHOE**, CEO, Nike (from the Foreword)

"*Winning on Purpose* is full of lessons for building customer loyalty and achieving more by treating others better. Fred Reichheld is a true pioneer in his field, and his practical ideas earn a high Net Promoter Score."

—**ADAM GRANT**, *New York Times*–bestselling author, *Think Again*; host, TED *WorkLife* podcast

"Fred Reichheld has again delivered a compelling and remarkable piece on winning through customer loyalty. We are fortunate to have worked with and learned from Fred for many years. 'Do the right thing' and read the book!"

—**ANDREW C. TAYLOR**, Executive Chairman, Enterprise Holdings (parent of car rental brands Enterprise, National Car Rental, and Alamo)

"Net Promoter is more relevant than ever in the digital world. We use Reichheld's tools every day to help us deliver on our promise to 'Put Members First' and to provide an unparalleled experience to our community of millions around the world. Such a compelling read—this book is fantastic!"

—**BRAD OLSON**, Chief Business Officer, Peloton

"*Winning on Purpose* continues Fred Reichheld's legacy of high-impact, practical guidance on keeping a company focused on its customers. His actionable approach engages employees at all levels of an organization on delivering what matters. Fred's thinking has influenced our organization for decades, and he has raised the bar once again."

—**TIM BUCKLEY**, Chairman and CEO, Vanguard

"Fred Reichheld is a great storyteller, and *Winning on Purpose* is partly a business book and partly a memoir highlighting important lessons about what it means to live a good and worthy life and to run a good business. This book shows how NPS provides companies with both a moral compass and a powerful tool for success."

—**ZEYNEP TON**, professor, MIT Sloan School of Management; author, *The Good Jobs Strategy*

"Fred Reichheld has shown definitively that putting customers at the core of your business is the key to enduring success. *Winning on Purpose* reveals the essence of Net Promoter's huge impact—treat people the way you want to be treated. An enlightening and moving book."

—**RAM CHARAN**, business adviser to CEOs of many startups and top companies; author; and member of seven boards

"What is the true purpose of a business? As Fred Reichheld powerfully illustrates in this important book, it is not to increase profits and shareholder value but to enrich people's lives. *Winning on Purpose* shows how doing the latter leads to the former. Required reading."

—**JEANNE BLISS**, founder and President, Customer Bliss; author, *Chief Customer Officer 2.0*

"Long-term growth is no hidden secret—it's all about your happy customers being your biggest marketing weapon! Reichheld has written a powerful guide on how your business can thrive—by creating a culture to put your customer's needs and happiness first. A must-read."

—**MARSHALL GOLDSMITH**, *New York Times* bestselling author of *Triggers*, *Mojo*, and *What Got You Here Won't Get You There*

"Reichheld has changed the business community forever, first with Net Promoter and now with Earned Growth. NPS has been the key metric we've used to keep ourselves focused on providing incredible customer experiences. Earned Growth now provides the accounting twin to leverage the power of survey-based NPS. Every entrepreneur should read this book."

—**DAVE GILBOA**, cofounder and co-CEO, Warby Parker

"At Schwab, we have been guided by Fred Reichheld's thinking for almost twenty years. His Net Promoter concept serves as the compass guiding our purpose and client-focused strategy. *Winning on Purpose* confirms Fred as the unquestioned leader in his field. It's a must-read for any businessperson pursuing sustainable success."

—**WALT BETTINGER**, President and CEO, Charles Schwab

"*Winning on Purpose* delivers a compelling and convincing digital-age update of the already-powerful Net Promoter System. But it offers much more, providing a motivational guidebook for purpose-driven leadership. Fred's stories demonstrate the benefits of treating people right, and the new data he reveals helps clarify the moral duties of business leaders in a customer-centered world. There could not be a better time for this book. I cannot wait to share it with my colleagues!"

—**BARBARA HIGGINS**, Chief Customer Officer, Duke Energy

"In *Winning on Purpose*, Fred Reichheld takes Net Promoter to the next level, explaining why leaders must reshape their strategies around customer love and loyalty in order to win—not just for customers but for all stakeholders. His work is backed not only by decades of first-hand experience but also by fresh data and insights illuminating the underlying economic advantages of truly great companies. *Winning on Purpose* will help investors identify long-term business winners."

—**ANDY CROSS**, Chief Investment Officer, The Motley Fool

WINNING ON PURPOSE

WINNING
ON
PURPOSE

THE UNBEATABLE STRATEGY

OF LOVING CUSTOMERS

FRED REICHHELD

With Darci Darnell and Maureen Burns

Bain & Company, Inc.

HARVARD BUSINESS REVIEW PRESS

BOSTON, MASSACHUSETTS

HBR Press Quantity Sales Discounts

Harvard Business Review Press titles are available at significant quantity discounts when purchased in bulk for client gifts, sales promotions, and premiums. Special editions, including books with corporate logos, customized covers, and letters from the company or CEO printed in the front matter, as well as excerpts of existing books, can also be created in large quantities for special needs.

For details and discount information for both print and ebook formats, contact booksales@harvardbusiness.org, tel. 800-988-0886, or www.hbr.org/bulksales.

Copyright 2021 Fred Reichheld and Bain & Company, Inc.

All rights reserved

Printed in the United States of America

10 9 8 7 6 5 4

No part of this publication may be reproduced, stored in or introduced into a retrieval system, or transmitted, in any form, or by any means (electronic, mechanical, photocopying, recording, or otherwise), without the prior permission of the publisher. Requests for permission should be directed to permissions@harvardbusiness.org, or mailed to Permissions, Harvard Business School Publishing, 60 Harvard Way, Boston, Massachusetts 02163.

The web addresses referenced in this book were live and correct at the time of the book's publication but may be subject to change.

Library of Congress Cataloging-in-Publication Data

Names: Reichheld, Frederick F., author. | Darnell, Darci, author. | Burns, Maureen (Maureen Farrell), author.
Title: Winning on purpose : the unbeatable strategy of loving customers / Fred Reichheld with Darci Darnell and Maureen Burns (Bain & Company, Inc.)
Description: Boston, MA : Harvard Business Review Press, [2021] | Includes index.
Identifiers: LCCN 2021025748 (print) | LCCN 2021025749 (ebook) |
    ISBN 9781647821784 (hardcover) | ISBN 9781647821791 (ebook)
Subjects: LCSH: Relationship marketing. | Customer loyalty. | Consumer satisfaction. |
    Marketing research. | Word-of-mouth advertising.
Classification: LCC HF5415.55 .R435 2021 (print) | LCC HF5415.55 (ebook) |
    DDC 658.8/12—dc23
LC record available at https://lccn.loc.gov/2021025748
LC ebook record available at https://lccn.loc.gov/2021025749

ISBN: 978-1-64782-178-4
eISBN: 978-1-64782-179-1

The paper used in this publication meets the requirements of the American National Standard for Permanence of Paper for Publications and Documents in Libraries and Archives Z39.48-1992.

NPS® and Net Promoter® are registered service marks and Net Promoter System^{SM}, Net Promoter Score^{SM} and NPS Prism^{SM} are service marks of Bain & Company, Inc., Satmetrix Systems, Inc. and Fred Reichheld.

This book is dedicated to
Adelaide, Clare, and our coming generation of
grandchildren. May they gather regularly to ring the
Loyalty Bell in celebration of generations past and present,
honoring our shared legacy of love and loyalty.

Contents

Foreword

John Donahoe
CEO, Nike, Inc.

I have known Fred Reichheld for almost forty years. We met at Bain's Boston office, where I held my first job out of college. My desk was located near Fred's office, and he would regularly engage us junior staffers in friendly conversations, which often ended up with him extolling the transformative power of loyalty. Today he is still at Bain, still preaching about loyalty—but from a far deeper well of experience and insight. Indeed, over the decades he essentially invented the field of loyalty economics and created the now ubiquitous Net Promoter System. I always referred to him as the Godfather—of loyalty. Since the relevance of his work has grown even more important in the digital age, I suppose we should call him the DG—Digital Godfather of loyalty.

The tools and frameworks Fred developed have helped me achieve practical results throughout my career, beginning with my time at Bain. During my term as Bain's CEO, we became the world's first company to implement Fred's brainchild, the Net Promoter Score, and enthusiastically supported its development into a full management system. In my subsequent CEO jobs at eBay, ServiceNow, and Nike, Fred's concepts and inventions continued to help my teams win. And while his engaging stories and arguments have sometimes sounded more moral than managerial, they have always helped my teams deliver results. Let me go a step further and say that in a time when so many in our society view capitalism with such suspicion, we surely need to carefully consider our moral duties as business leaders. Fred's approach can help make that practical. At the same time, just because some of Fred's chapters have high-minded titles such as "Honor the Golden Rule," don't be fooled into thinking this book won't help boost your growth rate. Indeed, Fred's road map to customer capitalism delivers the basic tools, measures, and processes that every business leader (and every team member, board member, and investor) will need to win in this increasingly customer-centered world.

There's more. This book provides fresh revelations for business history buffs, as Fred recounts the story (never before revealed in such detail) behind Bain's near meltdown in the early 1990s. He was one of the dozen or so frontline partners who signed an oath to lock arms and rally behind Mitt Romney to salvage the firm from financial collapse. Through his forty-four years at the firm, Fred experienced firsthand the brilliant innovations that Bain's founders contributed during their seventeen years at the firm as well as the nearly fatal flaws that took years of innovative resolve to mend after their departure. Why tell these stories now? I believe they help us understand how Bain became a truly great place to work—the best in the world during the past decade, according to Glassdoor—in part by teasing out and embracing the fundamentals underpinning NPS. Bain is indeed a very special place and well worth studying, because its evolving story can help every leader elevate and inspire his or her team toward greatness.

And I mean *true* greatness. As Fred explains in his manifesto at the end of the book:

> Great companies help people lead great lives—they are a force for good. Great leaders build and sustain such communities. They inspire team members to forge lives of meaning and purpose through service to others—service not merely satisfactory, but so thoughtful, creative, and caring that it delights customers and enriches their lives.

The book is both timely and timeless. Fred begins by updating the stories of a few great companies—such as Apple, Enterprise Rent-A-Car, and Chick-fil-A, which are companies he has been writing about for decades—because they have sustained their great performance over time. These updates provide clear evidence that businesses built on virtue are resilient. They can cope with the flocks of black swans that so often descend on business leaders. In the past year alone, we've had to confront pandemic lockdowns, worldwide recession, racial reckonings, and an armed assault on the US Capitol. You will also read fresh new stories of digital revolutionaries that are using Net Promoter philosophy and tools to shape winning strategies, companies such as Airbnb, Warby Parker, Peloton, and Chewy. By the time you finish the book, you will surely have a new understanding of what it takes to build a great business.

To be clear, this book is no mere recap of Fred's greatest hits. I consider *Winning on Purpose* to be his most important work to date. It reveals fresh breakthrough insights and clarifies the moral responsibilities of leadership as the world transitions from financial capitalism to customer capitalism. The book also provides deep and convincing evidence that the primary purpose that guides all great organizations is to enrich the lives of customers—hence, "winning on purpose." If you do nothing else, read Fred's Customer Capitalist Manifesto, quoted above and written in full in chapter 9, which distills his arguments to their very essence. Be sure to study the charts in chapter 5, which demonstrate that only companies that win the love of their customers can sustainably deliver superior returns to investors. And be sure to get familiar (and comfortable) with Fred's Earned Growth Rate, his powerful new metric that will help unlock the next burst of progress in the NPS revolution.

I hope that you will enjoy and find practical value in *Winning on Purpose* as much as I did. It is the right book at the right time.

Preface

The Genesis of Net Promoter

Just a few weeks before my sixty-fifth birthday, I awoke from an anesthesia-induced sleep to hear my doctor pronounce six dreaded words: *"You have a large malignant tumor."*

Talk about a bracing wake-up call. Later that day, I followed the nurse's instructions to hold my breath and remain motionless while the unyielding gantry glided me through the CT scan machine. As barium-contrast dye pumped through my veins to ferret out just how far my cancer had spread, it struck me that no matter what the radiologist discovered, my clock was ticking. As usual, my head was full of ideas that I wanted to share. But this time was different. If I failed to get those thoughts down on paper, and if I reached the end of my road sooner than expected, those ideas would disappear along with me.

So, it was the diagnosis of a potentially life-threatening cancer that first got me focused on writing this book. After a week of scans and tests, my team of physicians sat me down and explained that my treatment regimen would take more than a year, with multiple surgeries bracketed by months of chemo and radiation. They introduced me to the notion of survival curves—that is, what percentage of patients with my condition could expect to be alive in two or five years. Again, that kind of conversation really focuses the mind. It makes you think very hard about what you most want to get accomplished while you still have the chance. The more I thought about it, the more I became convinced that I simply had to get this book written.

If you're like me, under normal circumstances procrastination comes pretty easily—especially when you think you probably have another decade or two of good health ahead of you. In addition, I really don't enjoy the writing process. It's the mental equivalent of strenuous calisthenics—yes, you know it's the right thing to do, but actually *doing* it is no fun at all. Luckily, I got my wake-up call while there was still time to take action.

So, what are these ideas that seemed so important to me—to the extent that I was willing to devote the rest of what might be a foreshortened life to a task I really don't relish? I hope this book will make the answer very clear.

I have spent most of my forty-four-year career at Bain & Company focused on one subject: understanding the role that loyalty plays in building and sustaining great organizations and then developing tools and frameworks to help leaders nurture that focus. In my several published books, dozens of articles, and hundreds of speeches—thousands if you include the dinner lectures my poor family has been subjected to over the years—I have had plenty of opportunity to clarify and communicate my thinking. Meanwhile, the viral transmission of Net Promoter has spread my ideas to countless thousands of organizations around the globe. Pretty cool! So, it might be reasonable to assume that there was little more I could say about the subject. A reasonable person in my situation might resolve to fight through the daunting regimen of radiation, surgery, and chemotherapy and then retire to the garden, secure in the knowledge that the necessary seeds have been well planted.

So again, why another book on the subject? Well, first, while I am pleased that so many companies have embraced NPS, I am deeply troubled how badly most of them are implementing it—achieving only a tiny fraction of the system's potential impact. Second, some people presume that as more customer interactions shift to digital solutions, NPS becomes less relevant. In fact, many of the most successful digital revolutionaries rely heavily on our NPS framework, combining digital signal analytics with surveys to ensure that their digital solutions deliver such an appealing experience (with the right human touch) that customers become Promoters.* Finally, far too many practitioners are corrupting NPS by making the score a target rather than a measure that inspires learning and growth. I hope that by reviewing the genesis of NPS—its core principles, its

---

*As a rule, I'll capitalize Promoter, Passive, and Detractor in this book when they refer to components of NPS.

underlying purpose, and some practical advice—I can help resolve these misunderstandings.

Special Days That Opened My Eyes

The germination of NPS began during a few eye-opening days that changed my understanding of what it means to win in business, how to measure success (in both business and life), and the relationship between love and loyalty.

One of those special days came when I traveled from Bain's Boston headquarters to meet with Andy Taylor at his company's headquarters in Clayton, Missouri, a suburb outside St. Louis. The company was Enterprise Rent-A-Car. I'm sure that many of you have rented a car from one of Enterprise's seventy-six hundred branches in the United States and abroad.

I already knew that there was something special about Andy and his company, but I hadn't quite been able to put my finger on what it was—and this was the main reason I was in Clayton that day. I had been a strategy consultant at Bain & Company for a couple of decades by that time, so I was certainly impressed by the methodical way Andy had grown his family business from a local leasing company into the world's largest car rental firm. Enterprise had raced by its larger entrenched rivals—such as Hertz and Avis—despite operating in a low-margin, low-growth, and capital-intensive industry. As a privately held company, Enterprise had no need of outside investor equity, and this broke most of the rules about microeconomics and corporate strategy that I'd been taught at business school. But I suspected that there was more going on, and I wanted to learn what it was.

By that time Andy was already a billionaire many times over, with plenty to do other than talk to the likes of me, and he could easily have sidestepped my interview request. Instead, he welcomed me and was extremely generous with his time. In response to my probing questions to discover the secret to his firm's remarkable success, he patiently explained that there was no magic behind Enterprise's growth. "Fred," he told me, "there is only one way to grow a business profitably. You make sure your customers are treated so well that they come back for more and bring their friends."[1]

In the ensuing twenty years, I have come to understand that Andy was right. If you care about sustainability and what I call "good profits"—more on that later—that's the *only* way to grow a business.

Of course, this begs the question of *how* you make sure your customers are treated that well. When I asked Andy what he was most proud of during his tenure as head of the firm, he pointed to a fat binder on a nearby bookshelf. He explained that it was a list of every employee at Enterprise who had earned more than $200,000 that year. I'm sure that book is much thicker today in light of the firm's continued remarkable success.

Another thing Andy mentioned that I will never forget: "Fred, when your name is on the door as the leader or owner of a company, when customers aren't treated right, you need to take it personally—it is your *personal reputation* that is being hurt. When I hear friends and neighbors talking at cocktail parties or neighborhood barbeque gatherings about their Enterprise experiences, I know they are really talking about my extended family and how we influence our neighbors' lives."

Perhaps you've noticed that unlike many of its competitors, Enterprise generally stays away from nuisance fees, such as additional driver fees for your spouse, exorbitant late fees, and abusive markups on the gasoline they use to refill your tank. Yes, these are tricks that may boost the corporate bottom line in the short term. But over the long term, they surely diminish customer happiness and damage the company's reputation.

If Andy had a secret weapon—if he had a competitive insight that others in his industry hadn't tuned in to—it was this: *Those cocktail party conversations, those anecdotes told over the backyard grill, will make or break your reputation—and your business.* As those conversations are magnified through social media, Enterprise's advantage grows exponentially.

• • •

On another one of my special days, I was fortunate enough to spend time talking with Bob Herres at his office in San Antonio, Texas. After graduating from the US Naval Academy, Bob had risen through the ranks to become vice chairman of the Joint Chiefs of Staff under President Ronald Reagan. When I met Bob, he was CEO of USAA, the insurance and financial services giant that has grown from a tiny niche insurer of autos for military officers into a member of the *Fortune* 200. You've almost certainly seen USAA's ads on TV in recent years, with military families—actual customers—singing the company's praises.

Bob arranged a tour for me of USAA's enormous headquarters, which is one of the largest office buildings in the world—so big we needed a golf cart to get around. One unforgettable scene unfolded in an unlikely place: one of the company's kitchen commissaries, which by the late afternoon was stacked to the ceiling with freshly boxed meals. The chef explained that these were evening meals that employees could bring home to their families. Single parents in particular appreciated the time that they could now spend with their families rather than having to shop and cook. I had a lively conversation with the chef, who was particularly proud of the innovative meals his team had prepared that, he told me, not only appealed to young children but were also nutritious. Based on this and a number of other encounters I had that day, it struck me that USAA was caring for its employees' happiness and well-being in the same way that really good generals care for their troops. Bob taught me that the job of a leader is to ensure that the team is on the right mission, that they understand it and have the resources required to succeed, and, most important, that they know their leader will do everything possible to take care of their safety and well-being. Great leaders wake up in the morning worrying about that, and they go to bed worrying about it.

My USAA education didn't stop there. A number of times after that first visit, Bob reached out to be helpful. We talked several times on the phone about his leadership philosophy and the role that loyalty played in building a great organization. Bob even volunteered to fly to Boston to help me teach an executive seminar on loyalty at Babson College Executive Conference Center. During that visit to the Boston area, he took me out to dinner with our spouses. I noticed that his questions and answers both at the seminar and at dinner seemed aimed at helping me in my work rather than making himself or his company look good. At one point, I asked his longtime secretary if Bob was this generous with everyone. "Not everyone," she said without hesitation. "But when Bob spots someone doing work he believes is important, he just finds ways to be helpful. He invests in those people."

That lesson stuck with me. When you find someone who's working to make the world better or an organization full of such people, you should look for ways to help them succeed. You invest in those relationships, and through those investments you multiply your personal impact. This has to do fundamentally with *loyalty*. Bob understood loyalty not only in the context of risking your life in combat but also in the daily decisions and priorities you make that brighten the days of your customers and colleagues in a financial services business. Loyalty means investing time and resources in relationships. That's how you advance the principles on which those relationships are founded. That's how you make the world better.

USAA stands out as a pioneer in digitizing episodes across the customer journey (no surprise, since the company has no branches and has a customer base that's spread out all around the world). For example, USAA's digital banking team invented mobile online deposits for checks. Despite its digital sophistication, USAA never uses digital bots or algorithms to extract additional value from customers, only to serve them better. And that word gets around. Remember those cocktail parties and neighborhood barbeques, today complemented by social media, YouTube, and rating sites? Customers and employees learn to trust that the company will always act in their best interests. Of course, USAA has to match or exceed its competitors with sophisticated analytics and underwriting acumen. But it is the company's determination to use both human and digital capabilities to enrich the lives of its customers and inspire its employees to embrace that sacred mission that has made USAA a force to be reckoned with in the insurance industry.

• • •

A third day that stands out in my mind as especially instructive was the time I visited Chick-fil-A to help moderate a discussion on leadership succession with the company's executive team. Truett Cathy, the company's founder, set the tone for the visit immediately, inviting me to stay at his country house that night and making waffles for us all the next morning.

Let me make clear from the outset that I was concerned about Truett's position on how the Golden Rule applies to LGBTQ rights. I am the father of four children, two of whom are gay and proudly married. Truett was entering his ninth decade of life, a product of the Old South and a devout

Southern Baptist; I was a middle-aged Harvard-educated Unitarian from the North. So, we certainly didn't see the world the same way. I confess that as I flew from Boston to Atlanta, those differences weighed on my mind.

I'll never forget the tour that Truett took me on, driving me around town to visit a few of the dozen or so foster homes he sponsored and visited regularly. (I began this tour with some trepidation because Truett was definitely a senior citizen, but he turned out to be a surprisingly solid driver.) He was greeted warmly at each stop and obviously knew and cared about the families he sponsored. We talked candidly as he drove from place to place, and at one point he explained to me the Southern Baptist tradition of adopting a passage from the Bible as one's life verse. For him that verse was Proverbs 22:1, which in essence says that a good name is more valuable than silver or gold. He told me that he tried his hardest to live by that rule in both his personal and professional lives.

I remember thinking to myself at the time, *well, that might be the right verse for just about anyone.* I still think so today. Your reputation is indeed your most valuable asset. It defines the kinds of opportunities that will come your way while you're alive, and it may well be the only thing that outlives you. Every time you treat someone right—the way you would want to be treated if you were in their shoes—you are building your reputation and making the world a better place, one life at a time. This, of course, is the Golden Rule, a near-universal standard. Any behavior short of that Golden Rule standard diminishes your reputation and makes the world a little worse.

One lesson I took away from that day with Truett was that the sooner you figure out your purpose, the more time you have to deliver on it so you really can leave the world a better place than you found it. It also struck me that we need a better way to measure progress toward that purpose so you can gauge progress, learn from both successes and mistakes, and set the stage for further improvements down the road. Truett shared with me the thing that most energized him was turning a person's frown into a smile. His influence on NPS is apparent when you consider the score's underlying arithmetic (NPS = % smiles minus % frowns). Over the past decade, I have been pleased to see Chick-fil-A make important progress in affording to gays the love that (in my humble opinion) is consistent with an enlightened understanding of the Golden Rule. As a result, even more frowns are turning into smiles.

Like Enterprise and USAA, Chick-fil-A continues to grow and prosper in near-miraculous fashion. With no need to tap into public equity markets, this former niche regional chain of chicken sandwich shops has grown to become the world's third-largest restaurant chain in revenues (trailing only McDonald's and Starbucks), with more than twenty-five hundred locations in the United States and Canada. Financing this growth with internally generated cash flow—notably after donating a substantial portion of profits to charity each year—does seem like something of a miracle, especially when you consider that store operators make a onetime investment of ten thousand dollars up front and often earn several hundred thousand dollars per year—sometimes much more.

I think again of Andy Taylor's fat binder in which he took such pride. Truett and Andy were very different people, but they shared a common mission: helping their partners succeed and prosper through solving customer problems in such a way that frowns turn into smiles.

• • •

For me, these three episodes taught and underscored several vital lessons. First, my understanding of the economic forces governing business was deeply flawed. The financial model taught at business school and refined by my early years at Bain simply couldn't explain these three companies' astonishing self-financed growth. To understand their true economics, we had to uncover and quantify an underlying, overwhelmingly powerful force: *loyalty.*

Second, we had to get our arms around the fact that the leaders of these firms—each an incredibly successful entrepreneur—thought of themselves as servants to their companies' frontline teams. They were extremely generous to team leaders (imagine a restaurant manager earning several hundred thousand dollars per year!) and celebrated their successes visibly and happily. They cared for their team leaders' well-being by ensuring that they could live great lives and build prosperous careers—*when their teams treated the customer right.*

And this was a third and intimately related lesson. These companies embraced a purpose that was far more inspiring than profits or growth. Those things were beneficial by-products. The core mission was delivering happiness to their customers—solving their problems and turning frowns into smiles. By achieving that mission, these firms don't need to buy growth with costly advertising and marketing gimmicks. Instead, they earn growth by ensuring that team members treat customers (and one another) right. They eschew nuisance fees, gotcha-pricing tactics, tricks, traps, and fine print because these would be inconsistent with their purpose. When customers feel such loving care, they come back for more and bring their friends. That in turn fuels sustainable and profitable growth.

Personal Implications

While this is primarily a business book, these lessons have deeply influenced my personal life. By sharing a few personal stories, I hope their universal relevance will become apparent and help guide individuals—in every kind of organization, along with their customers, members, employees, and investors—toward better choices and more successful lives.

For example, I try to buy from firms that earn the highest NPS (read: customer-love) ratings. Life gets much more *fun* when you're dealing with suppliers who love their customers. When I finally jettisoned my bank after years of tolerating nuisance fees and mediocre service, I shifted to the bank with some of the highest customer scores in the industry: First Republic Bank. Now, I actually look forward to visiting my branch or phoning and emailing my banker. During the height of the Covid-19 crisis, she happily offered to walk out through the snowy parking lot to notarize documents while I sat (safely masked) in my warm car. These documents, by the way, were unrelated to my banking business. Life got *so much better* when I switched to a bank that believes its primary purpose is delighting customers.

My family has also benefited directly from understanding which companies most love their customers. For example, I have worked with Bain & Company since 1977, where many of the practices you will read about in this book were invented. Through Bain's analysis, I knew that Apple earned outstanding scores from both customers and employees. When my son Bill graduated from college and began trying to land his first full-time job in the midst of a recession, I encouraged him to consider applying to a local Apple Store. To make a long story short, he did and was hired. It couldn't have worked out better. As a result of his time at Apple, he has been indoctrinated in a culture and management process that takes seriously its mission to enrich the lives of customers and employees. In my estimation, the value of the skills Bill has developed in that community far exceeds the value he would have gained from earning an advanced degree in business or economics.

Bill has learned firsthand how it feels when a company cares for the well-being of team members. For example, Apple encourages its employees to save and invest, knowing this is a vital life skill that many young people have not yet acquired. First, the company promotes savings with its generous 401(k) plan. Over the past decade (which is about when Bill joined the store team), an employee contributing fully each year (into the Vanguard Total Stock Index Fund) would have built a balance over $100,000. To make saving and investing even more attractive, Apple also offers a stock purchase plan enabling employees to automatically invest up to 10 percent of their paycheck in Apple stock at a price equal to 85 percent of the closing price at the beginning or end of each six-month period (whichever is lower). If that hypothetical store employee who joined with Bill participated fully in the stock purchase program, her or his Apple stock balance would have grown to $300,000. Considered together with the person's 401(k), she or he would have accumulated savings of $400,000—quite a nest egg for ten years of work in an Apple store!

Of course, not every employee can afford to save 16 percent of their paycheck, but with such programs in place, many employees saved much more than they might have otherwise. And more important than any financial benefit, every employee benefits from the opportunity to spend time hanging around with good people—that is, the kind of people whom Apple tries to hire and whose inherent goodness is reinforced through Apple's recognition and reward systems that celebrate enriching the lives they touch. In Bill's case, he ended up marrying a wonderful coworker at his store (thank you, Apple!). Most of their friends are store colleagues or alums.

Truly, their lives have been enriched by the relationships built and lessons learned through their time at Apple.

Of course, to a father few things are as important as happy children. But for me there was another fringe benefit of viewing Apple from the inside: seeing the company not through the eyes of its advertising campaigns or its write-ups in the press but instead through the eyes of its employees. What I saw made me double down on my investment in Apple stock. That too turned out to be a very happy decision.

The Lessons Never End

You will see on the title page that Darci Darnell and Maureen Burns have joined my writing team as coauthors. Their editing judgment and steady stream of suggested improvements rose far beyond the level appropriate for behind-the-scenes editors, so I am pleased that they have joined me in a more public role. In one of our book development sessions, Maureen reminded me that when I originally created NPS, it stood for "Net Promoter Score." Then it evolved into a set of solutions that we came to call the "Net Promoter System." As we were digging into one of the chapters of this book, she remarked that today we are really talking about the soul of NPS. She recommended we refer to it as the *Net Purpose Score/System*. Darci concurred, noting that NPS implemented correctly reveals how consistently a company lives up to its purpose of loving customers. Thank you, Maureen—and Darci.

WINNING
ON
PURPOSE

Know Your Purpose

Then Live It

What is my purpose?

For almost any individual or company, this is a loaded question. For the individual, it carries philosophical and religious overtones and compels us to probe our very reason for existence. Every person needs to answer it for themselves and then, hopefully, live their lives accordingly.

But when it comes to a company, this book will make a bold argument: there is only one purpose that consistently wins. Sure, there are lots of possible purposes that seem appealing: become a force for good, be the lowest-cost and most efficient provider, become the largest in our industry, be the technology leader, be a great place to work, deliver happiness to our customers, reduce pollution, become a model of good governance, maximize shareholder wealth, improve equity and social justice, and so on. But the most resilient and sustainably successful firms consistently select one primary purpose: *enrich the lives of their customers*. Then they run their business accordingly.

This is not a widely shared point of view. According to a recent Bain & Company survey, only 10 percent of business leaders believe that the primary purpose of their firm is to maximize value for customers.[1] Many companies still operate in the old-school financial capitalist mindset in which maximizing shareholder value is front and center. In recent years, even more have attempted to adopt a balanced scorecard of accountabilities to multiple stakeholders: customers, employees, suppliers, investors, the environment, and society. But over the past four decades, I have observed that those firms that put customers first can deliver superior results—not just to customers but also to all these other constituencies.

You will see compelling evidence in chapters 2 and 5 that companies that best love their customers also deliver the best returns to shareholders. By making customers happy, they can make investors happy. The opposite strategy surely fails, because when firms put investor interests first, they often do things that alienate customers (think excessive late fees, overdraft fees, flight-change fees, etc.).

Of course, many firms today want to become more customer-centric, so there's nothing radical in that idea. But they aren't willing to elevate customer happiness to become their primary purpose, so they struggle to achieve meaningful progress. The truth is that despite today's profusion of customer-centric rhetoric, most businesspeople still believe that the primary purpose of business is profits. That's not surprising, given that we measure company success, pay bonuses, and determine career promotions based primarily on financial results. Why? Financials provide the most reliable audit-worthy information, so they drive planning, decision making, and accountability, and they command investor attention. Even though many leaders now recognize that we live in a world that rotates around customers rather than investors, their organizations, control systems, and governance processes were all designed to operate in that old profit-centered world.

Today's winners—including giants such as Apple, Amazon, T-Mobile, Enterprise Rent-A-Car, and Costco and digital revolutionaries such as Warby Parker, Peloton, and Chewy—have managed to adopt a customer-centered mindset. Their leaders have inspired teams to put customer interests first and foremost, above those of all other stakeholders.

Net Promoter shines a bright light that reveals the forces separating winners from the pack. By using NPS, firms can gauge progress against customer purpose. Customer centricity can advance beyond the puffery of public relations platitudes to the scientific rigor of measurement. The preface noted that Truett Cathy knew intuitively that what inspired him (and his organization) was turning frowns into smiles. NPS elevates this to a measurable and manageable process—indeed a science. As you will see, NPS can not only help customers choose the right suppliers but also help job seekers find the best place to work. And NPS can help investors beat the market—by a country mile.

The Dreaded Cold Call

When I was an MBA student, I dreaded getting cold-called by the professors.[2] Decades later, I felt that same adrenaline surge one morning when I got a phone call out of the blue from a Harvard Business School (HBS) professor named Boris Groysberg. After introducing himself, he explained that he sat on the board of his children's school, where it seemed that the head of the school was using NPS feedback very effectively. Groysberg was also a director at First Republic Bank, which recently had begun rolling out NPS. He explained that based on these two accidental exposures, he wanted to learn more about best-use applications for NPS. Where was it most successful, and where was it less effective? We agreed to meet for lunch at the HBS faculty club several days later.

Over lunch we compared life experiences, and Groysberg eventually shared his surprise that despite NPS's widespread adoption in the greater business world and my own connections to the school and its publishing arm, there had never been an HBS case study written about NPS. In fact, most faculty members preferred to keep a safe distance from my work. Why? I told Groysberg that the faculty must have pigeonholed NPS as a marketing tool—a marginally improved measure of customer satisfaction and therefore not of interest to executives in the corner offices.[3] But Groysberg, who focused on leadership and organizational strategy, saw much greater potential impact for NPS and wondered aloud if I could suggest a company that was using NPS to its fullest effect.

Toward that end I introduced him to FirstService Corporation, a Toronto-based property-services provider with some $3 billion in annual sales on whose board I serve. That introduction led in turn to the first HBS case study about NPS. The study focused on California Closets, a subsidiary of FirstService that has used NPS in a variety of ways. The case study captured a number of innovative applications for marketing segmentation and strategy, some of which you'll read about in future chapters. But at its heart, the case is about *mission*—how you inspire employees to treat customers right.

I sat in on a couple of the initial classes in which Groysberg taught the new case; he was masterful at helping the class recognize the many challenges to consider when implementing NPS, which stoked an animated discussion among the students. Toward the end of the class Groysberg asked me to comment on the origins of NPS, and then we finished up with a lively question-and-answer segment. Next Groysberg led me to a studio downstairs, where he interviewed me to create content for a supplemental teaching video. One theme of that interview was whether it had been wise to make NPS an open-source solution. I explained how that decision helped achieve rapid adoption and innovation but also created some confusion about its most effective application. NPS is currently being used by companies to measure brand equity, reduce customer churn, test out digital innovations, segment markets, and evaluate channels. However, as noted, the most important role for NPS is the framework it provides (along with an ever-expanding toolbox) to help leaders build and nurture a customer-centric culture in which progress is gauged against a company's primary purpose: *enriching customer lives*. In my view, I told Groysberg, this is where NPS can help companies solve some serious shortcomings in our capitalist system and forge its next stage of evolution.

The End of Capitalism as We Know It

The evidence is clear that dissatisfaction is surging against traditional capitalism, which I refer to as financial capitalism. In recent years, that dissatisfaction has been voiced by not only typical antibusiness radicals but also middle-of-the-roaders. A Gallup poll in 2018 found that the number of Americans with a positive view of capitalism had declined to 56 percent (and 47 percent among Democratic voters). The majority of respondents under thirty years of age preferred socialism over capitalism.[4] Even the capitalist glitterati attending the annual World Economic Forum in Davos, Switzerland, have expressed concern about the current system. Michael Bloomberg echoed this distress in his 2019 Class Day address at HBS.[5]

The blue-chip CEOs who comprise the venerable Business Roundtable have clamored for change. There seems to be a mounting demand for enlightened CEOs to hold themselves accountable for creating value for *all* stakeholders: customers, employees, communities, the environment, society, and so on.

Yes, these kinds of arguments are emotionally appealing, but the problem is that *being accountable to everyone means you are accountable to no one.* Being equally accountable to everyone is virtually impossible, just as optimizing value along multiple dimensions simultaneously leads to mathematical chaos. Even the most powerful of supercomputers balk when they're asked to maximize multiple dimensions of a complex system such as a business organization. They spit out some version of this error statement: *indeterminate solution.* Linear programming algorithms can't cope unless all variables except one are treated as constraints for which minimum hurdles can be specified; only one *single* dimension can be maximized.[6]

Of course, it's not just computer models that stumble when multiple goals for maximization are put forward. Complexity trips up humans too. That's why the best leaders work hard to simplify team objectives so they can focus their creative efforts productively.[7] This begs the obvious question: What is the single dimension that a business should optimize in its quest for greatness? I'm willing to entertain the argument that at one time in history, perhaps up to about the early twentieth century, maximizing shareholder value (famously promoted by Milton Friedman) was the correct theory and legitimate goal of the firm. But today, with oceans of capital sloshing around the globe in search of a slightly better-than-average return, capital is *not* the truly precious and constrained resource.

Today, targeting the maximization of shareholder returns, especially short-term returns, leads quickly to mediocrity and decline. Why? Customers are not loyal when they don't feel loved. But additionally, talented employees are the precious and constrained resource, and few people today embrace enriching shareholders as their life's work. Almost every company is desperately seeking the talent required to move more processes to digital platforms and to take advantage of cloud computing—and we've seen ample evidence that people in this Millennial and Gen Z talent pool want to work only for companies with an inspiring purpose.

So, should we embrace employee happiness as the central objective and line up behind their favorite purpose du jour? Labor unions and many progressive politicians naturally endorse this point of view. The problem is that many of the things that make employees happy—lots of vacation time, evading those demanding customers who insist on innovative solutions, avoiding the stress of competition and taking risks, sidestepping the need for uncomfortable change and adoption of better processes—are the very things that make customers *unhappy*, which quickly smothers their loyalty and over time eviscerates corporate growth and prosperity. And truth be told, those things make employees happy only in the short term and fail to engender the kind of loyalty that employers need.

Take a look at one of those "Great Place to Work" lists. They rarely mention delivering great customer experiences as a central criterion underpinning workplace rankings. Instead, they focus on cool fringe benefits: great cafeterias, ping-pong tables, free smoothie machines, and so on. But the sober truth lies in their collective name: these are benefits at the *fringe* of work life. I argue that beyond competitive salaries and benefits, what makes a company a great place to work is when it puts workers in the position to do great things for customers—again, building lives of meaning and purpose.

What will be the next stage in the evolution of capitalism? I believe we have already entered the age of "customer capitalism." While I am certainly not the first person to use this term, I believe this book provides the first comprehensive explanation of the full system, including its guiding philosophy and underlying economics, along with the metrics and managerial processes required to win in this customer-centered world.[8] You'll find my Net Promoter Manifesto in chapter 9, which distills the book down to its quintessence: detailing the seven core principles that business leaders must follow to build a sustainably prosperous business in this age of customer capitalism. Once again, the exemplars of customer capitalism do not attempt to extract maximum profits from every customer and employee to boost share prices and dividend streams. Instead, they focus on the vital role of kindness, generosity, and love in dealing with their customers and employees.

Did you hang up on those three nouns? Let me underscore them: *kindness*, *generosity*, and *love*.

So many self-help books today focus on actions you can take to make yourself happier and more successful. But by and large, they ignore the most vital question you must answer in order to earn happiness and success: *What is the primary purpose of your life?* If your answer is anything like mine—that is, to enrich the lives of others and to make the world a better place—then you need to think carefully about which relationships (individuals and organizations) deserve your investment of precious time and resources, *your loyalty.* You need to make sure they embrace and embody a concordant purpose. If they do, you can focus your energy on helping them prosper. And you can measure progress by how consistently you actually live up to the Golden Rule, which is the surest guidepost orienting you toward a life of meaning and purpose.

This is one of the key lessons that I want to convey through the stories and arguments in this book: be sure to *invest your loyalties wisely.* In the following pages I'll explain how to spot the right companies, those that are worthy of investing your time, your energy, your resources, and your reputation—in other words, your loyalty. The rules of thumb, tools, and frameworks I've developed—with the invaluable assistance of my Bain partners—can help you make better choices by clarifying the best organizations to buy from, work for, and invest in.

The Evolution of Net Promoter

My earliest work focused on quantifying the economics of loyalty, but that soon shifted to understanding how companies earn loyalty. I was already starting to think and talk in terms of *enriching the lives of customers* as the highest purpose for a business. But to test the results of embracing that purpose, we needed a practical method to gauge success and failure. In 2002, I began to develop Net Promoter to fill that void. It was inspired in large part by the customer-feedback process that Andy Taylor used at Enterprise, which he generously explained to me in great detail, but I took it further (shrinking his two questions about satisfaction and likelihood to repurchase to one question about likelihood to recommend) so it could be used by companies in any industry to improve their customer loyalty.

As Net Promoter has grown and evolved—accelerated by open-source innovation—one negative consequence has been confusion about what it really stands for. Far too many people presume that the central component of NPS is a specific metric based on a survey question that asks about likelihood to recommend. That's certainly not what I intended when I created NPS. As I discuss later in this chapter, the first name I considered for the system was "Net Lives Enriched." That's still probably a better descriptor for the system. Net Promoter is essentially a philosophy that posits that our success should be measured by our impact on customers. Did we enrich their lives? In other words, did we brighten their day, lighten their load, ease their suffering, and make them feel loved? Did we reduce the number of frowns and increase the number of smiles?

NPS divides those outcomes into three categories: Promoters (smiles), Passives (meh), and Detractors (frowns). *Promoters* are customers who are so pleased with their experience that they come back to buy more and recommend your brand to family, friends, and colleagues. They feel like they got more than they paid for, which when you think about it is one definition for "having your life enriched." Their enthusiastic loyalty makes them extremely valuable assets who help grow the business and its reputation. *Passives* are customers who feel they got what they paid for but nothing more. They are merely satisfied, not loyal assets with lasting value. And finally, *Detractors* are customers who are disappointed with their experience and feel like they got less than they paid for. Their lives were actually diminished by their experience with you, so they have become liabilities who may well diminish your growth and reputation.

We launched Net Promoter using a survey based on one scoring question (likelihood to recommend) followed by one or two follow-up questions explaining why that score and how to improve. The advantages of simplicity far outweighed the disadvantages. This score (which indicates success or failure at the core purpose) and the system of management around it have blossomed and developed. The world is tired of surveys, so today leading practitioners derive many Net Promoter insights through advances in big data analytics. Observing real-time customer behaviors (digital signals) provides more timely and accurate identification of Promoters, Passives, and Detractors. But surveys still play a critical role in probing more deeply into root causes and testing alternatives; in fact, survey results are used to train mathematical models to distinguish signals from noise.

One thing that has *not* changed with the digital revolution is that when you have truly enriched customers' lives, they want that experience for their loved ones and recommend you to friends and family. This single insight helps illuminate whether you have achieved your Net Promoter purpose.

The Power of Recommendation

Originally, we chose the question "How likely would you be to recommend us to a friend?" because it predicted subsequent loyalty behaviors of individual customers (such as repurchase, increased share of wallet, actual referrals, and so forth).[9] Those are the factors that drive loyalty economics. Over time, I learned more about why someone's *likelihood to recommend* is so revealing. When people recommend a product or service, they are effectively cobranding their own reputation with the recommended company. If a friend acts on their recommendation and ends up being unhappy, this reflects badly on the recommender's judgment and trustworthiness. The CEO of a *Fortune* 100 company shared with me his reaction when his next-door neighbors acted on his recommendation to visit his favorite Caribbean resort. The CEO felt anxious that entire week, worrying whether his neighbors were having a good time. (He even checked online to monitor the weather at the resort each day.) He was deeply relieved when the neighbors' kids reported that the vacation had been fun.

But a personal recommendation goes even deeper. In essence it is an act of love, aimed at improving the life of a friend or family member. Good people will not enthusiastically recommend a company that they know pollutes the environment, abuses its employees, or mistreats its vendors. An enthusiastic recommendation reflects more than the quality or value of a brand; it probes into the heart and soul of a business and its core purpose, reflecting important truths regarding how we feel about an organization's governance, its impact on the community, the environment, and social justice. Perhaps that is why German industrial giant Siemens now reports NPS as an explicit Environmental, Social, and Corporate Governance (ESG) sustainability metric.[10]

As noted earlier, I originally considered calling this system "Net Lives Enriched," since that is the core purpose our system measures: looking at all the lives you touch, how many are enriched, and how many are diminished. But I blinked. Instead, I opted for terminology that I thought would appeal to practical business leaders focused on bottom-line results. Surely they would understand the enormous value of Promoters—who drive profitable growth—along with the crippling cost of Detractors. So, I decided to call the system Net Promoter and, together with the help of my Bain colleagues, introduced this customer-centric management process to the world.

It worked. The subsequent rate of adoption has been astonishing. Since its conception in 2002, the Net Promoter System—and especially its eponymous score for gauging progress—has become the world's leading management system for putting customers first and measuring progress based on customer success. *Fortune* devoted a feature article to NPS in 2020 with this conclusion by *Fortune*'s senior editor-at-large, Geoff Colvin:

> All this devotion for a particular measure of customer sentiment? It may seem bizarre, but the phenomenon is real and growing. At least two-thirds of the *Fortune* 1000 use the Net Promoter Score, including most or all of the financial service companies, airlines, telecom companies, retailers, and others. Quietly, steadily, without anyone much noticing, NPS has moved into the C-suites of most big companies and the owners' offices of thousands of small ones—extending its reach deeply and broadly through the global economy. Skeptics and enemies have largely been vanquished. It is now used in every developed economy and many emerging ones. It's pored over in all types of organizations, not just businesses; in Britain, the National Health Service uses it. As organizations everywhere obsess over the customer experience, NPS's advance across industries and countries is, if anything, accelerating.[11]

The NPS phenomenon has also spread beyond the *Fortune* 1000, gaining traction among startups, small and medium-sized businesses, and nonprofits.[12] And tomorrow's leaders are taking note as well. A senior Stanford Business School professor told me that 60 percent of Stanford students already know about NPS when they show up for their first MBA class; by the time they graduate, that number climbs to nearly 100 percent.

A Road Map for Reading This Book

One key contributor to the rapid and far-ranging spread of NPS was our decision to make it open-source, thus freeing practitioners to experiment and adapt it to their own needs for both customer and employee feedback. As a result, our ideas have been shaped, refined, and customized to fit the increasingly digital challenges of thousands of organizations around the globe, making NPS the predominant framework for measuring customer experience.[13] But as with any open-source system, some putative innovations turn out to be harmful. Throughout subsequent chapters, I will try to resolve confusion surrounding the core purpose of Net Promoter and call out some of these destructive approaches—especially those that corrupt the score by converting a useful *measure* into a less useful (and less trustworthy) *target*. I will also illustrate the best practices across a variety of dimensions through practical company examples. In the final chapter I summarize the current state-of-the-art system, Net Promoter 3.0 (and provide a detailed checklist of NPS 3.0 components in appendix A).

The first two chapters illustrate what it means to have a winning purpose and how pursuit of the right purpose can lead to greatness. Chapters 3 and 4 explore what it means to love customers and how great leaders inspire their teams to embrace that mission. Chapter 5 explains why loving your customers leads to the best outcomes for investors and offers evidence that wise investors should insist that leadership teams prioritize loving customers as their primary purpose and that they upgrade to customer-based accounting so they can report reliable data on progress. I will introduce a new metric I've named Earned Growth Rate as a complementary gauge to buttress Net Promoter (and will include more technical issues around that metric in appendix B). Chapter 6 explains how the Golden Rule provides the moral and philosophical foundation for successful business communities and illustrates how leaders can nurture such communities. Then, in chapter 7, we explore how companies innovate and move beyond mere satisfaction to deliver a stream of remarkable customer experiences. Chapter 8 illustrates practical systems that can reinforce customer-centric cultures and put principles ahead of profits. Chapter 9 advises that humility is in order for most business leaders—because they have so much work to do before they can hope to approach the full range of best practices defined in Net Promoter 3.0—and that their organization's primary mission should be loving customers.

Good Profits

I once believed that loving customers and earning their loyalty provided a functional niche strategy useful only to a few firms (mostly private) in a limited subset of industries, especially those in which customer acquisition costs were high. Well, I was wrong.

The deluge of NPS feedback over the past decade reveals that in today's world, organizations that go beyond satisfaction and treat customers with loving care are building the only growth engines that can prosper sustainably in fully competitive industries.

Yes, free markets and financial capitalism have contributed hugely to advancing democratic ideals and raising living standards around the world. But the failures of old-school capitalism are increasingly apparent. In the coming chapters, I will refer to "good profits" and "bad profits." Bad profits are giving business a bad name; they result from exploiting customers and thus weaken support for capitalism. Good profits are earned by creating Promoters. No apology is necessary for generating a sizable net worth when that is accomplished through living the Golden Rule and enriching customers' lives. Wealth earned through creating Promoters is a formula that makes the world better.

One billionaire company founder you'll hear more from in subsequent pages once told me that "we don't deserve any profit until we have made our customers happy." I can almost feel Wall Street cringing. But as I'll try to demonstrate in the following pages, this radically moral approach provides an unbeatable strategy that helps all constituents, including investors, win. Customer capitalism wins because it strives toward the right purpose. It holds businesses leaders and their teams accountable to the highest standard in human affairs: *Love thy neighbor as thyself.*

CHAPTER 1

Lead with Love

The Unbeatable Purpose

When Steve Grimshaw joined Caliber Collision as CEO in 2009, that chain of sixty-eight auto body shops operated in only two states. By early 2020 it had expanded across the country to more than twelve hundred locations, and its revenues had rocketed from $284 million to almost $5 billion, making it far and away the US industry leader.

Then in March 2020, the black swan known as the Covid-19 pandemic flew into town, causing cars to sit parked in garages and driveways—where, of course, they tend to get into far fewer collisions. Industry revenues plummeted 55 percent, and many competitors shuttered locations to remain solvent. Caliber decided to sail directly into this headwind. It kept every one of its shops open and found a way to weather the crisis, despite a substantial decline in revenues.

Steve explained this choice to me. "At Caliber," he said, "we don't put profits first; we put people first." Instead of shutting down stores in response to the industry downturn, the company drew down a portion of its $300 million credit line. Then Caliber used excess capacity in the stores to upgrade its service and delight more customers. As a result, its Net Promoter Scores jumped to unprecedented levels, far exceeding industry norms. Insurance carriers noticed and began referring a higher share of business to the company.

What accounts for this remarkable and resilient performance? Steve explained, "Fred, people work hard for a paycheck, they work harder for a good boss, and they work hardest for a meaningful purpose." I asked him to describe Caliber's meaningful purpose. He told me his team had thought long and hard about their purpose and engraved the answer in their mission statement:

> When our customers come to us, their lives have been disrupted. They've been in an accident, which is a distressing ordeal. Then they experience the angst of having to find an honest and efficient repair shop. They are worried about insurance coverage and out-of-pocket expenses. Their work schedules have been upended, and they face the hassle of finding alternative transportation while their vehicle is in the shop. Their life is in chaos. So we decided our purpose should be to help get each customer's life back in order—*to restore the rhythm of their lives.*

So, Steve and his leadership team looked for ways to boost store volumes in a way that would restore that rhythm and at the same time inspire Caliber's employees. Caliber announced that throughout the Covid-19 pandemic, it would cover the deductibles (up to $500) for all first responders and frontline medical personnel. That meant substantial savings for every police officer, firefighter, ambulance driver, doctor, and nurse who needed collision repair. What a powerful way to say "thank you" and to inspire your teams and soak up excess capacity!

It's clear that when a company keeps teams gainfully employed during a downturn by helping them delight customers, the company ends up with happy customers and employees. But what about the investors? The private equity firm that hired Steve as Caliber's CEO paid $165 million for the acquisition. Today, just over ten years later, Steve estimates that Caliber's market value is approaching $10 billion, which represents something like a fifty-two-fold return on the private equity firm's investment, or almost a 50 percent annual return when compounded over a decade. Sweet!

Steve built a culture at Caliber based on always doing the right thing, which meant, among other things, always treating people right. "How our employees feel on the inside," he says, "is how they treat customers on the outside." So, every leader attends training courses to help them ensure each team member can experience what it feels like to treat customers (and teammates) right. The name of one of Caliber's advanced leadership development programs is particularly appealing to me: *Leading with Purpose.*

Caliber has also developed measures and systems to reinforce the cultural values that are taught in leadership training. To ensure that frontline team members could savor the full impact of their wins with customers, Caliber execs installed a weekly stand-up huddle process by which each branch reviews its customer numbers. During those huddles, Steve reported, "the team reviews the handful of metrics that gauge how well that branch has lived up to our purpose. By far, the most important of these metrics is their Net Promoter Score." All along the way, individual team members get shout-outs for "getting caught doing the right thing."

The Caliber story demonstrates a classic pattern you will see repeated throughout this book: there is one (and only one) purpose that generates long-term prosperity for a business and benefits all stakeholders. That purpose is *to enrich the lives of customers.* But remember, only 10 percent of business leaders believe that the primary purpose of their company is to enrich the lives of their customers.[1] To cast that troubling fact in an even more negative light, a dismaying 90 percent of today's executives dismiss the unbeatable advantages of a customer-centered purpose.

Nevertheless, the winning formula is relatively straightforward. Leaders who win on purpose attract and inspire good team members by helping them find meaning and purpose through brightening the days of their customers. When employees and their teams get recognized and rewarded for enriching their customers' lives, this reenergizes the purpose-driven flywheel, accelerating sustainable growth and economic prosperity. Simply stated, this is the path to both personal and organizational success. And as you will see in the chapters that follow, this purpose-based strategy is resilient to recessions, pandemics, and the increasingly regular black swan events that expose the fragility of less compelling approaches.

Purpose in the Digital World

Winning on purpose works beautifully in Caliber's gritty business of collision repair, even though that might not be the first industry in which you'd expect to find an example of virtuous employees providing loving care for their customers. (Think of the body shops in your own past!) So, could this same approach also work in a twenty-first-century digital business populated mainly by software engineers, coders, and systems designers, most of whom rarely interact directly with customers? The answer is "yes," and this became clear to me as I observed the successful evolution of one of the software industry's most admired companies.

Scott Cook and I joined Bain around the same time in the late 1970s. I stayed to consult and write books; he departed to found the financial software giant Intuit, which he built into an impressive loyalty leader with a market cap over $100 billion. Intuit's resilience is most impressive when you consider how few software companies managed to transition successfully from the era of shrink-wrapped boxes sold by mail order or through computer stores to the digital download era and all the way to cloud-based apps. I remember chatting with Scott at Intuit's headquarters in Mountain View, California—more or less the heart of Silicon Valley—shortly after I conceived of Net Promoter. He was so excited that he insisted we walk across the parking lot (in the middle of a rainstorm) to go tell his CEO about my new concept.

I'm not sure if the Net Promoter System would have ever taken off the way it did had it not been for Scott's early enthusiasm and his commitment to finding innovative ways to integrate the system into the core processes that made Intuit great for its customers. Intuit was a pioneer in using Net Promoter to guide annual budgeting and capital allocation processes. In addition, Intuit was the first company I know of to regularly report to investors its NPS for each business line, *benchmarked to key competitors*. Scott bravely shared his goal: that every business line would lead its competitors' NPS by at least ten points. In the NPS universe, that's a lot of points.

I think Scott became one of Net Promoter's earliest adopters because he saw the possibility that it could help him manage an essential element of his company's purpose: to solve customer problems and make them happy. I'll always remember the way Scott described the primary purpose of his organization, a quote that I've already foreshadowed in the introduction: "We don't deserve any profit until we have made our customers happy." Back when Intuit was still young, he believed that Net Promoter could help the company live up to that credo. He remains convinced of that in today's digital world, as Intuit continues to play a leading role both in its industry and in the Net Promoter community.

The Intuit credo constitutes a remarkable departure from the traditional capitalist notion of caveat emptor—buyer beware—that ranks profits for investors far ahead of customer interests. Of course, profits sufficient to attract investors are necessary to make a business sustainable, but profits measure *value extracted*, so to customers and employees they are inherently selfish and uninspiring, which in turn creates other problems. For example, old-fashioned capitalism puts a company's employees in a precarious position. They are supposed to care more about profits than treating customers and colleagues right. They are supposed to endorse the idea that caring for customers can take a back seat to feeding the (insatiable) appetite of investors. And by and large, they know that this makes no sense especially in the long term.

What's the alternative? A new cynosure: enriching customer lives through products, services, and experiences so remarkable they afford employees lives of meaning and purpose. When leaders decide that their primary purpose is to put employees in a position to enrich the lives of customers, they are aligning the ambitions of their companies with those of their teams. When Scott says, "We deserve profits only after customers are happy," he is pointing toward a new North Star—a new way of setting a course. Especially for public companies that historically have navigated mainly toward profits, it's a radical shift indeed.

This is not an easy or obvious transition, and it won't happen without relentless determination at the top. Leaders who decide to make this leap must come to grips with a plethora of tools and practices that are based on (and reinforce) the old profits-above-all paradigm. This paradigm continuously infects and reinfects firms, even those led by determined people such as Scott Cook. Why? There are lots of reasons. The old recidivist mindset spreads virally through business schools that are looking backward, journalists who aren't doing their homework, and transferring employees whose only work experience has been in firms that operated on traditional profit-centered principles. New hires (and new board members) join the Intuits of the world and unconsciously spread practices and processes that stifle customer-centered leadership. The drumbeat of financial reporting—and accountabilities tied to financials—can easily drown out the call to *do the right thing for customers and colleagues.*

In other words, living the right life is an ongoing challenge. But as we'll see in the following two stories—from the opposite ends of the NPS spectrum—it's an investment that's well worth making.

NPS, the Wrong Way

Let's start with the disheartening story. On the first stop of a recent car-shopping trip, I was impressed with the dealership's fancy new showroom: a glass palace replete with snack bar and leather sofas. I knew going in that this particular auto manufacturer and its dealerships boasted about their embrace of Net Promoter. Toward that end, they had implemented software company Medallia's state-of-the-art customer feedback technology platform, which is used by Apple and other leading Net Promoter practitioners. This system provides relevant customer feedback scores and comments directly to each employee's smartphone to enable real-time learning and improvement. So, at my auto dealership the table seemed to be set for a satisfying customer experience.

Wrong. In fact, my car-shopping adventure at this dealership was maddeningly old school, more reminiscent of a root canal than a delight-filled, life-enriching experience. At his first opportunity, the salesperson—let's call him Joe—disparaged the website I had used to research a fair price for the new car. Then he made an offer for my trade-in that was far below that website's estimate of its true value. I stayed relatively cool and told him that on both ends of the deal—trade-in and purchase price—I was only looking for a median deal. (In my younger days I would have insisted on something in the best quartile, but I guess age has mellowed me.) Even so, we spent the next hour dickering back and forth. The negotiation tactics were dishonest and manipulative, aimed at tricking me into paying the highest possible price ("just one moment while I confer with my manager") while reimbursing me as little as possible for my trade-in ("gee, now that we see it again in the daylight, we realize that it's in pretty good condition, after all").

It was an irritating, time-wasting process that ate away at both my patience and his dignity. Despite it all we finally agreed on a deal, and the next thing Joe said nearly took my breath away. "Of course, Mr. Reichheld," he began, putting on his most earnest face, "you know that you will be receiving a survey about your experience today. And at *our* dealership, only a score of 10 out of 10 is a passing grade." I must have been spotted rolling my eyes, because a few minutes later the clerk at the cashier's window who had overheard the conversation reinforced the point. "I hope you realize how seriously management takes this survey," she said. "Joe really will get in a lot of trouble if he gets a score less than 10."

Within a few days I received a survey not from the manufacturer, as I was expecting, but instead from the dealer. It turns out that many dealers try to get out in front of the manufacturer's survey with a preliminary "practice" survey of their own to ensure that their customers will give them all 10s when the subsequent "real" survey arrives. Despite my irritation with the whole process, I really didn't want to get Joe in trouble by slapping him with low scores—after all, most of the problems I encountered were the result of the systems and incentives created by management and thus beyond his control—so I simply ignored the dealership survey. But, of course, that wasn't the end of the story. Next I received a barrage of messages by phone and text imploring me to fill out the survey and to get back to them *right away* if I felt I couldn't give them a 10 on every question.

Well, I value my time, so I ignored those messages, which were nothing more than a silly exercise in gaming the system. They obviously didn't care the slightest little bit about getting honest feedback and learning how to improve how they did business. They just wanted to be sure that if I did bother to respond to the *real* survey, from the manufacturer, I would score them a 10. And sure enough, next came that real survey, which I also chose to ignore. I was fatigued by the whole experience—especially the survey antics—and had no energy to keep playing this game.

After the fact, I found myself wishing I had the opportunity to ask Joe how he feels when he gets a 10 from a customer. Is it in some way gratifying, or is he simply relieved? Failing that, I did the next best thing: I asked the dealer group senior executive who at the time was responsible for that location what Joe would have said if he had the courage to be completely honest. In response, the senior executive first explained that, as I suspected, the dealers are simply marching to the drumbeat of the manufacturers, who have little faith in tools such as closed-loop follow-up, root-cause diagnosis, or test-and-learn systems, which are the kinds of tools that make Net Promoter possible. He confided that most dealership managers watch scores but don't even bother reading customer comments. What the manufacturers *do* care about is winning a J.D. Power Award, mainly for its perceived advertising value. So, they built a system to punish dealers if they receive low scores that would disqualify the brand for an award.

Then the senior executive answered my question more directly. "Fred," he said, "that salesperson certainly wouldn't have said anything about feeling good about his life. Most likely he'd have said something like 'Thank goodness I dodged another bullet, and I get to keep my job another day.'"

So, the answer is *no*. Receiving a 10 at that dealership doesn't generate positive energy among employees; it mostly alleviates fear. Management posts the scores for each salesperson on the wall of the team meeting room. During weekly reviews, anyone receiving a low score feels the heat. Any salesperson with two or more low scores in a week is at risk of being fired. And yes, most scores *are* 10s, but it's a system rigged with begging for forgiveness, pleading and browbeating, and occasional bribes of free car mats or oil changes—and nobody's fooled by it.

In other words, Net Promoter surveys, even when delivered with a state-of-the-art technology platform, can't magically transform the low-grade hell on earth that so many of us experience on visits to our local Auto Mile. That requires a change of heart from leadership and a new way of thinking about what Net Promoter is really trying to measure and why.

NPS, the Right Way

Now let's turn to the second and more inspiring story. It focuses on Apple Retail, which now operates more than five hundred stores worldwide and was an early adopter of the Net Promoter System. I have done a number of favors for Apple over the years, including appearing onstage at a couple of its worldwide store management meetings. In return, Apple invited me to visit its flagship store on Boston's Boylston Street for a morning of filming and interviews. This was highly unusual: the Apple retail stores, like the larger company, operate under a pretty thorough veil of secrecy. So, I was very pleased to get a rare behind-the-scenes opportunity to observe Apple teams putting Net Promoter into action.

I arrived an hour before the scheduled 10:00 a.m. opening time. The team began its day with a stand-up huddle, dubbed the "daily download." This turned out to be a high-energy affair, focused almost entirely on issues relevant to enriching the lives of customers and employees, which is the explicitly stated core mission of Apple Retail. The team leader didn't talk about sales targets or what the store had to do to "make its numbers." Instead, he reviewed the Net Promoter feedback received from the prior day's customers. Team members shared ideas for solving a range of customer problems, and the leader summarized some ideas that might delight even more customers that day. He reminded the team of some retail basics—looking customers in the eye, shaking hands when appropriate, and so on. Finally, there were several minutes of formal recognition for team members who had received "Promoter" comments from yesterday's delighted customers. Since this was a stand-up meeting, the ovations were standing ovations.

This may strike the reader as a bit corny or formulaic or forced. But to my eye, in real time it was none of those things. It seemed to me that the team members who received shout-outs were energized and inspired by that recognition. And it's only a short step to infer that those employees were inspired by their mission as well: *enriching lives*.

After the huddle, team members dispersed to their various assignments. I made my way down to the basement team room to interview the associate with the highest Net Promoter Score in the Boston store, which at the time was earning some of the very highest Net Promoter Scores among Apple's flagship stores.

This young woman—let's call her Alice—soon struck me as the distillation of the best aspects of the millennial generation. For example, she seemed far more interested in mission than in the size of her paycheck and more focused on purpose than on how quickly she would get promoted. Her role at that time was an "Apple Creative"—that is, a teacher who helped customers learn how to get the most out of their Apple products. She began by describing her upbringing, emphasizing the impact that her education at a Quaker school in Cambridge had on her. There, she said, she came to understand that the Golden Rule—treat others the way you would like to be treated—is the best foundation for a healthy community and a good life. I asked her for an example of how she put that rule to work. She thought for a moment and then responded. "I struggled with ADHD in school," she said, "and I had trouble concentrating in boring classes. That experience made me focus on finding ways to make learning exciting and fun for all my students."

By "students," Alice meant her customers. She said that she listened carefully to her customers' comments and feedback to be sure she was able to put herself in their shoes. Early on she realized that many of her customers found technology intimidating, so she discovered ways to make those customers feel safe and comfortable. She made a point of telling them that there is no such thing as a stupid question. When they occasionally asked her about something she didn't know, her response was usually along the lines of "Well, that's a great question. Let's go find out together." Then she and her customer would walk over to consult with another employee in the store who had deeper expertise in that particular subject.

Alice told me that she got most of her job satisfaction from seeing the positive impact she had on her customers' lives. She explained that one major advantage of Apple's Net Promoter System was that it tracked how well she was doing, *each day*, at enriching customer lives. Net Promoter enabled her to gauge how consistently she was living up to the Golden Rule that she had embraced years earlier as a life standard. She wasn't apprehensive about getting this kind of visible, rolling "report card"; in fact, she welcomed it. She was proud when Promoter comments scrolled across video monitors in the break room, thereby making her positive impact visible to all team members across the store. (By that point the Boylston Street store had more than five hundred employees, few of whom would get to see firsthand the smiles on her customers' faces.) And Alice knew that her store leaders studied these scores—as did her market manager, as did Apple execs in faraway Cupertino.

I asked Alice how it made her feel when she got a 10 from a customer. She pondered and then she said something I'll never forget: "It makes me feel like I'm living the right life."

My initial reaction was one you might expect from someone who was forty-plus years older than Alice: a mix of skepticism, empathy, and maybe even a little frustration ("Ah, Alice; you'll learn soon enough that the world doesn't always reward that kind of idealism!"). But then I realized that although I might have used different words, *I felt exactly the same way.* When the question is asked honestly and if in response to that question someone decides to give you a 10—in other words, an unqualified recommendation that they would want their loved ones to have a similar experience—this is incontrovertible evidence that you have brightened their existence. I'll go further. It's not too much to say that in earning your 10, you have found and embodied a little greatness—in the sense that Martin Luther King Jr. intended when he observed that *everybody can be great because everybody can serve.*

Living the Right Life: The Net Purpose Score

One common denominator that a lot of us human beings seem to share is the desire to live a life of meaning and purpose—to make this world a better place. With a bit of reflection and even without the benefit of a mind-focusing cancer diagnosis, most of us come to realize that the surest path toward this goal is enriching the lives of the people we touch. The trouble is that this goal seems so elusive—so amorphous, rarely urgent, and generally impossible to measure—unless, that is, you work at a company where the Net Promoter System rigorously tallies each day the portion of lives each employee enriches (Promoters) and subtracts the portion of lives diminished (Detractors).

When I walk into an Apple store, I can feel the positive energy and vibe from that community of employees. They are not simply trying to sell me another iPhone, although they're very good at that (Apple has far greater sales per retail square foot than anybody else).[2] They are also striving to brighten the day of another customer—and by so doing live the right life.

To some extent, the argument that customer and employee happiness are inextricably intertwined and are linked to organizational success seems self-evident. How could they *not* be mutually reinforcing? And yet, too many companies fail to connect the dots or connect them badly. In my view, the typical Apple store (along with its customers and employees) is getting far more benefit from its Net Promoter System than the typical car dealership. This was not by accident but instead was by design. Apple designed its system to energize frontline employees and help them learn how to innovate to enrich customer lives. (Alice received daily digital feedback from customers' smartphones, not just scores but also comments and suggestions that helped her track and manage her progress.) By contrast, most car companies design their systems not to help frontline dealer salespeople learn how to enrich customer lives but instead to help their corporate team control their sometimes unruly dealers.

Regrettably, the Net Promoter System at most companies resembles that of my local car dealership rather than Apple's. The leaders of those companies have missed a golden opportunity. But there's no reason why they can't get it right. In the chapters ahead, I will review the best practices that consistently inspire teams to delight customers. Many of the choices involved in designing an effective Net Promoter System hinge on the answers to seemingly small questions. For example, should employees ever mention impending surveys and desired scores to customers? Should individual employee results be shared with peers? Should individual employee score results drive recognition, compensation, or promotion? Who should be responsible for closing the loop with unhappy customers? Can we replace bothersome surveys with customer behavior data that signals their status as Promoter, Passive, or Detractor? Should there be a target score or benchmarks for score improvement? Who should have ultimate accountability for customer scores?

The choices made in response to these seemingly small choices accumulate into *enormous differences* in results. But the most important decision of all is this: What is the primary mission toward which leaders are navigating with NPS? NPS helps employees consistently enrich the lives they touch—in other words, lead the right life. That is the purpose of great organizations. Designed and deployed correctly, NPS can become an organization's Net Purpose Score and gauge progress toward living that purpose.

CHAPTER 2

Aim for Greatness

Everybody Can Be Great

The setting was a large living room in a suite atop the Four Seasons Hotel in Palo Alto, California. We had hired a camera crew to record a roundtable discussion of CEOs from highly regarded Net Promoter pioneers: eBay, Charles Schwab, Bain & Company, Intuit, and Rackspace.[1] I had been worrying that having all of us wired for sound and seeing cameras dodging between reading lamps as they sought better angles might feel a bit awkward. Might this stifle our conversation?

I needn't have worried. The members of this self-confident group ignored the technological intrusions and immediately leaned in to share their experiences.

The wide-ranging discussion that followed clarified for me that these leaders were using NPS not simply as a tool for measuring customer loyalty; they were also employing NPS as a practical moral compass for their organization. In my last book, I had already profiled the nearly incredible NPS-based turnaround led by Charles Schwab (who came out of retirement) to get his eponymous brokerage firm back on track. When Walt Bettinger was tapped to be the next CEO, he continued to effectively utilize the NPS framework. At the Four Seasons session, Walt updated us on how NPS had evolved at his company, concluding that NPS made it safe for his people to always do the right thing.

In other words, Bettinger viewed NPS feedback as a solid point of reference—a sort of objective moral backstopping—that his teams could use to support their actions and decisions. Rackspace CEO Lanham Napier made another comment that lodged itself in my brain. "I think of NPS as a GPS [Global Positioning System] for greatness," he said. "It lets our teams know how often they are achieving great results for our customers."

The heads around the room were all nodding, because the CEOs understood his vantage point and perspective. Helping a team know when they have touched greatness—by providing extraordinary service to others, embedded in a process that helps them learn how to do it more consistently—is one of the most important gifts a leader can provide. I appreciated Napier's comparison of NPS to GPS, because GPS locates our current position, and—combined with cloud-based network apps that integrate feedback from other drivers—can show us the best route forward. Metaphorically speaking, NPS too can reveal our current position relative to greatness. And when enabled by predictive algorithms that integrate feedback signals from similar customers, NPS can illuminate our best path forward toward greatness—defined as "enriching customer lives."

Let me return here to a subject I brought up in chapter 1. When I introduced NPS in a 2003 *Harvard Business Review* article, I thought it made sense to emphasize the hard-nosed economic and financial advantages that NPS unleashes. After all, I was an economics major in college and at that point had worked twenty-five-plus years at Bain, which prides itself on delivering measurable financial results for clients. From this perspective, Promoters represent the firm's core assets, exhibiting loyal behaviors that generate cash flow: they come back, expand purchases over time, refer their friends, and provide constructive feedback. I confess that in 2003 I treated the inspirational side of Net Promoter as extra credit—icing on the corporate cake, so to speak—out of concern that too many business leaders might dismiss this inspirational dimension as flimsy and soft. Instead, I positioned Net Promoter as a way to increase the corporation's *financial* net worth, which is what I thought would make the system most compelling and accessible to the average businessperson.

NPS as Moral Compass

This positioning proved unnecessarily narrow. Leaders such as Walt Bettinger and Lanham Napier valued Net Promoter not only because it helps an organization remain centered on its primary purpose—enriching customer lives—but also because it serves as a practical moral compass for employees. Maybe this customer-centric business movement would have advanced faster if I had taken a bolder stand, focusing less on building financial net worth and more on the more fundamentally important goal of building human net worth.

Recall that Martin Luther King Jr. quote: "Everybody can be great, because everybody can serve." By that standard, meaningful service to others surely should be the true measure of greatness and our ultimate goal. But because "meaningful service to others" has traditionally been devilishly difficult to measure, we have typically defaulted to more easily measured financial metrics for gauging greatness.

This is true on the individual level as well as the corporate level. Let's start with individuals. The annual *Forbes* list of billionaires for too long has served as the compendium of our society's exemplars of great success. But are these wealthy magnates really our most worthy role models? I would say "no." Financial net worth provides a wholly untrustworthy measure of personal greatness. Consider the historical examples of people such as Abraham Lincoln, Clara Barton, Mahatma Gandhi, Nelson Mandela, Mother Teresa, Martin Luther King Jr., Jonas Salk, and Albert Einstein. These are individuals who had unexceptional financial net worth and yet created enormous human net worth.

Conversely and sadly, too many people built great financial net worth by abusing their customers, employees, and partners. I'm thinking, to name a random few, of Chainsaw Al Dunlap, Jeffrey Epstein, Harvey Weinstein, Theranos founder Elizabeth Holmes, and the Sackler family, whose Purdue Pharma empire shamelessly fostered opioid addictions and deaths; the list of bullies and cheats goes on and on. They are all black-belt masters of value extraction rather than value creation. This is an important point. Relying on profits as our gauge of greatness is often misleading, because profits quantify value extracted from customers and employees rather than value created for them. If our primary goal is to create customer Promoters, then profits cannot serve as our North Star.

The pursuit of financial success as the ultimate corporate objective often leads not to greatness but instead to abusive and manipulative practices that diminish the dignity and well-being of customers and employees. Consider the legal but morally questionable practices of traditional financial capitalist companies that make profit their overriding purpose. You could make your own list: car rental firms charging punitive late fees, payday lenders preying on financially vulnerable populations, brokers pushing complex and risky investments to retirees, some hospitals tripling their prices for uninsured patients, and many health clubs selling hard-to-cancel subscriptions to customers they know won't use them.

Redefining Greatness

Most of the business literature on "excellence" or "greatness" treats financial net worth as the one true goal—the alpha and omega of capitalism. Certainly the most celebrated contemporary analysis of corporate greatness is *Good to Great* by Jim Collins.[2] That book has sold more than five million copies and remains a staple of the executive bookshelf. Collins identified his "great" companies based purely on financial criteria. His eleven exemplars of business greatness, listed in figure 2-1, were chosen without regard to the firm's primary purpose or human net worth created, but simply through the lens of financial capitalism. These firms generated superior shareholder returns after previous periods of average performance.

But when we examine their performance in the years *following* the book's publication, these companies were far from stellar. Why this dramatic reversal of fortunes? The answer is complicated and varies from company to company. Collins himself studied that decline and published his findings in a subsequent book; he blamed the downfall of those companies on hubris and the mentality of buying growth at any cost.[3] But I think there is more to it. Those firms (like most companies today) gauged their success using the metrics of financial capitalism—primarily profits.

FIGURE 2-1

Exemplar companies

Good to Great	The Ultimate Question 2.0—NPS leaders	
• Abbott	• Amazon	• MetroPCS (now T-Mobile)
• Circuit City	• American Express	• Southwest
• Fannie Mae	• Apple	• State Farm* (Life Ins.)
• Gillette	• Chick-fil-A*	• Symantec (now Norton)
• Kimberly-Clark	• Costco	• Trader Joe's*
• Kroger	• Facebook	• USAA* (P&C Insurance)
• Nucor	• Google	• Vanguard*
• Philip Morris	• JetBlue	• Verizon (Internet)
• Pitney Bowes	• Kaiser Permanente*	
• Walgreens		
• Wells Fargo		

* Not publicly traded

When profits become purpose, it becomes too easy for large and powerful firms to boost their financial performance by shortchanging customers and employees. This is value extraction, not value creation, and since value extraction doesn't show up in audited financial statements, this kind of abuse can go undetected for months or even years, at least by the investor community.

Customers and employees notice right away, but it may take them a while to react. Once customers have integrated a provider into their lives—for example, by putting all their billing information into a bank's automated bill-pay solution—they are quite vulnerable to value extraction by that provider. Meanwhile, employees who have invested many years with one firm are likely to find that switching to a new job entails substantial costs, and these too may be viewed by profit-driven managers as exploitable exit barriers.

Actually, I'm a big fan of Jim Collins's work and remember agreeing with most of what he wrote in *Good to Great*. Nevertheless, the simple fact is that the *Good to Great* companies were not resilient and started to slide shortly after they were anointed. Bain teams examined the total shareholder return (TSR) of these firms in the decade following that book's publication. We didn't take the lazy man's benchmark—the readily available S&P 500—because that index rotates companies on and off its list, is cap-weighted, and ignores dividends. To create a more accurate standard, we

FIGURE 2-2

Total shareholder return (TSR) vs. US median

Cumulative total shareholder return indexed vs. US public firms (median) for the decade beginning January 1st of each book's year of publication

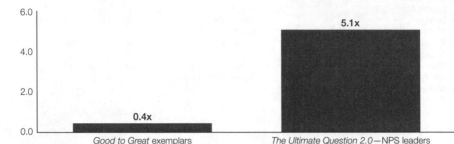

Source: CapIQ

Note: Cumulative TSR represents total return assuming investment from 1/1/2001–12/31/2010 for GTG companies and 1/1/2011–12/31/2020 for NPS Leaders companies; Altria and Philip Morris: upon split on 4/28/2008, assumed reinvestment proportional to the deal terms; Gillette: P&G acquired Gillette in 2005 for $57B—TSR reflects reinvestment into new P&G, in 2019 P&G wrote off $8B of Gillette value; Facebook: TSR since IPO for the period 5/18/2012–12/31/2020; MetroPCS: assumes TSR for MetroPCS through TMUS acquisition in 4/30/2013 and re-evaluates TMUS TSR since IPO for period 5/1/2013–12/31/2020; Public US firms represent ~1,400 and ~1,600 publicly traded companies in US with revenue >$500M listed as of the start of each respective time period.

gathered data on share-price appreciation plus dividends paid for all US public companies.[4] We then performed the same analysis for the NPS leader companies from *The Ultimate Question 2.0* for the decade after that book's publication. The lists of company exemplars used in each book are displayed in figure 2-1.

In figure 2-2, we compare the TSR performance of the *Good to Great* companies versus the TSR of the NPS leaders identified in *The Ultimate Question 2.0*. In each case, we quantified TSR for each group relative to the median stock market return in the decade following each book's publication.

As you can see, the *Good to Great* companies delivered only 40 percent of the median market performance, while *The Ultimate Question 2.0* NPS exemplars delivered 510 percent of the median return. In other words, the firms that appeared great through the lens of financial capitalism made their investors very unhappy over the decade following their anointment, while investors in companies that looked great through the lens of customer capitalism delighted their investors in the decade after their NPS superiority was revealed.

Meanwhile, let's not forget the six NPS leaders that are private, subsidiaries, or mutually owned and for which we can't use the stock market as a gauge. These firms are sending signals of equally impressive performance (and maybe even better). For example, Chick-fil-A has now expanded to 2,500 stores to become the third-largest US restaurant chain, Vanguard has mushroomed to $7 trillion in assets under management, and Trader Joe's is so popular that, at least at my local store, there is usually a line of cars waiting to get into the parking lot. There is not a single clunker among the NPS leaders.

In figures 2-3 and 2-4, we break out the performance of our two collections into the individual firms. And as you can see, only three firms of the eleven in the *Good to Great* collection managed to beat the stock market median. The reason I chose to benchmark medians was to avoid

FIGURE 2-3

Eight of the eleven *Good to Great* companies lagged the US median (1/1/2001–12/31/2010)

Cumulative total shareholder return indexed vs. US public firms (median)
(1/1/2001–12/31/2010)

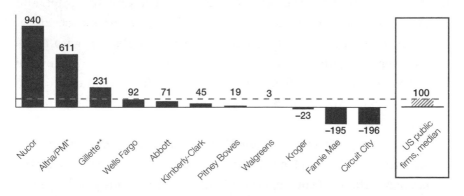

Source: CapIQ

Note: Cumulative TSR represents total return assuming investment from 1/1/2001–12/31/2010; all US firms represent all publicly traded companies with revenue >$500M as of 1/1/2001 (N = 1407).

*Altria and Philip Morris: upon split on 4/28/2008 assumed reinvestment proportional to the deal terms.

**Gillette: P&G acquired Gillette in 2005 for $57B—TSR reflects reinvestment into new P&G; in 2019 P&G wrote off $8B of Gillette value.

FIGURE 2-4

All eleven NPS leaders beat the US median (1/1/2011–12/31/2020)

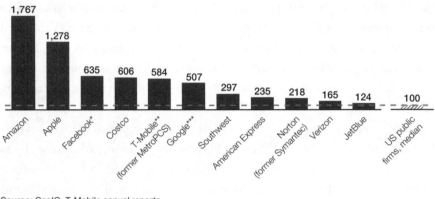

Cumulative total shareholder return indexed vs. US public firms (median)
(1/1/2011–12/31/2020)

Source: CapIQ, T-Mobile annual reports

Note: Cumulative TSR represents total return assuming investment from 1/1/2011–12/31/2020; all US firms represent publicly traded companies with revenue >$500M as of 1/1/2011 (N = 1594).

*Facebook: TSR since IPO for the period 5/18/2012–12/31/2020.

**MetroPCS: assumes TSR for MetroPCS through TMUS acquisition in 4/30/2013 and re-evaluates TMUS TSR since IPO for period 5/1/2013–12/31/2020.

***Google parent company Alphabet Inc. used.

overweighting the disastrous performances of Circuit City (bankrupt) and Fannie Mae (essentially bankrupt, placed in government receivership).[5] Several other *Good to Great* exemplars got slapped with enormous government fines for mistreating their customers. Two or three of the firms are indeed excellent, but overall, has this turned out to be a collection of admirable and resilient companies? I know where I come down.

Contrast the performance of *The Ultimate Question 2.0* collection. All eleven firms beat the stock market median over the decade following the book's publication. Of course, everything is clear in hindsight, but hindsight couldn't help us when we selected the list of NPS leaders in 2010. All we knew was that these firms had so loved their customers that they transformed into loyal promoters—which undergirded these firms' superior Net Promoter Scores. And this single insight accurately foreshadowed their future performance.

Lessons Learned

Again, *Good to Great* contained many insights. Jim Collins's particular genius enabled him to draw useful lessons even from his soon-to-be-defrocked exemplars of greatness. Many of these lessons are indelibly imprinted in today's common business wisdom and MBA curricula, and rightfully so. Get the right people on the bus, focus where you can be the best in the world, make that strategic flywheel spin, pursue Big Hairy Audacious Goals, become a level 5 leader, and so on—all excellent ideas. But even Collins's insightful analysis and vivid articulation of his findings couldn't help his exemplars extend their successful runs. Their formula proved fragile and failed the test of resilience.

My takeaway will be familiar to you: A company can't be great without embracing a great purpose. In this way, I believe that the Net Promoter framework complements the lessons from *Good to Great*—and perhaps fills in some weak spots. *Good to Great* employed a financial capitalist mindset, defining greatness in terms of financial results. I recommend measuring greatness against the standard of a winning purpose. While Collins emphasized that leaders must concentrate where they have passion, Net Promoter posits that the primary purpose worthy of passion—and the one that consistently wins—centers on enriching customer lives. One important insight that *Good to Great* overlooked is that Collins's famous flywheel won't keep spinning unless it is powered by loyalty economics. You will see evidence throughout this book supporting this perspective.

I am sadly confident that some of the NPS leaders we identified in 2010 will not maintain their lofty perches. Competitors will innovate superior customer-enriching solutions and displace them. But we—and they—*will see this transition coming* as their relative NPS results weaken. By focusing on this gauge of greatness, by measuring their success based on their relative Net Promoter Score, I expect that some firms will be able to reverse their decline before it is too late. Investors who are wise enough to monitor NPS will also be able to anticipate these declines and take action. Amazon, for example, regularly benchmarks its NPS versus competitors in every category where they compete—and always includes new entrants. Founder and chairman Jeff Bezos constantly reminds his team never to ignore the small and apparently insignificant players. Why? In part because Barnes & Noble once ignored Amazon as a small, insignificant player—and look what happened.

Customer Capitalism: A New Theory of the Firm

What should our response be when a financial metric such as profits or TSR can't be relied on to correctly identify great companies? It may be time to rethink our basic conceptions about the role of the firm and what kind of corporate results would epitomize "greatness."

I believe that firms that practice customer capitalism—putting customer interests first—have the best chance of achieving sustainable greatness. When employees understand that their surest path to sustainable personal happiness and fulfillment comes through enriching customer lives (and helping their teammates do the same), then we have a theory of the firm that holds water in today's world. And it's not a theoretical proposition; we have plenty of evidence right in front of us. Firms that make customers feel loved are winning; they are outpacing and outgrowing the competition.

Look again at the list of NPS leaders on the right-hand side of figure 2-1. Almost without exception, these are onetime niche players that have grown into leviathans. How and why? All too often, journalists and analysts interpret the success of these firms through old financial-capitalism lenses. Shortly after Apple's market cap surpassed the trillion-dollar mark, for example, the *Wall Street Journal* ran an op-ed explaining that the key to Apple's success was its financial structure and supply chain management. Nothing—literally *nothing*—was said about its world-class customer-centric growth engine that has earned the company millions of Promoters. When its valuation surpassed $2 trillion in the summer of 2020, once again the financial pages were full of financial explanations like Apple's stock buybacks. There was, however, not a peep about safeguarding customer data or treating frontline employees with dignity and respect.

This turns out to be a stubbornly blind eye. At the end of his March 2019 live-streamed announcement of new services from Apple—and just after hugging Oprah Winfrey—Apple CEO Tim Cook reminded the audience it was not the glitz and glamour that really made Apple special. "At Apple,"

Cook said, "the customer is and always will be at the center of everything that we do."

The following day, the *Wall Street Journal* ran an article on Apple's new offerings titled "Apple Pitches Values along with Credit Card, News and TV Plus—but Will People Buy It?" The snarky subhead challenged the notion that corporate values can create real value by asking "How does being a beacon of social responsibility help the iPhone-making paragon of capitalism?" The article disparaged the idea that Apple's relentless innovation, its zealous protection of consumer privacy, and its commitment to inclusion, equality, and environmentalism and always putting customers first could provide a solid platform for its economic future. Obviously, it *had* to be about hard stuff such as finance and procurement, right?[6]

Nonsense. It's time to let the scales fall from our eyes and acknowledge that financial capitalism is giving way to a new era of customer capitalism in which corporate purpose is to enrich the lives of customers and in which the leader's primary responsibility is to help employees live that purpose and thus lead great lives.

And one more time: long-term investors also win big in customer capitalism. I know this for a fact, because I have been investing in companies that put customers first for more than a decade. And as you will see, my results have been impressive by any standard.

F.R.E.D.'s Purposeful Theory of Investing

Based on my theory that the best growth engines are fueled by customer loyalty, I have been investing in NPS leaders for many years. These companies live by the Credo of F.R.E.D. (*F*oster *R*ecommendation, *E*liminate *D*etraction). To showcase the results of this investment strategy, I created the F.R.E.D. Stock Index (FREDSI), which tracks TSR for the portfolio of companies that achieve the highest NPS in their industry sector—in other words, the customer-love winners. I began the index with the eleven NPS leaders identified in the research for *The Ultimate Question 2.0*, listed in figure 2-1.[7]

As Bain research probed additional industries and discovered clear NPS leaders, I added those firms to the index on January 1 of the subsequent

FIGURE 2-5

FREDSI beats the stock market

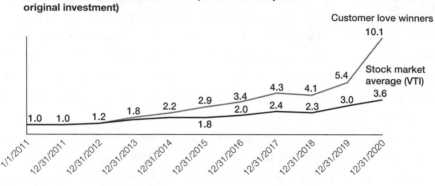

Cumulative total shareholder return (shown as multiple of original investment)

Customer love winners

10.1

Stock market average (VTI)

5.4

4.3   4.1   3.6

3.4   3.0

2.9   2.0   2.4   2.3

2.2

1.8

1.2

1.0   1.0   1.8

1/1/2011 12/31/2011 12/31/2012 12/31/2013 12/31/2014 12/31/2015 12/31/2016 12/31/2017 12/31/2018 12/31/2019 12/31/2020

Source: CapIQ

Note: FREDSI covers all NPS Leader companies for the period 1/1/2011–12/31/2020; in addition, FREDSI also includes Texas Roadhouse (1/1/2011–12/31/2020), Discover and FirstService (1/1/2015–12/31/2020), and Tesla and Chewy (1/1/2020–12/31/2020). FREDSI is calculated as the equal-weighted average cumulative return for each year.

year. Texas Roadhouse joined the index in 2010, and both Discover Financial and FirstService were added in 2015. In 2019, Bain performed an NPS X-ray across the auto industry and found that Tesla had built nearly a ten-point lead versus runner-up Subaru. In pet supplies, Chewy outpaced the competition by twenty-eight points. So, we added both firms in January 2020. I plan to drop firms from the index if their NPS slips to a distant runner-up status, but that has yet to happen.

We rebalance the portfolio each January to give equal weighting to each company so the index won't be dominated by meteoric success stories such as Amazon and Apple. In figure 2-5, you can see why I'm so confident that putting customers first does not come at the expense of investors.

The FREDSI consistently beat the stock market (using Vanguard's Total Stock Index as its benchmark).[8] Its annual returns exceeded 26 percent, which with compounding nearly tripled the stock market's cumulative TSR over the decade. To calibrate how remarkable the FREDSI's performance has been, consider this: the very best return across the universe of mutual funds and exchange traded funds tracked by Morningstar barely reached 19 percent over the decade, seven points lower than the

FREDSI. I asked leading private equity expert Steven Kaplan, professor at the University of Chicago's business school, how the FREDSI compared to funds in that sector. He confirmed that my 26 percent annual return outperformed the vast majority of private equity funds over that decade while avoiding the risky leverage and illiquidity inherent in those funds.[9]

Remember, we didn't build this index after the TSR results were already clear, through a backward-looking portfolio construction. We spotted customer-love winners up front based on their industry-leading NPS. The extraordinary performance of the FREDSI indicates that investors should welcome customer capitalism. You'll see even more evidence of this in chapter 5.

Back to the Apple Store: Defining Great Leadership

Now, let's return from the world of financial investments back into the personal world. I want to share one last story before we move on to chapter 3, which focuses on interacting with customers. Let's pick up where I left off, after my interview with Alice in the basement of the Boston Apple Store. I went back upstairs to the sales floor, where a team member interview was being videotaped for a training video. The interviewee, whom I'll call Janine, was asked to explain what made her happy working at Apple.

"I know it sounds pretty lame," Janine replied. "Enriching customer lives with technology products. But that's what we do here." She then told a story about an elderly customer whom she taught how to build an online store so the customer could display her artwork and process transactions at local art shows. That customer, obviously overwhelmed by all the confusing new technologies that seemed to be second nature to young people such as Janine, began her training session at the Apple Store. But the two of them—Janine and the artist—stuck with it. And in the weeks and months after her coaching session, that customer not only found it possible to earn a living through her art but also became the go-to expert among her artist colleagues—a resource who was sought out by young and old alike to help them sell their artwork online. She came back to the store to tell Janine how it had worked out, and Janine told the story to us.

I was standing behind the video camera next to the Boston store manager. As Janine wrapped up her inspiring story, the manager leaned over to me and confided, "This is what I like best about my job. When I see my team members getting recognized for enriching customers' lives, I ask myself, what better gift could I give my team, what could possibly be more rewarding as a leader?"

That neatly sums up the revelation of this chapter and a main focus of this book: leaders and organizations are great when they help team members lead great lives. That's the purpose that energizes *everybody* in the organization.

CHAPTER 3

Love Your Customers

The Quintessence of Customer Capitalism

Toward the end of my cancer treatments, I noticed an American Express sign posted at the cashier's station near the hospital discharge desk. The sign read: "We love our customers."

Love? *Really*? Is that how a business should feel about its customers?

My initial reaction was that some advertising copywriter had gone a little loopy. But upon deeper consideration, I have come to believe, yes, this is exactly the way a business should feel about its customers. Even the most hard-nosed businesses—those in the most ferociously competitive low-margin industries—need to love their customers, because in this age of customer capitalism, love offers the most resilient winning strategy.

Now, I readily admit that love can seem like a pretty ephemeral, abstract, and imprecise idea. For example, people use the same word, *love*, to describe the way they feel about their favorite ice cream, their country, their dachshund, their mother, and their spouse. So, for our purposes let me define the term: *Love is the state of caring so much for a person that most of your own happiness from the relationship derives from increasing that person's happiness and well-being.*

This kind of loving wisdom underpins the Golden Rule—"love thy neighbor as thyself"—which provides the foundation for all good relationships and good societies. I argue that it is also the kind of love that underpins good business. When you put overriding emphasis on enriching the lives of customers, those customers come to trust that you will act in their best interests. When you earn your customers' trust, they openly share their needs and vulnerabilities. They provide honest feedback, which helps you design and deliver optimal experiences. They integrate your products and services into their daily lives and thus depend on (and contribute to) your continued prosperity. They treat your employees with dignity and respect. These factors turbocharge your loyalty growth engine, accelerating you past the competition, using the most efficient and sustainable fuel ever invented: happy customers coming back for more and referring their friends.

In the case of American Express, this is demonstrably true. Its customers felt the love, which explains why American Express earned such stellar Net Promoter Scores over the years. My personal experience as an American Express customer has been excellent indeed. When I think of all the good things American Express has done for me—from providing a sufficiently large credit line that more than covers my international travel needs, protecting me from car rental firms thirsty for bad profits (American Express covers any insurance gaps, so I can waive all those overpriced insurance offerings), and protecting me in merchant disputes to helping me score dinner reservations at the hottest restaurants—I have to say that American Express has definitely enriched my life.

One airline is not the least bit shy about expressing its love. Southwest Airlines paints its heart logo on every plane and adopted the New York Stock Exchange trading symbol LUV—a bit of a play on words, since the airline was founded at Dallas's Love Field. But as Southwest's then president Colleen Barrett explained to me over lunch one day, this commitment to what she unabashedly called "love" was no marketing gimmick. In fact, it reflected the airline's core philosophy of living by the Golden Rule. To accentuate her point, Colleen gave me a big grandmotherly kiss in front of our NPS Loyalty Forum.[1] And to accentuate that point to all its passengers, Southwest avoids baggage fees, flight-change fees, and all the other exploitation tactics dreamed up by their less-loving competitors.

And consider the love gospel embodied by the Apple retail stores, as described in chapter 2. When Apple Store founder Ron Johnson designed those fabulously successful retail outlets, he was inspired by Jesus's advice to "Love thy neighbor as thyself," which Johnson considers to be the essential message of the Bible. He explained that his goal was to "design a store based on love." He proclaimed that purpose by printing it on every employee badge: "to enrich the lives of employees so they can enrich the lives of customers." Then he designed the operation to emphasize service and education above sales. To make sure customers were feeling loved, he invested in real-time customer feedback and avoided commission-driven compensation typical in electronics retailing.

The hotel giant Marriott International has been running TV ads for years asserting that "treating others like we'd like to be treated has always been our guiding principle." When I asked some of Marriott's senior executives to give me evidence that they were indeed serious about this commitment, they shared several illustrations of putting the Golden Rule into practice. For example, when business collapsed at many of Marriott's properties after the 9/11 terrorist attacks, many employees could not work enough hours to qualify for health insurance. Marriott's executives extended coverage to these employees, using the rationale that employees were like family—and you wouldn't let family members lose their health insurance for reasons completely beyond their control. The executives made a similar decision after two devastating hurricanes—Irma and Maria—struck Puerto Rico in 2017. Local employee disaster relief funds were quickly depleted, so the company stepped in and covered the shortfall.

The Golden Rule and customer love are relevant not just when disaster strikes. Far from the headlines and the public eye, for example, Marriott uses the Golden Rule in the design of its training programs. Frontline employees role-play a variety of challenging situations, such as the predicament presented by a guest at the pool whose children are acting up and annoying other guests. The trainer asks team members to imagine what it might feel like to be in that stressed-out parent's shoes. What can we do about it other than demand that the guest get the children under control or, worse, ask the offending family to leave the pool area? Together, the employees brainstorm solutions that might solve the problem in a way that would make the parent and the children feel good about themselves. Among the winning suggestions was offering a coloring book and a box of crayons to the bored child or offering to hold the baby, thereby giving Mom a chance to pay more attention to the older children.

But consistently living up to the Golden Rule isn't easy, especially for a public company for which the relentless drumbeat of quarterly profit reports tends to set the priorities. Marriott is a case in point. As I write this, the company along with other hotel brands is tangling with a group of state attorneys general, one of whom has filed a lawsuit challenging the industry's resort and destination fees as deceptive practices. Legislation has been introduced at the federal level to outlaw these noxious fees, which have become so widespread that even hotels in distinctly nonresort locations—such as Nebraska—charge them.

I encountered these annoying (and in my opinion deceptive) tariffs at one of Marriott's properties when I made a reservation online for a family vacation in the Caribbean. The website claimed that weekly charges would be $1,500. Once the rooms were booked, however, these extra fees ballooned the price to $2,300. I did not feel well loved at that moment!

One of Marriott's senior executives told a LinkedIn interviewer that this was a really tough issue: "None of us as consumers necessarily love it . . . [but] I don't think they are going away."

Well, actually, they *could* go away and sometimes do. One of my fellow board members at FirstService, Erin Wallace, once ran operations for Disney World in Orlando. I asked her if Disney charges these loathsome resort fees. After all, Disney World really does qualify as a resort, right? She said no, her Orlando operation didn't charge them. She also noted that the Disneyland Resort Hotels in California had levied resort fees for many years, but a new leadership team eliminated the fees. This pleased Erin a good deal, because she considered the practice to be a stain on Disney's brand and reputation.

So, here's my uncomfortable takeaway: When even outstanding companies such as Marriott and Disney struggle to stay out of these kinds of traps—bottom-line friendly and customer-hostile gambits—it must be impossible for more typical companies to live up to Golden Rule standards and consistently love their customers. After all, most companies utilize pricing algorithms that scientifically optimize revenues, never distinguishing between good and bad profits. The problem is that those artificial intelligence models can't fathom love—artificial or otherwise. They never incorporate the long-term costs of diminished customer trust and loyalty when those customers feel unloved. Nor do they take into account the long-term effects on the dispirited employees who are compelled to enforce these unloving policies. It would be depressing indeed if the accelerating shift toward digital interaction portends a darker era, a digital winter in which love is no longer relevant.

Love in the Digital Era

Fortunately, as I'll demonstrate below, the Golden Rule and customer love remain vitally important even as automation overtakes the world. But in the mad rush to digitize customer interactions and replace expensive employees with efficient bots, some firms are herding their customers toward a bleak and soulless digital journey.

Imagine a dystopian world run by profit-seeking drones, bots, algorithms, and predictive models. As human service is replaced by digital frontlines, how can leaders ensure that their customers feel loved? Bain's NPS Prism data indicates that 80 percent of today's US bank transactions are now automated or digital, further isolating bank executives from their customers. The theory is that big-data analytical tools enable executives to understand their customers—and indeed, some of these data tools are most helpful in predicting why a customer is behaving like a Promoter, a Passive, or a Detractor.

But here's the hard truth: Only when this data is effectively combined with the voice of the customer and the voice of frontline employees can customer-loving leaders build winning solutions. So, the question becomes how to best integrate NPS feedback with big data to keep leaders connected to customer needs and concerns. We can learn from some excellent role models that have successfully combined the best elements of digital with human warmth, empathy, and personalization, companies such as Warby Parker, Chewy, Peloton, and Airbnb. These are cutting-edge, technology-rich companies that still nurture communities with humanity in which customer love and the Golden Rule still guide decision making.

Warby Parker, the digital purveyor of custom eyeglasses (with more than 120 stores aimed at augmenting their customers' digital experience) puts the Golden Rule at the top of its list of stakeholder priorities: "We treat customers the way they'd like to be treated—with warmth, helpfulness, empathy, and incredible service." I asked co-CEO (and cofounder) Dave Gilboa how the company measures progress against this lofty standard. He agreed with my notion that to bring vitality to a purpose you must be able to measure progress toward it, and he explained how they do that at Warby Parker: "We measure our Net Promoter Score. We want to build a brand that customers love, and that score helps us understand the long-term health of our brand—and the company."

Another element of the company's love strategy is to provide free eyeglasses to those in need. The company distributes a free pair of brand-new glasses for every one purchased by a paying customer—more than eight million pairs, to date, which are now helping disadvantaged school children to see their books and blackboards and enabling vision-handicapped workers to perform their jobs. Warby's strategy of love and charity—which I'll return to in subsequent chapters—has resulted in a remarkable digital-era success story. Only ten years after its founding, investors now value this privately held company at $3 billion.

What other compelling examples of digital companies building customer relationships full of meaning and engagement are out there? Consider online pet supply retailer Chewy, which proclaims, "At Chewy, we love pets and pet parents. We view pets as family and are obsessed with serving pet parents by meeting all of their needs and exceeding expectations through every interaction."

Operating without stores—and therefore with no face-to-face customer interactions—Chewy has had to be inventive. The emotional connection begins with the search bar on Chewy's website, which once said "Find the Best for Your Pet." To ensure those "best for your pet" items get delivered fast, Chewy built and stocked eight fulfillment centers spread across the United States. Chewy's interactions with customers on the phone and the web are viewed not as costs to be eliminated but instead as opportunities to wow. So, the company staffs those eight centers 24/7/365 with reps who love pets. Chewy even built a large internal wow team responsible for dreaming up and executing remarkably thoughtful and kind solutions. As only one compelling example, the team often sends flowers to a bereaved owner when a pet passes away.

This customer-love strategy is no secret. In fact, Chewy published it for all to see in its 2019 SEC filing in preparation for its initial public offering.[2] "We strive to provide exceptional service every time (*customers*) interact with us," that filing said. "Our highly trained and passionate customer service representatives ('CSRs') are available to provide the type of tailored, knowledgeable service and guidance that customers can usually find only at the highest quality neighborhood pet stores. Our high-quality service and customer satisfaction are demonstrated by our Net Promoter Score, which we have calculated to be 86 for fiscal year 2018."[3] Superior NPS provides evidence the customers are feeling the love—as does the firm's rapid growth, which has resulted in a market cap now exceeding $30 billion.

Peloton provides another illuminating example of how a digital platform can earn customer love. Peloton's mission is to use technology and design to "connect the world through fitness, empowering people to be the best version of themselves anywhere, anytime." Well, that sounds pretty loving to me. At the top of its list of core values is *put members first*. When asked by the *New York Times* to explain how the firm so quickly amassed legions of loyal fans, CEO and cofounder John Foley said, "We've created an experience that people just love so deeply."[4]

The *New York Times* provided this analysis: "Peloton does not sell just a simple piece of hardware. Instead, the company spent tens of millions of dollars creating an inviting experience, complete with brand-ambassador celebrities and high-end retail locations."[5] I have heard from a surprising number of Peloton community members that their experience has been more than life-enriching; it has been life-changing. And by the way, the company's market cap now exceeds $25 billion, despite the costly challenges of the firm's safety-related recall of its treadmill product.

Finally, Airbnb provides another compelling example of how a thoughtfully designed digital platform can empower a worldwide community—in this case, of guests and hosts. To emphasize the central role of love and Golden Rule treatment, the founders of Airbnb wove the love theme into the firm's heart-shaped logo. Founded by Brian Chesky, Nathan Blecharczyk, and Joe Gebbia in 2008, the online platform has transformed the travel industry (Airbnb's US listings today represent about 20 percent of lodging industry capacity). Sure, Airbnb utilizes bots and algorithms, but they contribute to the creation of a community of hosts who treat their guests with loving care. In fact, prior to the Covid-19 pandemic, the firm organized gatherings of local hosts to help them share tips for delighting guests—for example, the smell of just-baked chocolate chip cookies almost always makes guests feel most welcome.

The platform now claims more than 4 million hosts and 150 million users.[6] Investors have been impressed by all this love; Airbnb's market value also exceeds $90 billion, despite the collapse in travel volume due to the pandemic.

Love, Costco Style

Now let's spend a day with another company where I had my eyes opened: Costco Wholesale Corporation, the enormously successful Washington-based chain of warehouse clubs.

MIT-Sloan professor Zeynep Ton generously arranged some time in her office for me with Jim Sinegal, Costco's cofounder and longtime CEO. Then we joined Ton's classroom session, which that day featured a discussion with Jim, who was accompanied by the store manager and the butcher department manager of Costco's Waltham, Massachusetts, outlet. After the class we joined the students on a field trip out to the Waltham store, where Sinegal led us on a guided tour.

In the course of preparing for my time with Jim, I had reviewed some old stock analysts' reports I had filed away back when we originally discovered that Costco had earned the highest NPS rating in retailing. Those analysts roundly criticized Costco for paying too much to its frontline employees and for setting the prices for its goods too low. So, it seemed fair to ask Jim about those criticisms and, more generally, how he felt about Wall Street's relentless focus on profits. "Fred," he said, "if you try to run a business following advice from Wall Street, you won't be in business very long."

Jim went on to elaborate on the theme: "Our first responsibility is to obey the law. Our next responsibility is to our customers. After that, we take care of our employees, and we respect our suppliers." Not until he got to the end of this list did he mention his shareholders. "The shareholders are last in line?" I asked, eyebrows slightly raised. "Yes," Jim responded without hesitation. "But keep in mind, too, that since we went public in 1985, our total shareholder returns have far exceeded those of the S&P 500."[7] "Our culture is our most important asset," he continued. "It's based on doing the right thing. Put yourself in the member's shoes. Be *fair*."

How does Costco prosper by doing the right thing? Part of the answer lies in the company's membership model. Annual membership fees essentially lock in the firm's required profits at the beginning of each year. With that foundation in place, every subsequent decision can be taken with an eye toward maximizing love for customers. Sinegal noted that Amazon, Costco's Washington neighbor, had copied the Costco membership approach with Amazon Prime: one of the biggest success stories in Amazon's pretty spectacular history.

Here is one of the stories Jim shared in Ton's classroom. The story has two chapters. First, Costco's buyers negotiated a great deal on Calvin Klein jeans. The retailer followed its long-standing pricing policy of marking up everything 14 percent except its private label Kirkland brand, which gets marked up 15 percent. This policy not only minimizes complexity in running the store but also earns trust from customers, who can rely on Costco never to play games through high-low pricing and promotion gimmicks. Well, the price that Costco negotiated on the Calvin Klein jeans was so low that the standard 14 percent markup translated into a retail price of $29.99. Since these same jeans were priced at $59.99 at major retailers, Costco's jeans sold like hotcakes and quickly disappeared from the shelves.

Then Costco learned that an additional one million pairs of jeans were available because a foreign buyer's letter of credit failed, and Calvin Klein now needed to find another outlet. This time the Costco buyers negotiated an even lower price, which made possible a retail price of $22.99, including the standard 14 percent markup. The sages of Wall Street got wind of this and began complaining that Costco's management was acting irresponsibly. The stores had already sold out the product at $29.99. So, why not price this new lot at *least* at $29.99 and keep the extra $7 per pair to boost profits? The autopilot policy of 14 percent markups, the sages complained, was leaving at least $7 million on the table.

Jim stuck to his guns. Later in that MIT classroom he offered this explanation: "Our members trust us to pass along every saving to the customer," he said. "Any exception to this—well, it would be like taking heroin. Once you start it, you can't stop doing it. And it would change the whole nature of the company."

Then, Professor Ton, whose book *The Good Jobs Strategy* closely aligns with my own thinking, asked Jim, "So why not take that extra $7 million and increase employee compensation?"[8]

Sinegal responded that Costco already has one of the best compensation programs in retailing, with average hourly pay running at around $24.[9] If employees saw their company flouting the 14 percent markup rule, he said, they'd know it wasn't truly committed to always doing the best thing for its members. The Motley Fool once asked Jim to define "competitive advantage" and to identify Costco's biggest competitive advantage. His answer: "Well, the competitive advantage is that you've got loyal customers who believe in you."[10] And—I would add, by extension—you have employees who believe in your customer-centric mission.

My family and I love doing business at Costco. It's fun to discover remarkable bargains at the store. Costco's returns policy is incredibly generous. My daughter once purchased a two-pack of electric toothbrushes. One failed to work correctly, so she brought it back to the store. She was pessimistic about her chances because she had thrown away the receipt. Not to worry, said the woman at the service desk; Costco maintains digital purchase records for every member. She found the transaction on her computer, credited the full purchase price, and told my daughter to keep the second toothbrush if it was working correctly.

What else does Costco do for our loyalty? I bought a fire table from Costco.com in preparation for outdoor socializing during the Covid-19 winter. When I noticed its price dropped by $150 the following month, I went online and requested a $150 credit—which Costco issued within a few days. When we travel, we use Costco's travel service because it not only guarantees the best rates but also protects us from nuisance fees such as car rental extra-driver charges. Our daughter bought her honeymoon trip to Bora Bora through Costco. Last and certainly not least, we also invested in Costco stock many years ago, and that has turned out to be a very good decision.

Jim Sinegal retired as CEO in 2012. It's certainly fair to ask if Costco is still living the same moral philosophy today in his wake. A recent annual report provides this update: "Our unwavering 'do the right thing' philosophy led us to another strong year." No surprise here. If you add up all our family purchases from Costco and Amazon, the NPS leaders in retailing, you would find there is not much budget left over for the rest of the retailing industry—where, unfortunately, love is often hard to find.

Discover-ing Love

Discover Financial Services unexpectedly popped up on my radar screen when it surpassed American Express for NPS leadership in the credit card industry—not just once but several years in a row.

Why was this a surprise? Well, I had been an American Express customer for more than forty years. I knew American Express as a most formidable company with a stellar track record of earning customer loyalty. How could it have slipped a couple of points behind this relative upstart, Discover?

I had no direct experience with Discover as a customer, but I certainly had noticed its TV advertisements. Those spots depicted a humorous interaction between one of the company's phone-service representatives and a customer, with the roles being played by lookalike actors. The tag line—*we treat you like you'd treat you*—pretty much paraphrases the Golden Rule in updated language. As I began my research into this relatively new (to me) NPS superstar, I went back through some old annual reports. Here is what I found in the 2011 statement from the CEO:

> At Discover, everything we do starts with a focus on the customer. . . .
>
> When it comes to customer service, our approach is very different from companies that regard service primarily as an expense. In contrast, we regard customer interactions as opportunities to strengthen relationships, reinforce rewards, encourage usage, and build loyalty.
>
> Great customer service starts with hiring the right employees, training and developing them, and then engaging customers in meaningful conversations. Customer service for our

cardmembers is handled 100% by Discover employees at U.S. locations, which we regard as a competitive advantage. We have also invested to ensure cardmembers have the best online experience in the industry. Our goal is to serve customers any time, any place, and in any way they want to interact with us.

I noticed a familiar name at the bottom of that statement. David Nelms had been a member of one of my early Bain teams—a standout talent who contributed to some of our original loyalty economics research many years ago. I reconnected with David shortly before he retired after fourteen years as Discover's CEO. As we talked, it became very clear that "we treat you like you'd treat you" is much more than an advertising slogan; in fact, it anchors many of Discover's decisions and priorities. I asked David for some examples that would illustrate how Discover put customer interests first. Specifically, I wanted to know if Discover so loved its customers that it had minimized or even eliminated the kinds of abuses that are so widespread in the credit card industry. He responded by citing the following facts:

- Discover was the first major card company to completely do away with annual fees—on every one of its cards. If profit is your sole motivator, then an annual fee makes sense, but if your purpose is treating customers right, then such a fee is counterproductive.

- Discover eliminated breakage for rewards, so customer points are never wasted. "Breakage" is industry lingo for rewards or rebates that customers have qualified for but don't get used before their expiration date. Many loyalty programs are designed so that up to half of the value of the points earned by customers never gets redeemed, the logic being that marketers can entice customers with rewards worth twice the apparent value if only half will ever get redeemed. Discover banned this sneaky, anticustomer manipulation.

- As David Nelms's annual report introduction emphasized, all Discover customer service is handled by employees based in the United States. By the time of our conversation, most competitors had either outsourced customer service to third-party vendors or offshored their servicing to low-wage locations such as India or the Philippines. Discover had tested offshore resources and learned that while costs declined, so did the quality of service experienced by their customers, most of whom live in the United States and prefer the cultural familiarity and language skills of US-based employees.

- Discover makes enormous investments to develop effective digital solutions for the simple customer interactions, thus reducing call volumes, which frees up employees armed with outstanding support systems and training to deliver great service on those remaining complex situations.

- Service reps are encouraged to explain all options clearly so customers can choose the best solution for them rather than something that might be more profitable to the company.[11]

- It is easy to reach a human for customer service twenty-four hours a day, seven days a week, and the relevant phone numbers are prominently displayed on Discover's web pages and in its literature. Some competitors try to steer customers into lower-cost digital solutions by hiding these phone numbers. Discover lets the customer choose but continuously upgrades digital options so they become preferable to customers, especially for simpler interactions.

- Discover sends customers an email the day before they incur late fees so customers can avoid a penalty for simply losing track of the date.[12] David said that he got pushback on this decision from his CFO, who warned that late fee revenues would decline by $200 million annually, but David overruled that objection as profits-first thinking.

- The first late fee is automatically waived for new customers.

- Discover was the first to offer a free "freeze-it" function (through phone, online, or via its phone app) to stop unauthorized charges against lost or stolen cards and also offers free alerts to help card members protect their identity.

- Discover monitors the dark web for abuses of customers' Social Security numbers and offers free alerts to customers whenever a new account is opened in their name.

- FICO credit scores are provided free (without affecting a person's credit score), right there on the customer's statement, online, and on the mobile app; there is no irksome thicket of promotional gimmicks to click through.

- Information on factors that might improve one's credit score is provided for free.

- Discover does not sell bad debts to collection agencies, even after they become total charge-offs. As David asked rhetorically, "You wouldn't do that to a family member, right?"

I'll stop there, but you get the idea. No wonder Discover earns the highest Net Promoter Scores in the credit card industry. Kate Manfred—recently promoted to chief marketing officer and a seasoned financial services exec—offers this perspective: "The culture here is really unique. We start with the consumer and solve for their needs—not our profit targets. I've been in a lot of boardrooms where the P&L is the ultimate objective. Here, caring for our customers' happiness and well-being is the ultimate objective."

Kate recalled her surprise when she attended her first annual planning meeting at Discover. At most companies, she explained, people are asked to put forward ideas and proposals that are then assessed in terms of how profitable they might be. At Discover, the ranking system is very different: "Instead of proposals being ranked based on how much money they could make us, our teams prioritized the things that would most delight customers or fix things that most bothered customers. Then we'd try to figure out how to make those investments affordable."

Current CEO Roger Hochschild reinforced this notion, noting that Discover's executive team had recently become intrigued by the services provided by a company called LifeLock. For a hefty fee, LifeLock protects its customers against the growing threat of identity theft and fraud. "But we didn't set out to exploit our customer fears and then sell those services at a high price," Roger told me. "Instead, we tried to figure out how many of those features we could offer our customers for free."

At this point, I'm picturing two crowds of people running in opposite directions. One comprises my readers, some of whom are probably rushing to fill out applications for Discover cards. (They won't be alone; roughly 20 percent of all US households already have one.) The other crowd consists of potential investors running for the nearest exit. How can all this love for customers—I hear them asking—possibly leave sufficient scraps of value for shareholders?

Well, this is one more example of the economics of loyalty overwhelming traditional financial thinking. "Fred," David reminded me in one of our conversations, "you and I both know that loyal customers far outperform their FICO scores."[13] In other words, loyal customers are *far more profitable* to the companies whose products or services they purchase than the standard risk models might indicate.

Let's dig deeper. The cash-generating assets of a credit card business, like most businesses, are customers. When customers put your credit card on top in their wallet and therefore spend more with it, those assets increase in value. Add to that higher retention rates—which means you have no leaky bucket for marketing to refill through expensive promotions and acquisition campaigns—and lower credit losses than the relevant FICO scores might predict, and you end up with *far better financial outcomes* than Wall Street would otherwise expect. The upshot is that from 2011 through 2020, Discover generated the highest total shareholder return (TSR) in the industry—85 percent greater than the Vanguard Total Stock Market Index Fund (VTI).

In figure 3-1, I've ranked the TSR for the largest US credit card players and compared them to the TSR for Vanguard's VTI. Credit card revenues dominate the business mix of Discover and American Express but account for smaller portions of the other players. Stock performance is the result of each firm's entire portfolio of businesses. But the pattern you see here will be repeated throughout this book in a variety of industries. Leading NPS players in each industry usually deliver the best returns to shareholders, and only the handful of players with superior Net Promoter Scores manage to beat the stock market average reflected by Vanguard's VTI.

FIGURE 3-1

Only NPS leaders beat the stock market average (VTI)

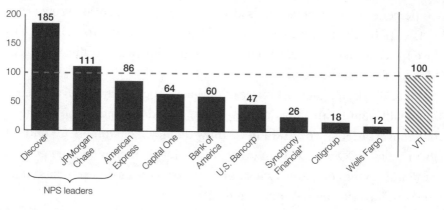

Cumulative total shareholder return indexed vs. Vanguard Total Stock Market Index (VTI)
(1/1/2011–12/31/2020)

Source: CaplQ

*Synchrony: TSR since IPO for the period 1/8/2014–12/31/2020; VTI represents the Vanguard Total Stock Market ETF (ARCA:VTI).

Love in the Age of Smartphones

If you went looking for an industry that is almost completely addicted to sneaky and abusive "hotel resort fees"–style charges, you'd have to consider mobile telephony providers.

While many of these bad practices have since been acknowledged and rectified, for years customers regularly encountered big and unpleasant surprises when they opened their monthly bills. For example, roaming fees could run into many hundreds of dollars on top of the standard monthly contract fees. My provider finally offered a roaming-protection plan, of sorts, so that when I travel outside the United States I pay "only" $10 a day on top of my normal charges. Yes, this is certainly better than the highway-robbery rates I had been hit with previously, but it still seems pretty aggressive—even abusive. My standard unlimited usage plan costs $45 per month, or $1.50 a day, so $10 daily represents a 667 percent markup! If I travel outside the United States on a thirty-day

FIGURE 3-2

John Legere's customer-love strategy ignited T-Mobile growth

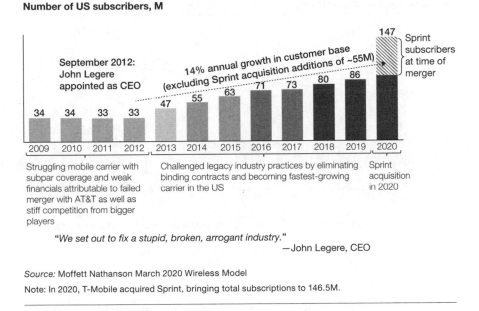

Number of US subscribers, M

September 2012:
John Legere
appointed as CEO

14% annual growth in customer base
(excluding Sprint acquisition additions of ~55M)

147 — Sprint subscribers at time of merger

| 34 | 34 | 33 | 33 | 47 | 55 | 63 | 71 | 73 | 80 | 86 | |
| 2009 | 2010 | 2011 | 2012 | 2013 | 2014 | 2015 | 2016 | 2017 | 2018 | 2019 | 2020 |

Struggling mobile carrier with
subpar coverage and weak
financials attributable to failed
merger with AT&T as well as
stiff competition from bigger
players

Challenged legacy industry practices by eliminating
binding contracts and becoming fastest-growing
carrier in the US

Sprint
acquisition
in 2020

"We set out to fix a stupid, broken, arrogant industry."
—John Legere, CEO

Source: Moffett Nathanson March 2020 Wireless Model

Note: In 2020, T-Mobile acquired Sprint, bringing total subscriptions to 146.5M.

---

extended trip, my monthly bill runs $345 instead of $45. Hmmm. This does not make me feel loved.

Fortunately, along came T-Mobile. In 2013, T-Mobile purchased MetroPCS. Then the combined company invested to upgrade its network and proceeded to modify or abandon every one of its industry standard anti-customer policies, one after another. By so doing, T-Mobile demonstrated to customers how it felt to be loved—and the market responded. The company's impressive growth since then is illustrated in figure 3-2.

Another way to measure the success of former CEO John Legere's customer-centric strategy is to track the company's NPS improvement relative to competitors'. Figure 3-3 illustrates the impressive rise in T-Mobile's Net Promoter Score, which surged from the back of the pack in 2013 to industry leadership by 2020.

That dramatic climb to leadership—34 points over five years—is a truly remarkable accomplishment. I asked Callie Field, a sixteen-year T-Mobile veteran who is currently executive vice president and chief customer

FIGURE 3-3

T-Mobile NPS improved from worst to first

Wireless provider NPS (2013–2020)

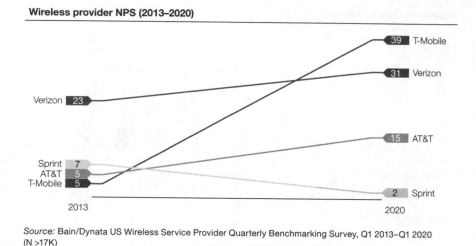

Source: Bain/Dynata US Wireless Service Provider Quarterly Benchmarking Survey, Q1 2013–Q1 2020 (N >17K)

experience officer, how the company managed to achieve this leadership ranking. She explained, "When John Legere came on board, our position was precarious. Our network was weak, our technology lagged the competition, and our customer churn was the worst in the industry. We saw no other option. We decided we were going to love our customers better than anyone else." Legere traveled around the country, visiting with frontline employees in the stores and customer service centers and asking what T-Mobile could do to make its customers happier—and also what the company could do to make it easier for its reps to deliver a great customer experience. He took good ideas home to his chief marketing officer, Mike Sievert (recently promoted to CEO as Legere's successor) and Callie, who together designed what Callie describes as "our Un-carrier revolution." The list of customer-loving enhancements is impressive:

- T-Mobile radically simplified its rate plans—including simple unlimited plans on all devices—and also offered simplified plans for business customers.

- T-Mobile dropped contracts that locked customers into their carriers.

- T-Mobile made upgrades easier and offered no-contract family plans.

- All international roaming charges were removed. (Ahhh!)

- T-Mobile purchased and swapped high-quality blocks of spectrum capacity to improve network performance.

- T-Mobile began offering a host of attractive freebies, including a free iPhone, free music streaming, and free in-flight calling and texting with Gogo.

- T-Mobile implemented an automatic rollover of unused data and introduced a simplified rewards program built on the principle of no points breakage.

- T-Mobile eliminated resort fee–style billing tricks whereby an advertised $40 unlimited plan might balloon up to $50 on the customer's monthly statement as a result of hidden taxes and fees. In other words, T-Mobile's advertised price incorporates all taxes and fees so that—absent any changes requested by you—your invoice is the same as the advertised price of your package.

- T-Mobile reorganized its service centers into a team of experts to better serve specific customer segments, ensuring that customers are handled by the same team whenever they call, thereby improving continuity and quality of service.

- And finally, those local teams began closing the loop with customers, contacting every Detractor to learn what went wrong and how to solve those problems.

T-Mobile cleverly started referring to itself as the "Un-carrier," and this list of bold actions suggests that it earned the nickname. Simply stated, T-Mobile abandoned just about every abusive policy its industry ever invented. Not only were these radical changes good for customers, but they also set the stage for happier employees.[14]

You can probably anticipate my last paragraph in this section. This long list of simplifications, freebies, and givebacks must have hurt T-Mobile's returns to investors, right? Well, no. The hidden economic forces of loyalty absolutely overwhelmed traditional financial analysis, rooted as it is

FIGURE 3-4

T-Mobile wins for investors (industry's top TSR)

Cumulative total shareholder return (1/1/2014–12/31/2019)

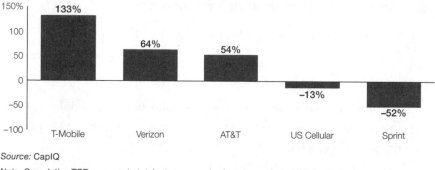

Source: CapIQ

Note: Cumulative TSR represents total return assuming investment from 1/1/2014–12/31/2019; 2019 is used as the end year due to T-Mobile's acquisition of Sprint in 2020.

in the outdated financial-capitalism paradigm. In figure 3-4, you can see that from the end of 2013 through the end of 2019, T-Mobile's TSR of 133 percent was by far the best in its industry.

Love Is PURE

One afternoon after I had delivered a keynote at an insurance industry conference, an audience member approached me and asked if I knew about PURE Insurance, a relatively new company that closely adhered to my loyalty-based principles. I was skeptical but reached out to my broker, who confirmed that PURE was a very special company. The more I learned, the more I understood that PURE was indeed my kind of company—and I have since switched all of my policies to PURE and recommend the company to my friends.

What was the story, here? PURE's founders saw a substantial segment of risk-averse, relatively high–net worth customers who required multiple lines of coverage for home, auto, umbrella, and so forth and were being overcharged and underserved by existing carriers. CEO Ross Buchmueller structured the firm to maximize value to policyholders (PURE refers to customers/policyholders as members, similar to Costco). Pricing included a surplus contribution to create a capital pool that reduced reliance on outside investors, a bit like the mutual structure utilized by Vanguard and USAA. This enabled PURE to focus completely on delivering a truly exceptional experience.

PURE then coached its members on what steps they should take to protect themselves and their property—for example, by installing backup generators, water shut-off devices, burglar alarms, and so on. In my case, PURE helped me find the best generator supplier to equip my home on Cape Cod—where we often lose electricity during storms—and helped negotiate the best price and then reduced my premium substantially once the generator was installed. Why? To help me reduce my risks and my premiums and make me feel *loved*.

Members love this approach. In-force premiums have grown to more than $1 billion. The majority of the company's new members are the result of referrals from existing customers. (Again, more word-of-mouth comments means fewer advertising dollars required, plus referred customers generate lower losses.) PURE's member retention rate is a staggering *96 percent*. Insurance industry experts will appreciate how amazing an accomplishment this represents—high-growth companies adding lots of new customers (which typically have the highest rates of defection) almost never see these retention rates.

As a rule, even among committed NPS companies, annual reports and self-reported scores are not the best place to get a bead on how deeply a company embraces NPS. While many firms mention NPS somewhere in the chairman's letter, they reveal little about the process used to gather the information, their calculation methodology, or how they intend to improve. PURE, by contrast, regularly devotes two full pages in its annual report to its customer NPS, which has been steadily rising over the past few years to its current very impressive 71 percent. Rather than simply charting the historical NPS, PURE reports NPS ratings by tenure, customer segment, whether the member has filed a claim, whether members receive policies and bills electronically, product line, and so on. PURE explains how it gathers NPS feedback and how the method has changed (in 2019, for example, PURE shifted from an annual blast of surveys to surveying a rotating 25 percent of its customers each quarter). PURE also details the innovations that were introduced based on feedback from the NPS survey including, for example, more logical pricing on high limits of umbrella coverage, a new type of fraud coverage that also covers instances of cyberfraud, and higher sublimits on jewelry in the basic homeowner's policy.

Last year, as I filled out the Net Promoter Survey that I received from the company, I lodged a small complaint. I explained that I loved the company but was unhappy that its pricing for my auto coverage was slightly higher than that of my previous insurer. In response, I received this message:

> **From:** *Mary Loyal Springs*
> **Sent:** *Wednesday, May 1, 2019 10:29 AM*
> **To:** *Reichheld, Fred <Fred.Reichheld@Bain.com>*
> **Subject:** *PURE Insurance NPS Comment 483680743919*
>
> *Good morning Mr. Reichheld,*
>
> *Thank you for taking the time to fill out our annual NPS survey earlier this week. The feedback from this survey helps us understand what we are doing well, but more importantly, where we can improve.*
>
> *I noticed that you made a comment regarding PURE offering competitive coverage for your automobiles. I would recommend that you contact your broker to requote this line of business, because if it was moved to us, you would be eligible to receive companion discounts on your homeowner's policy. I did a quick quote in our system and am quoting annual savings of almost $800 annualized. Perhaps if we aren't exactly competitive on the auto, the savings on the home would make it worth the move— coupled with the convenience of also consolidating your insurance to one carrier.*
>
> *If there is anything I can do to assist you, or answer any questions you have about PURE, please do not hesitate to reach out.*
>
> *Thank you for your business and continued loyalty.*
> *Kind regards,*
>
> **Mary Loyal Springs** *VP, Member Experience*
> *701 E. Bay St., Suite 312, Charleston, SC 29403*

Not a form letter, an email blast, or a robocall: an actual response from a human! I was so impressed that I called Mary Loyal Springs on her direct line, using the number she provided.[15] She agreed to look into some of the NPS data I had seen in PURE's annual report, which revealed that one of the biggest improvements in NPS results occurs when customers renew at their fifth anniversary of joining the PURE family.[16] Why? One reason is that PURE favors its most loyal members by including a reduction in their insurance costs at that point so that customers who stay longer get a really good deal—roughly a 10 percent reduction in my case and about $850 for PURE's typical customer.

When Mary Loyal called me back—again, does that surprise you?—she confirmed that these loyal-over-the-long-term customers are still more profitable than the average customer, despite the reduced coverage costs they enjoy.[17] She further revealed that PURE developed an additional loyalty reward: members who have been with the company for ten years or more are eligible for annual cash distributions, further reducing their coverage costs.

And with evident pride, Mary Loyal volunteered that PURE was so deeply committed to rewarding customer loyalty that the company had published a treatise on pricing principles so that future generations of actuaries couldn't easily undo these policies and backslide to more typical industry practices. She included a link to an online posting of these pricing principles, which I visited. Here are some highlights:

- We will price to achieve long-term sustainability, not to maximize profit.

- Those who deserve a lower rate should receive one.

- We will never charge a new member less than we charge a renewing member with the same risk characteristics.

- If we ever have to raise rates significantly, we will ask regulators to allow us to immediately increase rates for new members and phase in the increase over time for existing members whenever possible.

- We must remember that loyalty is rewarded at PURE. . . . Regardless of their popularity in our industry, we will not use special incentives that offer new members a lower price than an existing member.

- We will be transparent with members regarding changes to their premium.

Can an insurance company love its customers? Obviously, yes. PURE has enriched my life. Since PURE is not a public company, we can't use TSR to demonstrate the economic superiority of its growth engine, but there is a clear signal indicating that industry insiders have been impressed. PURE was acquired by industry giant Tokio Marine in the first quarter of 2020. CEO Satoru Komiya explained the seemingly high $3.1 billion price, which was thirty-three times PURE's forecasted 2020 profit. "We are paying for PURE's big potential growth," he said.[18]

And I would explain that growth potential with two words: customer love.

Are You Feeling Loved?

The companies in this chapter and others like them earn primarily good profits—what I define as profits earned from Promoters: those customers who feel the love. These companies are customer capitalists, meaning that they love their customers and view adequate profitability as a requirement for sustainability. Their growth engines, fueled by love, run smoothly, cleanly, and efficiently. Love yields superior retention/repeat purchases, expanded share of wallet, new customers via referrals, and lower costs resulting from happy customers with fewer complaints and problems to solve.

And then there are all those other companies, the ones that embrace old-school financial capitalist thinking. They operate inefficient growth engines that are fueled by customer acquisition, and—to extend the metaphor—belch pollution in the form of disaffected customers and jaded employees who either defect or look for ways to settle grudges as they prepare for their eventual defections. These firms have to *buy* their growth and their profits. They overpay (or underprice) for new customers and underinvest in (or overcharge and underlove) loyal customers. The resulting churn is the enemy of efficiency and explains why so many firms struggle to achieve sustainable, profitable growth. They simply don't understand that sustainable growth will not happen without customer love. To prop up accounting earnings, they become addicted to what I call bad profits.

I called out these noxious practices in my previous books, but the truth is that bad profits remain commonplace. In fact, all too many companies continue to innovate new and creative forms of customer abuse. I've already discussed so-called resort fees imposed by hotels in locations that are decidedly not resorts.[19] But how about those car rental companies, first mentioned in the introduction during my discussion of Enterprise Rent-A-Car's business model? Not everybody has followed Enterprise's lead! Return your car thirty minutes late and you risk getting charged a whopping penalty. Thinking about having your spouse share the driving? Get ready to pay an additional driver fee. If you happen to encounter a toll road, get ready to fork over outrageous fees for electronic toll-payment devices. Rent a car for a week, encounter a single toll on a single day, and you'll get charged as much as a $7 device fee for *every day* of the seven-day rental period! And I'm sure you've noticed that car rental firms continue to turn refilling gas tanks into a game of roulette, where the odds are always stacked against the customer. Firms skillfully craft plans to ensure that the house wins: customers either pay for a full tank—and receive no benefit for fuel remaining at the end of the rental—or opt for the plan whereby they must refill the tank, and when they inevitably forget or bad traffic leaves no time to stop for a fill-up on their return trip, the rental firms charge three times the going market rate to top off the tank.

What else?

My former bank became addicted to bad profits. For example, when I ordered replacement checks at my longtime bank at the same branch I had used for more than thirty years, I noticed that the fee for these checks, which used to be free, had ballooned to $120. I was complaining about it to my youngest son that evening, and he told me that Costco offers replacement checks for any bank. So, I promptly cancelled the check reorder through my bank website and ordered the identical checks through Costco's website for a grand total of $14. Incidentally, Costco used the same check-printing company to fulfill the order as my bank.

I decided to go find another bank, which I soon did.

The bank from which I defected—the one with the $120 checks—hasn't even noticed yet that I'm gone. I represent one of its legions of hidden defectors. I'm still technically a customer. To retain access to my historic spending and bill-paying records, I left some money in the account—just enough to cover any legacy transactions and avoid any minimum balance fees. That bank wouldn't have to hire a detective to figure out what's going on. The number of my transactions through the old account has plummeted, my paycheck is no longer deposited there, and I no longer use that institution's ATMs. Yet I haven't heard a peep from them. That bank is currently running a big ad campaign and spending big money to stress its dedication to earning customer loyalty and trust. Good luck with that!

You heard about First Republic Bank in the preface and will hear more about its superior NPS results in future chapters. For now, let's just say that when I learned that First Republic had a branch in my neighborhood, I switched my business there, and life has been so much better ever since. The woman I deal with at the branch actually watches out for my best interests. When an automatic salary deposit failed, for example, she emailed to warn me that I would be charged a fee for insufficient funds and then helped to arrange a wire transfer from my brokerage that came through within twenty-four hours, sparing me that expense.

Imagine, a bank looking out for you so you can avoid fees! That's so much better than imposing an unreasonable fee and then forgiving the fee if the customer calls to complain. In truth, most customers eventually give up on phoning (because the bank ensures that it's too much of a hassle). Those aggrieved customers still resent those fees, though. That resentment builds and builds, and then an ATM doesn't work or something else bad happens, and at last the relationship ruptures. The aggrieved customer leaves. Maybe the bank notices, maybe not. Probably not.

Let's be truthful. One reason why customers get such bad service today is that they *tolerate* it. Sure, it can be uncomfortable to complain about bad profits, and sometimes it takes time and effort to switch suppliers. But unless you push back, you are guilty of enabling these bad practices and should feel partially responsible when the next customer in line gets similarly mistreated. I can't believe that I waited so long to switch banks; now, I kick myself for having been so lazy. Shame on us customers for settling, continuing to do business with firms that do not love us and never will. We are wasting precious moments of our time on Earth. We deserve better—and we can find it by searching out the suppliers earning the most enthusiastic recommendations from friends and family.

And my advice to business leaders: make sure you are building that kind of company.

CHAPTER 4

Inspire Your Teams

To Embrace a Life of Meaning and Service

Stop wasting our time, Romney. There is precisely *zero* probability that Bain Consulting can avoid bankruptcy."

That's what the Goldman Sachs adviser told Mitt Romney thirty years ago during the negotiations Mitt was leading in an attempt to rescue our consulting firm, then teetering on the brink. In the years preceding the crisis, a group of lenders had financed a founder-led employee stock ownership plan based on a lofty valuation, enabling the founders to pull more than $100 million out of the firm. And now the bottom was falling out.

We heard this sobering news from Mitt during an emergency Saturday morning partner meeting in the boardroom at Bain & Company's headquarters in Boston's Back Bay.

I suspect that the Goldman representative's language was actually far more colorful and that Mitt, being the good Mormon that he is, toned it down as he retold the story to us. I also suspect that the banker failed to understand that Mitt relished a seemingly impossible challenge and that advising him to throw in the towel would only push him in the opposite direction. For his Mormon mission service, for example, Mitt gamely accepted the task of persuading the French to give up their wine. (I'm happy to report that the mission didn't succeed.) Mitt later achieved renown as the savior of the Salt Lake City Olympics, governor of Massachusetts, presidential candidate, and US senator from Utah.

Back then, though, Mitt was a relatively young, relatively unknown manager in a very tough spot. There were about a dozen of us partners who had banded together to help save the firm, on the condition that Mitt would agree to help lead us out of this seemingly impossible situation.[1] Mitt had been a Bain & Company consulting partner prior to founding Bain Capital—a highly successful private equity Bain spin-off. We all signed a letter of commitment to stick with him for the next year or two, and Mitt in turn committed to lead our turnaround. I signed on, in part because I treasured the company that we had once been, and also because Mitt seemed like the one person with a deep insider understanding of our business situation who could win the trust of all the warring factions, including the founders, the banks, and us remaining employees.

The turnaround of Bain's consulting business surely represented the greatest leadership challenge Mitt had ever faced—and one of the most eye-opening periods of my life.

• • •

This chapter focuses on honoring your teammates, that is, your colleagues and employees. You'll note that I'm sticking with the hierarchy of constituencies that Costco's Jim Sinegal laid out for me. First, Jim said, you make sure you're always on the right side of the law, which can be taken to mean that you're not knowingly hurting your community or your environment. Next, you take care of your customers (my chapter 3), then your employees (this chapter), and then your shareholders (chapter 5)—in that order.

In this chapter, I'll draw heavily on my four decades of employment at Bain & Company. Let me explain why. Bain was always customer-focused—in fact, intensely so. The company's early chapter represents a pattern I've seen again and again in my consulting career: when a company's founding generation hits upon a powerful formula for delighting customers, that new venture starts to rock and roll, energized by heady growth. But at the same time, it's not always common at that stage for the company's leaders to focus on taking good care of their employees. In some ways, the exhilaration of rapid growth provides a crutch that enables uninspiring leadership practices to persist. That became increasingly true at Bain in its early years, and that's the primary reason why—in addition to exogenous factors such as a serious recession—the firm got into deep trouble.

But it's what happened *after* that deep trouble that earns Bain a place in this chapter. The firm not only survived that near-death experience but also returned to the top ranks of the consulting industry. Today, the firm has more than twelve thousand employees in sixty-one offices spread across thirty-seven countries, with worldwide revenues approaching $5 billion. And—most significant for our purposes—the firm today is almost universally recognized as a great place to work and is considered by some to be one of the best in the world.[2] On Glassdoor's list, for example, Bain is the only firm to rank among the top four firms every year since that company launched its list, ranking us number one in five out of the last ten years—including the 2021 rankings released as I was writing this chapter.[3]

The new leaders of the firm who lived through the near-death experience learned early in their careers that the only way to sustainably delight customers was to build and inspire a team that fully embraced the noble purpose of helping its clients achieve great results. Or to say it more bluntly, there is no way that a company can sustainably love its customers without creating inspired and committed teams who share that purpose.

How did Bain go from being a difficult place to work in the early 1990s to one of the very best a quarter century later? The new generation of leaders learned—the hard way—that no company can sustainably love its customers without honoring its teams. In the interest of presenting additional perspectives, I'll also dig into the recent histories of three other companies—T-Mobile, Chick-fil-A, and Discover—to explain how they have prospered in part through honoring their teams.

Bain: The Good Old Bad Old Days

Bill Bain founded Bain & Company in 1973 along with a handful of colleagues from the Boston Consulting Group. In its first decade or so, Bain grew rapidly—at an average annual clip of 50 percent—largely through word of mouth in the CEO community, which appreciated Bain's good counsel especially in the realms of strategy and cost-cutting.

I suspect that when I applied for a consulting job at Bain in 1977, I might have been the only person from my class at Harvard College to do so.[4] Signing up with a swashbuckling four-year-old company wasn't a particularly safe choice, but I sensed that this was a place where I would learn a great deal in a hurry. On that score, I was right. Unlike other consulting firms that were hired to work on narrow projects, often specified by the client—and not always defined well—Bain focused on the profitable growth of the whole company, which required building strong relationships with CEOs and other senior corporate leaders. For a young consultant, Bain provided an incomparable opportunity to have a substantial impact on major companies while you learned a ton and could earn good money.

What was Bain doing right back then? From my humble vantage point, it seemed like the firm's leaders saw their primary duty as building a community of extraordinary teams that could do great things for our clients. In our brightest years, our leaders focused effectively on ensuring that their teams were having a meaningful impact—helping clients generate superior results.

Bain understood from day one the central importance of delivering value to customers. Customer loyalty was the only way the firm could grow. It was a point of pride for us in our early years that we had no marketing. For many years, in fact, we didn't even have business cards. We believed that sales and marketing expenses were a tax that a company had to pay when it failed to deliver remarkable outcomes to customers. As a small startup firm, we knew this was a tax we could not afford, so we focused our energies on helping our clients achieve remarkable results. And I mean *focused*: we had no senior partners who served primarily as rainmakers, which would have meant that their time would have been spent acquiring new accounts rather than serving customers. None of us spoke at conferences; we didn't schmooze at industry gatherings. The only reason we grew so fast was that our clients loved our work so much that they bought more from us every year and referred us to their friends and colleagues.

Bain's focus on earning customer loyalty did not waver through the years, but something else did. Early on, our founders preached this gospel: *Impact, Fun, Profits.* Down in my basement, I still have a bottle of champagne from an early firm celebration. It sports a custom-printed label featuring those three words—Impact, Fun, Profits—arranged in a mutually reinforcing triangle. It all made sense to me. When you serve clients so well that you have a major impact on their success, that serves as the foundation for a fun work experience and generates profits for the firm, which in turn makes the whole process sustainable.

But the early formula came up short in terms of consistently honoring employees. I noticed that too many departing employees were treated as losers or even traitors. The founders believed that the employee's job was to make Bain great, and those defectors were failing in that mission. What I came to learn over the years is that truly great leaders are committed to helping employees lead great lives, and the gulf between these two philosophies gets clarified when the going gets rough. That's what happened at Bain. The leaders talked a good game about the vitally important "extraordinary community of teams," but when the business hit a downturn, those founders punched the layoff button. Newly hired consultants and longtime partners alike were unceremoniously dumped in order to keep the founders' bonus pool healthy. To me and other junior partners, it began to feel like our leaders had jettisoned "Fun" and "Impact" in favor of profits. It seemed that caring for the happiness and well-being of team members and building a community of extraordinary teams were no longer serious priorities.

It soon became apparent that our founders' primary purpose was to maximize their own personal wealth. The troubles began in 1984, when Bill Bain and his senior colleagues decided to cash out their holdings in the consulting firm to fund investments in their new spin-off, Bain Capital, and another similar entity called Bain Holdings. That's when they saddled the consulting firm with some $200 million in debt to fund the employee stock ownership plan mentioned above, a burden that began slowly driving the company into the ground. This process transpired in utmost secrecy so that nobody at Bain outside of the leadership inner circle understood the transaction or its implications.

All of this was perfectly legal, of course. Bain was a private company, owned by a small, tight-knit group of founders who prized their privacy and steadfastly refused to share data on the firm's revenues or profitability (even with us junior partners). They had every right to embrace maximizing shareholder value as their North Star, and given that it was *their* shares whose value was being maximized, I'm sure it all seemed appropriate to them. But when leaders focus on maximizing shareholder value—especially for their own financial gain—they cede the moral high ground. When teams no longer believe that their firm is guided by a higher purpose, they are no longer inspired to do remarkable things to enrich the lives of their clients.

Through their swelling ambitions for Bain Capital and Bain Holdings, Bill Bain's inner circle got distracted from the core mission of helping teams deliver great results for clients. They kept secret the economics of each client relationship, practice, and office, which impeded us from making wise decisions for the business and understanding the depth of our challenges. This breach of trust between the founders and the younger generations— who by the way were the ones working every day on the front lines with our customers—resulted in defections of some of our most talented colleagues. The firm's woes were further compounded by the crunching recession of 1989.

By 1990, when Mitt Romney agreed to try to rescue Bain, the firm could barely meet its payroll.

Insights and Innovations

We did manage the long climb back up out of our deep hole. Despite Goldman Sachs's bleak assessment—a zero percent chance of success—we were able to resurrect the firm and get it back to its roots: Impact, Fun, Profits. Surely a large part of the credit for that turnaround belongs to Mitt Romney, who immediately shared profitability data so every office around the world could adjust tactics and priorities. Mitt also scheduled our partner meetings for Saturday mornings in order to free us up to spend our weekdays fully engaged in client work (and symbolically remind us that dealing with our internal issues should not get in the way of our client work). As I look back, Mitt stands out as one of the most talented leaders I have ever encountered. But our whole team played important roles, developing a number of insights and innovations and building client relationships that enabled the firm once again to be a truly great place to work,

and thereby ensuring that it could once again attract and retain outstanding talent.

Let's begin with those insights (not necessarily in chronological order
but instead organized for clarity and their relative importance in the march
toward becoming a great place to work). For many years, Bain had conducted annually a so-called employee engagement survey. As we rebuilt
the company, most of us agreed that this annual process, while useful for
spotting our biggest challenges, had to be augmented with more frequent
real-time feedback to help teams make better decisions and gauge progress day by day and week by week. One challenge: through a long string
of well-intentioned tweaks, the annual survey had ballooned to more than
a hundred questions. So, a creative leader in our human resources department took on the task of distilling the survey down to its essence. After
lots of statistical slicing and dicing, he discovered that more than 80 percent
of the variation in team member happiness could be explained by how
much team members agreed with a single statement: *I feel valued, motivated, and inspired.*

Over the years, I have refined that to read *I feel like a valued member
of a team that wins with its customers.* For a time I thought that "I feel
like a valued member of a winning team" would suffice, but I think it is
wise to remind everyone that the only true wins result when the customer
is happy. Earning a valued role on a team that consistently delivers on that
mission—and receiving appropriate recognition and rewards—is what motivates our people. So, to get Bain back on track we structured ourselves
into very small teams (three to five members, typically) in which all members depended on each other. We worked hard to develop outstanding team
leaders who exemplified our core values. And we developed a rhythm of
practical feedback and learning processes to help teams evaluate their
progress.

We embraced the idea that the center—headquarters—existed primarily to serve the field. (Most organizations have it the other way around.)
Henceforth, the primary duty of our most senior leaders would be to help
frontline teams deliver great results for clients. One of the inherent challenges here, we knew, was to keep our most talented and accomplished
people out in the field directing the good work of those frontline teams:
working directly with clients. In most companies the most talented and

ambitious people get promoted, move to headquarters, and climb their way up to the C-suite. On their path to those corner offices, they are awarded powerful jobs running functional silos, which inevitably means that over time they tend to become removed from customers. This distance from the day-to-day service of customers makes it very difficult for them to know what decisions and policies are getting in the way of delivering great customer value or how best to help teams deliver great results.

Ultimately, we solved that problem by eliminating headquarters. We elect a managing partner every three years, and although an individual can serve up to three consecutive terms in that role, that has yet to happen. The managing partner continues to work in his or her home office, and we therefore can operate with no official headquarters.

In the same spirit, we ask our customer-facing leaders to play active roles in vital functions such as recruiting and training. For most of the major administrative roles—such as office head and practice leader or member of the compensation and promotion committee (which often represents the pinnacle of power in typical professional firms)—Bain reinforces the servant-leadership nature of these roles by rotating partners through these positions while they still devote at least half of their time to directly serving clients.

We compensate with this same philosophy in mind: client work generally pays better than administrative work. Again, this starts at the top. As Mitt prepared to turn over the firm leadership to the next generation of leadership, we agreed that the managing partner, as a servant-leader, should never receive the highest compensation in the firm. His or her job is to help partners deliver outstanding results for clients, not to boss people around and make the important decisions for them. I've emphasized the point here because it's a core idea: *The primary duty of our senior leaders is to help our frontline teams achieve success for their clients.*

The Power of Doing Huddles Right

We developed a process of regular team huddles aimed at enabling teams to gauge progress, spot problems early, and reset priorities as needed. Of course, lots of companies use huddles, but in my experience Bain huddles are different from most. Much like agile scrums, they are quick, typically held weekly or biweekly, and focus on helping the team identify, prioritize, and solve its own problems/opportunities. Our London office pioneered their development during a time when that office was really struggling with unhappy teams and high turnover. Huddles proved so successful that they spread organically, with leaders bringing the process with them as they were transferred to other offices around the globe. Eventually huddles became standard across all Bain offices around the world.

Rather than focusing on sales targets or operational priorities—which already get plenty of attention—our huddles focus the team on the elements we believe can *make work great*. These elements include, among others, how to handle a tricky client situation, how to protect team members from burnout, and what changes are required to honor our core values. Our teams prepare for huddles by responding to a very brief survey emailed to each team member the day before the huddle. Individual responses remain anonymous, but survey results are shared with the entire team in advance of the huddle. This kind of preparation means that during the huddle itself there's a shared base of knowledge, and the team can move quickly to the next level of diagnosis and action.[5]

Over time, we've seen some very effective process enhancements that have been adopted voluntarily by large numbers of teams. For example, many teams appoint a huddle captain, or ombudsperson, who can help lead huddles without the formal team leader being in the room (or on Zoom). This facilitates follow-up conversations—probing for root causes and possible solutions—that can also remain confidential.

I'll discuss several other advances in later chapters. For the purposes of this chapter, though, the most important dimension of the huddle is the handful of questions that guide the conversation. Every survey starts with the question "How likely would you be to recommend this team to an interested colleague?" (0–10). This question makes people think about the team's culture and values, quality of leadership, and ability to win. Next comes a statement (1–5 degree of agreement) about client impact: "Our team's work adds significant value to the client." Then we ask team members to rate the sustainability of the workload, their opportunity to learn and grow, and whether they feel respected and included. Finally, we encourage shout-outs for members who have gone above and beyond to help the team succeed. During a crisis or other transformational change, we add a question that helps gauge progress. For example, as the Covid-19 crisis emerged, we added this highly relevant question: "Our case team is actively discussing Work-From-Home norms and making appropriate use of available resources and tools" (1–5 degree of agreement). The survey tool also makes it easy for team leaders to drag and drop additional questions from a library of questions designed to help solve common problems— although always with the guideline of *keeping it short.*

In the beginning each team ran its own process, using a tool such as SurveyMonkey. Today we rely on a sophisticated digital survey management system that maintains the anonymity of the scores and comments that are submitted by individual respondents so that people feel safe to speak the truth. We *do* share aggregate team scores transparently to let teams know how they are performing vis-à-vis every other team in their office. Even more important, the monthly partner meeting in each office reviews a summary of the survey results, which rank-orders teams so that any problems are readily apparent. Office leadership reaches out to leaders of struggling teams to offer help and support.

That's a key point. We have worked hard to ensure that this process helps teams *improve* rather than being punitive. It's a way for team leaders who are in trouble to get out of trouble. Of course, our transparent team-scoring system inevitably puts some pressure on low-scoring teams because consultants are naturally reluctant to join troubled teams. On the other hand, as noted, teams with low scores get first dibs on the kinds of office resources that can help turn things around.

I asked one of our new consultants whom I had known since he was a youngster (and a playmate of my children) about his experience with the team survey results and whether he felt pressure from the team leader to artificially inflate the score. He responded that, in all honesty, he had been surprised at the effectiveness of the process. He had worked at another consulting firm prior to getting his MBA and had seen the dark side of team ratings in a competitive culture. He assured me that in his office, at least, the process was working effectively. In fact, the first team to which he was assigned upon joining the firm was one of the lowest-scoring in the entire office. *This doesn't look good*, he remembered thinking. So he was surprised when his team leader, rather than hiding or explaining away this result, used it as leverage with office leadership to put his team first in line for additional resources. In this case, those resources took the form of a set of workstations located together to help keep the team, which was staffed from multiple offices, coordinated and connected.

Focusing on Frontline Team Leaders

What single factor has the most impact on inspiring teams to strive for greatness? Of course, there are entire books written on this subject. But at Bain, we came to realize through our own experience that the frontline team leader sets the tone, models the values, sets the priorities, and balances individual needs with team needs. Given this critical importance, we select leaders with great care and invest heavily in their training and coaching. As noted, we developed the huddle process to help our team leaders get coaching from their members. Huddle scores arrive frequently and, like grades on homework assignments, are designed primarily for coaching rather than evaluation.

There's a second process we use with teams to help them evaluate their leader: a robust and trusted upward feedback process that takes place every six months. What makes it unique is what we ask, how we use that information, and how carefully we designed the process to make it trustworthy. Bain's approach to teams is somewhat unusual in that our teams disband and re-form frequently, so it is very possible that a consultant will get the opportunity to work multiple times with the same team leader. With that in mind, team members rate every leader with whom they have worked during the previous six months by answering one question: "How much would you like to work with this leader again?"[6] To provide coaching insights, we also ask respondents to list the things their leader should start, stop, and continue doing in order to improve.

For this process to work, everybody involved has to *trust* it, which is easier said than done. The team leader has to believe that the correct people are answering the question—meaning, among other things, that those people being surveyed were actually on that team for more than a few days and therefore know what they're talking about. In addition, the team leader has to believe that each of those "correct" people will get one vote and that those votes will be counted accurately. Equally, the people being surveyed have to be confident that their answers will remain anonymous, so they can be candid without fear of reprisal, and that leadership will use their input appropriately. Finally, leaders must trust their teams to provide thoughtful and constructive feedback. Again, not simple, but indispensable.

At Bain, we use this process to identify the most inspiring leaders, celebrate their successes, and share their best practices. We also provide lots of coaching to help laggards grow and improve. When Mitt Romney handed the reins of the firm to our worldwide managing partner, Tom Tierney, we collectively made a number of important decisions.[7] One that helped put us on a path toward making Bain a great place to work was deciding that *only the leaders who were rated highly by their team would be eligible for promotion.* When Tom and I recently reminisced about the Bain turnaround, he reminded me that one of his first tasks as managing partner was to manage out almost half of Bain's partners—those who were not inspiring their teams. Today the firm's promotion policy has evolved, but strong ratings on team upward feedback still provide a major asset in a promotion candidate's portfolio. Many otherwise qualified candidates get passed over because of weak team ratings.

Let me clarify this key point. Team feedback and upward ratings don't solely determine who gets promoted—in fact, there are many dimensions to a promotion-related decision that team members aren't in a position to evaluate. But the upward-feedback hurdle has to be cleared before the individual can even be considered for promotion. Why? One thing that teams most certainly *can* judge is how well their leader lives the organization's values and thereby is or isn't worthy of trust and respect. By delegating this considerable power to our people, we ensure at every level of the organization that only leaders who live our values can get promoted to positions of more power and authority.

A radical process? Yes and no. It's never easy for the senior leaders of an organization to cede control, especially if their personal fortunes are closely tied to the fortunes of the company. But I'll turn the question around and ask a skeptic to explain why this process, or something like it, shouldn't be adopted by *every* business that is serious about being a great place to work. Bain believes so deeply in the universal relevance of this process for building a great place to work that we have designed it into a client offering labeled "Net Promoter for People."[8]

Focusing on Results

Bain's mission has always prioritized getting results for our clients. In the early days, we focused on *economic results*—indeed, those were the exact words in our mission statement. We came to recognize that our mission should include other dimensions of results that are hard to measure with standard financials, such things as social impact, team experience, and client capabilities. In 2019, we officially removed "economic" to make official this evolution to our broader mission. I believe that embracing this broader mission led to important innovations that helped Bain become a truly great place to work.

For example, as a firm we invest heavily in causes that are important to our teams, supporting their volunteer efforts and social justice initiatives. We have scored a perfect 100 on the Human Rights Campaign's Corporate Equality Index for fifteen consecutive years. We have developed firm-wide plans to achieve zero net carbon and have committed $1 billion worth of pro bono services over the next decade to support social-impact initiatives. And on the local level, the partner in charge of each office delegates enormous responsibility to grassroots teams of frontline volunteers to design and run everything from office meetings to office renovations to summer meetings/office retreats and our Results Challenge, in which teams compete to win recognition for their exceptional impact on their clients' success.

How does this program work? Each year, case teams self-nominate their case for consideration. The nomination requires teams to demonstrate their proficiency in four main areas: true results delivered; an enduring client relationship; creating client Promoters; and inspired team. Office leadership selects finalists for the office competition. The final presentation is a momentous occasion. Theatrics, costumes, and celebratory music set the tone. Junior and support team members typically take the lead in presenting to the entire office, typically at the annual offsite meeting. They bring key points to life—results (financial or otherwise) achieved; impact on clients and key stakeholders (often delivered via video testimonials or verbatim quotes); approach for creating Promoters, including the client Net Promoter feedback (including scores and comments); huddle scores; and other milestones, such as individual promotions and life events—to underscore how inspired they were on the case.

An office-wide vote or a selection committee selects the winner. The winning team receives a stipend for a team event and an etched crystal award and becomes eligible for the regional competition. This process not only emphasizes the primary importance of delivering great results for clients but also exposes the firm's best work to a wide array of employees, who learn to recognize what great Bain work looks like.

In summary, we inspire our teams by hiring and training outstanding frontline leaders. We help them succeed by empowering team members to deliver outstanding value to their clients. Then we provide the tools (such as huddles, upward feedback, training, and so on) to help guide and gauge progress so they can learn how to get better every day. We strive to ensure that every person is inspired to earn a valued role on a team that wins with its clients.

It's probably worth underscoring that client Net Promoter Scores are kept separate from our compensation system. We believe that doing otherwise would dishonor our team members by placing them in a position whereby they might feel compelled to game their scores rather than seek honest feedback that illuminates how best to improve. Linking scores to bonuses would have a chilling effect on candor, would work against the process and spirit of the team, and would undermine the NPS philosophy.

To Enable Turnarounds, Leaders Must Honor Teams

The Bain turnaround was remarkable by any standard, but the vital role played by inspiring teams is a consistent element in most effective turn-arounds. For example, the remarkable reversal of fortune at the Charles Schwab Corporation, which I detail in *The Ultimate Question 2.0*, relied on this important ingredient. Nuisance and penalty fees had mushroomed to 25 percent of revenues. These bad-profit policies were irritating customers and dishonoring the employees who had to enforce them. CEO Walt Bettinger committed to eliminating all of these bad profits because he believed strongly that his teams had to be proud of how the firm treated its customers. Schwab has returned to its status as an industry leader in large part because Bettinger made good on his promise.

We saw a similar pattern at T-Mobile, where an entire industry was addicted to bad profits. By steadily eradicating those disgraceful tactics, frontline teams were energized and motivated to serve customers with pride. As noted in the previous chapter, CEO John Legere inspired his frontline teams by venturing out from his Seattle-area headquarters for regular visits with those teams. He listened carefully to their suggestions and took action. He supported Callie Field's proposal to radically reorganize the company around its customers, splitting customer service call center factories into 150 separate teams—each with its own leader and separate profit and loss statement. Each team was responsible for a set of specific customers, usually based on geography, so when customers called in for help, they would be dealing with customer service representatives with the same local accents, sports team affiliations, and local knowledge (including that particular stretch of highway where calls get dropped). And because T-Mobile understood the economic advantage of delighting customers, the company invested heavily in upgrading the employee experience.

Concurrently, T-Mobile's leadership reduced the size of the teams to ten customer service representatives per coach/leader.[9] That is far smaller than most phone centers, which operate with a factory mindset that is focused primarily on productivity. T-Mobile's smaller teams enabled coaches to spend more time helping each colleague. Leaders allocate twenty minutes every day to team e-huddles and skills development. Most phone centers (again, with their factory mindsets) would never consider cutting into productive hours like this—but then again, most of these operations don't understand the importance of honoring teams or loving customers. Those companies would also have a hard time understanding how T-Mobile can afford to pay six-figure incomes to phone center supervisors when they deliver great results on their profit and loss statements, which they understand result from happy customers coming back for more and bringing their friends.

Inspiring the Team at Chick-fil-A

Inspiring frontline leaders (their store franchisees) with outstanding compensation upside has also worked miracles at Chick-fil-A. While the company is private, it shares key information about its performance, including the number of store locations and revenues. The performance of each store is easily accessible by all franchisees. Economic transparency demonstrates trust and respect for teams.

Here's another important element in the Chick-fil-A story: Truett Cathy did not create the company to make himself wealthy, although it eventually turned him and his family into billionaires several times over. He viewed his role less as the owner and more as the steward of corporate resources, responsible for serving both his customers and the frontline teams who served them.[10]

Given this foundational perspective, it's not surprising that Truett designed his organization to provide maximum service and support to his franchisees (called store operators). These are the roles that deliver the firm's promise to its customers. Thus, Truett viewed maintaining top-quality frontline leadership as his highest priority and worked hard to honor his store teams by ensuring that the company recruited only the very highest-caliber person—in terms of both talent and character—for store operator positions. He understood intuitively that having outstanding talent running the stores and making local decisions to delight customers offered the best path to building a great reputation—and a great business.

So, Truett designed a system to attract and retain the best store operators. He provided unprecedented financial upside to store operators so they could achieve their personal financial goals while still concentrating on running a single store (or possibly two if they demonstrated this special capacity). There would be no delegation of store operations to second-tier staff and no race to climb the corporate ladder up to a regional job or national headquarters. Central headquarters and regional staff understand that their jobs exist to serve the store operators. To reinforce this message and to build empathy with the field, every headquarters employee works in a store at least one day each year. In order to join the field operations staff, candidates spend months training in stores so they deeply understand the needs of restaurant teams.

Selection of store operators is of paramount importance. I remember asking Steve Robinson, then Chick-fil-A's chief marketing officer, how he could tell if the interview candidate would be a good fit. He explained that he asked himself if he would feel elated to learn that his teenage son or daughter was going to work for and thus be shaped by this person. "We are looking for people," Steve told me, "who join our family—hopefully, forever."

Truett Cathy helped ensure the quality of store operators by purposefully constraining the number of new outlets that got opened. I remember vividly one of the biggest disagreements he had with his executive team during a planning retreat that I hosted for the company in my Cape Cod living room. The younger execs in attendance were keen to add many more outlets. The financials were great; the company had no debt and was generating cash at a very healthy clip, even after donating a substantial portion of its profits to charity. But Truett, standing on principle, stubbornly refused to heed the call for accelerated growth. As Steve Robinson recalled in his recent book, Truett "never let financial goals get in the way of personal relationships. In fact, Truett had an aversion to financial goals. To him, that would have been letting the tail wag the dog. . . . Disciplined growth allowed him to select Operators who shared his business philosophy and love for customers."[11]

In other words, Truett believed that the real constraint on *quality* growth was not financial. Rather, quality growth was achieved by the company's ability to attract and develop more great frontline leaders, and by providing appropriate incentives, *keep* them there and motivated to keep getting better. Franchise owners were required to put up a bare minimum of cash, $10,000, in contrast to the $1 million or more required to buy a McDonald's franchise. But in return, Chick-fil-A operators don't own the business assets and can't sell them or give them to their kids. The company retains ownership and control of the stores and, through the low upfront investment threshold, vastly broadens the pool of people it can draw upon to serve as operators.

Is it working? Most Chick-fil-A operators earn far more running their stores than they could earn in a job at headquarters. The company receives about twenty thousand applications a year for franchises and only awards about a hundred new stores annually. How many institutions do you know with a 0.5 percent acceptance rate?[12]

Bain measures NPS for quick-serve restaurant chains—and Chick-fil-A regularly tops that leaderboard, most recently earning an NPS of 60 in 2019. It's a virtuous circle. As *Entrepreneur*'s Matthew McCreary points out, "Chick-fil-A makes more per restaurant than McDonald's, Subway, and Starbucks combined, even while being closed on Sunday."[13]

Inspiring the Teams at Discover

I now want to return to Discover Financial Services (introduced in chapter 2), which caught my eye when it beat out American Express for NPS leadership in credit cards. Among the contributing factors to that surprise success, as I've explained, were the company's investments and systems and training to help contact center representatives deliver great service.

Let's dig deeper. At Discover, the frontline teams in the service centers see ample evidence that they are valued and appreciated. "They are not viewed as a cost center," then-CEO David Nelms told me, "but a profit center. They are our brand ambassadors. We pay very competitive salaries to start and then invest heavily in their training and in the technology to help them do a great job with customers."

Backing up one more step, Discover still has these jobs in the United States. Nelms noted that the cost-center mentality that prevailed with most of his competitors persuaded them to outsource their customer service operations to low-wage countries or force-feed automated solutions to deal with their customers. Nelms and his colleagues were convinced that it takes a knowledgeable, culturally adept, and caring employee to solve the kinds of complex problems that can arise in the credit card context. Outsourcing, offshoring, and automation weren't going to cut it. An unhappy customer on the verge of cutting up his or her card can only be won back through the intervention of a talented employee.

Current CEO Roger Hochschild told me that employee surveys over the years reveal that Discover's call center employees are even happier than the folks at headquarters—a rare occurrence. Bain research has found that in general, the further you go down the organizational chain of command (and closer to the customer), employee NPS ratings steadily decline. But as my research for an earlier book revealed, at loyalty superstar companies, employee happiness is pretty consistent across organizational levels.[14] This underscores the power of a headquarters team that is committed to servant leadership.

How exactly did Discover make its frontline teams feel so honored? Well, the company pays well and offers extraordinary benefits. Discover inspires its teams by providing exactly the same health care coverage options for its frontline teams as it does for its most senior executives. In this era when student debt is crippling the lives of so many young people, Discover offers a remarkable alternative, the Discover College Commitment, which covers tuition, fees, books, and supplies needed to complete select online degrees at one of three schools: the University of Florida (via UF Online), Wilmington University, and Brandman University. Employees can start participating their first day on the job. Discover offers academic counseling to help employees find the program that best fits their educational and professional development. Unlike typical education benefit programs, in which students pay course costs up front in hopes of receiving reimbursement months later *if* they earn a good grade, Discover pays 100 percent of tuition up front with no strings attached. It's a remarkably generous approach, implying a level of trust that one rarely sees in the corporate setting.

Visibility helps too. Phone reps at most companies would be shocked to get a visit from their company CEO and might conclude that bad things—perhaps even layoffs—were in the works if the CEO *did* show up.[15] At Discover, CEO Roger Hochschild visits each call center at least once each year, delivering four presentations throughout the day to cover all shifts. Typically, he updates teams on the company's progress and priorities and finishes with a lively question-and-answer session. There is clear evidence that leaders listen to their teams—and take action. To cite one fairly down-to-earth example, the reps did not feel that it was fair for workers on Sunday shifts to get higher pay than those who worked Saturdays, given that most people found working Saturdays equally undesirable. In response, management adjusted pay rates so Saturday's matched Sunday's.

Service center employees are paid to reinforce their inherent desire to treat the customer right. There are no commissions in the compensation structure at Discover—in fact, there is no traditional selling of any kind. "We feel that when customers call in for help," Roger explained to me, "the best way to sell them additional products is to deliver great service—then make it easy for them to learn more about our offerings on our website, app, and marketing communications."

To make sure I wasn't hearing just the headquarters perspective on call center happiness, I visited Discover's Phoenix call center and spent the day talking with rank-and-file employees. I came away convinced that yes, the employees feel like they are well cared for in terms of benefits, but their primary source of inspiration is that Discover helps them delight customers.

Donna Matthews, an eighteen-year veteran, enthusiastically cited the fact that she receives regular coaching that emphasizes doing the right thing for customers even if that might seem to work against Discover's bottom line. She gave this example: Whenever a customer calls in to request a cash advance—up to a $100 loan available at a local ATM, but with a $10 fee and interest rates often in the range of 22 to 24 percent—she checks her computer screen to see if that customer is eligible for a cash-back transaction at one of the local retailers up to $120, with no fee and no interest, if paid off with the Discover month-end payment.[16] "It makes us proud," Donna said. "It makes us look forward to coming in to work each day."

Phone reps are aware that Hochschild and his fellow headquarters-based executives listen to hour-long samples of call center customer interactions twice per month.[17] Their goal: to discover which technology investments and process changes might help the reps delight more customers. During these sessions executives discuss what they learned from their listening sessions, and based on those discussions set priorities for improvements.

This process helps explain how Discover has developed outstanding digital tools to support its employees and its customers. Again, this is an industry outlier. Most financial service firms have tried to make customer service center costs disappear by hiding their phone numbers from customers and steering them to cheaper digital solutions. As noted in earlier chapters, Discover opted to make its digital options so good that customers seek them out whenever appropriate—but at the same time, the support phone number is prominently displayed across the website so that whenever customers want to talk to a human, they can know how to easily reach an agent 24 hours a day, 365 days per year.

Think about what this means from a service rep's point of view. At other companies, many customers start their live conversation *angry*. They have fought with the automated voice response system or on the web have been shuffled off to a page of so-called frequently asked questions. If an increasingly frustrated customer is persistent, he or she finally gets hold of a human, who presumably has been hiding behind these unfriendly technological barriers the whole time! Not so for the Discover rep. The customer gets there effortlessly. The interaction is designed to be low-pressure and self-paced. The customer soon realizes that the rep is under no pressure to meet an average handle-time goal, which results in lower-key exchanges aimed at problem solving with much greater potential to result in customer delight.

Team leaders are promoted from within. These exemplars serve as role models and coaches to their teams. In addition, there is an extensive coaching and feedback system called iMatter that uses customer feedback to create coaching plans to improve service delivery and celebrate success. The iMatter system reinforces to team members that they can really make a difference in their customers' lives. As at Bain, this feedback is never linked to bonuses to minimize gaming of the system.

A final interesting dimension of Discover's approach to inspiring its employees is the way the company organizes its reps into teams. Whereas typical call center teams might range from twenty-five to thirty people, Discover prefers pods with the capacity to hold just sixteen agents. But given their flexible work scheduling, with plenty of time for individual coaching sessions, the typical team in action is closer to twelve agents. This happens to be similar to the size of a US Army Special Forces tactical team, a context within which soldiers are expected to demonstrate higher degrees of initiative, self-reliance, maturity, and resourcefulness. It also happens to be the size of Southwest Airlines' airport teams, which are much smaller than typical airline teams, and is also reminiscent of T-Mobile's customer service representative teams, described above.

What's the common thread? Smaller teams elevate the importance of each individual, underscoring that everyone's role is vital to the team's success. From the pure accounting perspective, big teams are great because they leverage an expensive chief across a small army of low-wage grunts. But Discover's experience argues that small teams provide the best way to inspire employees and love customers.

The Secret to Being an Inspiring Leader

When the primary purpose of a business is to enrich the lives of its customers, the leader's first responsibility is to help team members embrace and achieve this inherently inspiring mission—safely and sustainably. Team members are inspired when they can play a valued role on a team that consistently delights customers and can earn appropriate recognition and rewards when that mission is accomplished.

The very best leaders make sure their team members can earn standing ovations (tens) from their customers (and their peers). Experiencing that signal of love and affirmation is the secret ingredient that great leaders utilize to inspire their teams and provides the essential fuel for winning on purpose.

CHAPTER 5

Respect Your Investors

They Win Only When Your Customers Are Loyal

I n the summer of 2019, a Chinese entrepreneur bid an astounding $4.57 million for the privilege of having lunch with legendary investor Warren Buffett.[1] This news reminded me how incredibly fortunate I had been back in 1996 when a similar opportunity (perhaps an even better one) came my way. The price was surely better. I was treated to a round of golf with Jack Bogle, and the famously parsimonious Vanguard Group—which Jack founded—covered both my greens fee and dinner that evening.

Jack was a true superhero in his field and was widely admired for his respectful treatment of his investors. As a MarketWatch obituary in 2019 put it, "Jack Bogle even towered over Warren Buffett as the (world's) most influential investor."[2] Buffett himself didn't disagree, saying to CNBC that "Jack did more for American investors as a whole than any individual I've known."[3] So, you can imagine how cool it felt to spend an afternoon teamed up with Jack—by then already a legend—on the golf course at the St. Michaels Harbour Inn resort on the Chesapeake Bay's Eastern Shore.

Jack's golf game that day was not very impressive (mine never is). I noticed that his eyes kept watering, and I ventured to ask if he was suffering from seasonal allergies. "No, no," he replied, matter-of-factly. "I've got a new heart, and my body is struggling to get used to it." At that point, I'd heard about a series of experimental heart transplants that were being conducted in South Africa, but I assumed he was just joking around. Over dinner that night, though, I was startled to learn that he really *had* undergone a recent heart transplant and was already back playing golf, and the antirejection medicines he was taking were indeed giving him watery eyes.

I thought a lot in the following years about Jack's drive and determination. I decided that they were inseparable from his personal mission: to treat investors with the respect they deserve. He understood what was in his investors' best interest and built an entire company to provide that solution. His example came to frame my thinking on this subject. What does it mean to treat investors with respect? Does that conflict with loving customers as the firm's primary purpose?

· · ·

How did I come to be golfing and dining with Jack Bogle that day? Vanguard's newly appointed CEO, Jack Brennan, read my first book, *The Loyalty Effect*, and was intrigued by how it quantified the enormous economic advantages that can result from long-term customer relationships. Because this philosophy and its resulting economic advantages were central to Vanguard's strategy, Brennan called and invited me to speak at Vanguard's annual executive retreat in 1996. Given that Vanguard had so deeply influenced my perspective on how respectful treatment of investors will earn their loyalty, I immediately cleared my calendar to accept the offer.

I had been putting my savings in Vanguard's index funds since I graduated from college. Even though Vanguard was still relatively small at the time, I believed in its contrarian philosophy of long-term, buy-and-hold investing and not wasting energy trying to beat the market. My own research, starting in college and continuing through my Bain career, convinced me that Jack Bogle was right. So, spending a day with Jack and his team was a real treat. Over dinner, I asked him how large he thought Vanguard could grow. (The company was still a niche player at that time, with hardly any advertising.) "Fred," he responded, "*growth* is not our goal. Our goal is to deliver great value for our investors. Striving to grow big can get you in trouble." Although he said it differently, he was expressing the same clear philosophy that I had heard while riding in the passenger seat of Truett Cathy's car: that Truett's dream for Chick-fil-A was not to be *big* but instead to be *great* for its customers and employees.

But don't you need ambitious growth goals to grow? In a word, no. As of this writing, the Vanguard 500 index fund (its large-cap index fund) and its sister total stock market index fund (a second index fund that blends in some midcap companies) are the largest and third-largest funds in the world. Taken as a whole, the Vanguard Group is now the world's second-largest mutual fund company, with more than $7 trillion in assets under management. This exceptional growth has been achieved despite a miniscule budget for sales and marketing.

Vanguard's remarkable growth provides one more illustration of the efficient and sustainable power of loyalty-fueled growth engines. Vanguard is mutually owned by its client-investors, so all growth is financed with internally generated cash. Vanguard's enormous scale and broad availability today make it easy for any investor to diversify away all individual-company risk. By design, Vanguard's index funds mirror the market average return at bargain basement prices. My Vanguard Total Stock Market index fund, for example, charges only .04 percent in expenses. When I graduated from college, typical mutual fund expenses were 2.0 percent, or five thousand times higher than today's Vanguard price. This makes Vanguard truly a miracle—one lovingly designed to provide a remarkable product at a great price.

I begin this chapter with this Vanguard story for several reasons:

- It provides another example of how hanging around with good people (such as Jack and the Vanguard team) enriches your life.

- Vanguard illustrates that the best way to grow is not to buy growth with sales commissions and advertising but instead to earn it with the unbeatable strategy of loving your customers.

- The story demonstrates that there need be no tension between loving customers and delighting long-term investors (Vanguard's investors are its customers).

- Vanguard's success created a new baseline that every company must beat in order to deliver true value to their investors.

- I began my experiment of investing in F.R.E.D. Stock Index (FREDSI) companies (see chapter 2) through my Vanguard brokerage account, where the superior results were easy to see by comparing them to my Vanguard Total Market Index Fund.

This chapter will spotlight Jack Bogle's standard of respectful treatment of investors and will provide further evidence that customer-love winners make investors happiest. I will explore several resulting implications about the need for reliable Net Promoter Score data and for a complementary metric that deepens and buttresses NPS, a new invention that I call the Earned Growth Rate.

A New Standard of Respect for Investors

Due to the remarkable growth of Vanguard's index funds—which inspired a bevy of worthy competitors, including Fidelity and Black Rock—such investment options are now easily available to all investors. These funds diversify risk so efficiently that they provide a practical hurdle rate that a firm must exceed in order to make the risk of holding its single company stock worthwhile. For example, I am happy with my investment in the shares of an individual company (such as Amazon, Apple, FirstService, or Costco) only when they beat my Vanguard market index fund, which includes these stocks along with many other companies'. The logic is straightforward: if a single-company stock underperforms that index fund, then I would have been better off investing in the index fund. In fact, if my single-company stock merely matches the index fund, I have lost value, since the broad index diversifies away all the single-company risk. In other words, I assumed the risk of investing in a single company and received zero value in return.

Therefore, Vanguard's Total Stock Market Index provides a useful hurdle rate to test whether the exemplar companies I have used throughout this book delivered true value to me and their other investors. Figure 5-1 shows their cumulative returns for the decade ending December 31, 2020. The hashed bar on the right shows the Vanguard Total Stock Market Index, labeled "VTI." The chart shows the NPS superstars handily beat

FIGURE 5-1

NPS exemplars beat the stock market average (VTI)—delivering true value to investors

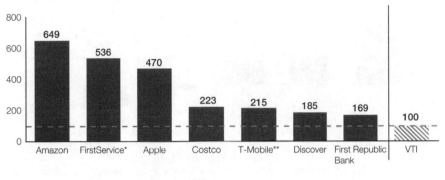

Cumulative total shareholder return indexed vs. Vanguard Total Stock Market Index (VTI) (1/1/2011–12/31/2020)

Source: CapIQ, FirstService and T-Mobile annual reports

*FirstService: TSR assumes all former FSV stock from Colliers/FSV spin-off shifted to new FSV shares in 2015; not currency adjusted (TSR adjusted to CAD/USD change 2010–2015 = 725%); if investor made no additional moves and followed deal structure (FSV 41.4%; CIGI 58.6%) return would be 619%.

**T-Mobile: assumes TSR for MetroPCS through TMUS acquisition in 4/30/2013 and re-evaluates TMUS TSR since IPO for period 5/1/2013–12/31/2020.

the VTI, thus delivering true value to their investors. This is compelling evidence that when companies successfully put customer interests first, they stoke the loyalty-growth engine because customers come back for more and bring their friends, which delivers superior results to long-term investors. This is the reason why long-term investors should *love* customer capitalism!

Loving Customers Is an Unbeatable Strategy That Wins for Investors

FREDSI provides persuasive evidence that investors win when companies love their customers.[4] Let's dig even deeper and scrutinize a few industry case studies to learn whether there are alternative (noncustomer-loving) paths that deliver superior total shareholder return (TSR) for investors.

FIGURE 5-2

Only T-Mobile delivered true value to investors (TSR exceeding VTI)

Cumulative total shareholder return indexed vs. Vanguard Total Stock Market Index (VTI)
(1/1/2014–12/31/2019)

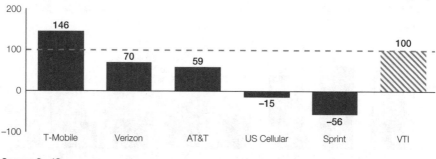

Source: CapIQ

Note: Cumulative TSR represents total return assuming investment from 1/1/2014–12/31/2019; 2019 is used as the end year due to T-Mobile's acquisition of Sprint in 2020.

In chapter 3, we saw that when John Legere became CEO and transformed T-Mobile into a purpose-driven customer-love engine, that company's performance skyrocketed. His team systematically purged bad profits by eliminating the tricks, traps, and gotcha fees, and his company delivered the highest TSR in the industry. Figure 5-2 reveals something even more intriguing: NPS leader T-Mobile not only delivers the industry's best TSR but is the *only player* whose TSR exceeded the VTI hurdle.[5] In other words, only the NPS leader delivered true value to its investors.[6]

Figure 5-3 gives the results of a simple regression calculation, which shows that more than two-thirds of the variation in TSR are explained by one single variable: NPS. This is impressive, since our NPS calculation was based only on feedback from US mobile subscribers, whereas the TSR for each of these companies results from their entire portfolio of businesses. For example, in addition to mobile telephony, Verizon offers wirelines, is a major internet provider, and offers cable TV packages. AT&T acquired media properties and DirecTV during this period. Despite the lack of perfect data (we don't yet have Net Promoter Scores for all those other business lines), the pattern in figure 5-3 certainly supports my theory that investors win when companies love their customers.[7]

FIGURE 5-3

US Mobile Telecom: customer-love wins

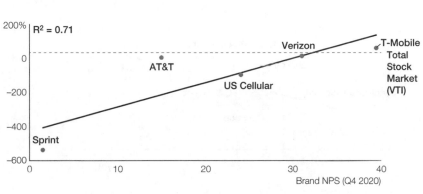

**Cumulative total shareholder return (ln)
(1/1/2014–12/31/2019)**

Source: Bain/Dynata US Wireless Service Provider Quarterly Benchmarking Survey, Q4 2020 (N = 20,034); CapIQ

Note: Cumulative TSR represents total return assuming investment from 1/1/2014–12/31/2019; 2019 is used as the end year due to T-Mobile's acquisition of Sprint in 2020.

Now let's return to the credit card industry, where we've seen Discover nose out American Express as the NPS champion through its extensive campaign of customer-friendly actions. When we plot each competitor's TSR versus NPS (figure 5-4), the pattern is similar to what we see in mobile telephony.

Once again, the ideal analysis would look at pure credit card TSR, but unfortunately there is no such distilled statistic; all of these companies participate in multiple business lines. While credit card operations do provide the lion's share of revenues for Discover, American Express, and Capital One, they represent only half of revenues at JPMorgan Chase and less than 20 percent at Bank of America.[8] That said, in my experience, a customer-centric culture tends to spread across all business lines, so a star NPS player in credit cards likely treats its customers well in its other businesses, such as mortgage loans and deposits. More important, the more frequently we observe this pattern of only the top NPS players delivering outstanding TSR, the more confidence we should feel that the FREDSI prescription holds water.

FIGURE 5-4

US credit cards: customer-love wins

**Cumulative total shareholder return (ln)
(1/1/2011–12/31/2020)**

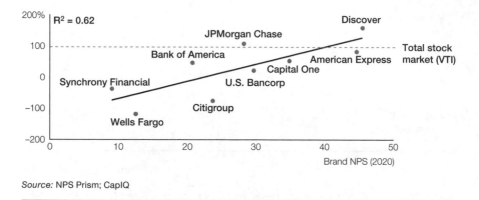

Source: NPS Prism; CapIQ

FIGURE 5-5

US auto: customer-love wins

**Cumulative total shareholder return (ln)
(1/1/2011–12/31/2020)**

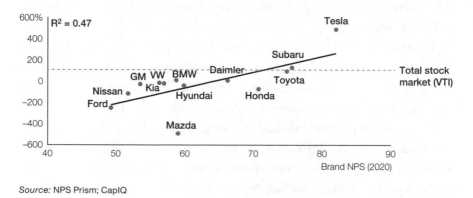

Source: NPS Prism; CapIQ

Where else should we look for that evidence? Well, we see a similar pattern in the US auto industry, as illustrated in figure 5-5.

Again, the relationship is surprisingly strong given that TSR results from these companies' worldwide sales, but we have NPS available only for the US market.[9] Tesla seems to be something of an outlier, with TSR even higher than its NPS leadership might explain. Many financial experts believe that Tesla's skyrocketing share price represents a speculative frenzy and is not realistic or sustainable. So, we also ran our analysis excluding Tesla. The results didn't change much; NPS still explains most of the variation in competitor TSR.

Share price aside, Tesla's NPS advantage indicates a truly impressive level of customer love. This is not only the result of its breakthrough product design. When I chatted a few years back with a Bain alum then serving as Tesla's head of US operations, he told me that I should feel proud because Tesla had adopted my Net Promoter System. It turned out that he and founder Elon Musk regularly reviewed the flow of customer comments and prioritized actions based on that feedback. For example, reports circulated of customers paying $1,000 to get a place in line to buy the new Model X more than a year before it would be delivered and then hearing nothing from Tesla for months and months after that investment. NPS feedback spotted the issue, and Tesla decided it needed a communication program to keep these new owners informed about progress. By forwarding emails with photos of the new line and sharing updates as well as reassuring owners that Tesla was still holding their spot in line, the company made these soon-to-be new car owners feel like special insiders.

There are a few other things worth noting as we ponder Tesla's superstar NPS status. It is impossible to deliver a great customer experience without a great product (or service design) at its core, and Tesla designed and manufactured a product that wows customers. Some competitor, somewhere, is sure to build an equally great product someday soon, but Tesla has created another advantage that may be even more sustainable. It is the only auto company that owns its own retail outlets, which are technically stores rather than traditional dealership franchises. This enables Tesla to deliver a seamless, integrated shopping, purchase, delivery, and ownership experience. (No haggling over price! No frustrating interludes while the salesperson pretends to extract concessions from his or her manager! No finance manager impugning the car's reliability to convince you to purchase extended warranty coverage or rust-proofing.)

Tesla achieves its prodigious growth with almost no advertising or promotional marketing gimmicks (no touts shouting *"Come on down!"*). I decided to test out the Tesla journey myself and went shopping for a car on its website. The process was delightfully simple. All you have to do is answer a few questions on the beautifully designed site, and your new car will show up in your driveway. Yes, Tesla's current stock price may be hard to justify, but it will be very difficult for existing auto brands to match Tesla's shopping, sales, distribution, and service advantages.

In industries such as restaurants, many brands (such as Chick-fil-A) are private, so there is no shareholder return to track. But we can examine the relationship between NPS and same-store sales growth—a key driver of profitability. The two charts in figure 5-6 show the power of NPS in the two major restaurant segments, casual dining (5-6a) and quick serve (5-6b). I discovered Texas Roadhouse (at the top right of figure 5-6a) on a comparable Bain chart just over a decade ago and was delighted to add it to my investment portfolio upon learning it was a public company.[10]

Take a minute at this point to review figures 5-3, 5-4, and 5-5, which chart TSR versus NPS for Mobile Telecom, Credit Card, and Auto. It should be clear from those displays that the only credible manner in which a company could improve its TSR would be to love its customers better—and improve its NPS relative to competitors'. But look again at the dotted horizontal line on each chart that represents Vanguard's VTI return for that period. To reiterate, that hurdle rate must be exceeded before true value has been provided to investors. The only companies that beat this hurdle are the NPS stars. In other words, *only customer-love winners delivered respectable returns (above stock market index funds) to their long-term investors.*

This is a mighty important insight and one that all investors should ponder. The implication is clear: wise investors should enthusiastically support company leadership in their quest to love their customers better. That kind of encouragement will end up yielding far better long-term results than pressuring executives to meet quarterly earnings targets. All our evidence points toward one conclusion: *Unless a company finds a way to make customers feel loved, it will struggle to deliver respectable returns to investors.* A great Net Promoter Score is not itself the objective, but a

FIGURE 5-6A

US casual dining: customer-love wins

Same-store sales cumulative growth (1/1/2011–12/31/2019)

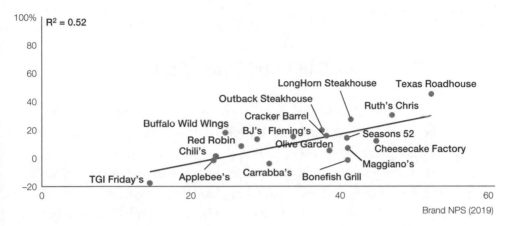

Source: Quick Service & Casual Dining Restaurants NPS Study (US, 2019); Restaurant Research, Thomson

Note: 2019 data used due to extraordinary impact on dining from 2020's Covid-19 pandemic.

FIGURE 5-6B

US quick service/fast casual dining: customer-love wins

Same-store sales cumulative growth (1/1/2011–12/31/2019)

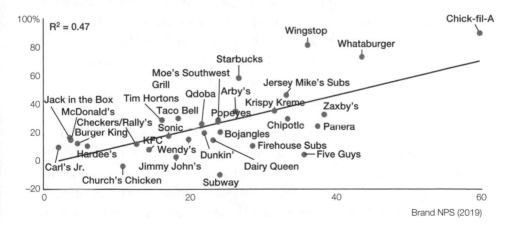

Source: Quick Service & Casual Dining Restaurants NPS Study (US, 2019); Restaurant Research

Note: 2019 data used due to extraordinary impact on dining from 2020's Covid-19 pandemic.

company's NPS relative to its competitors' seems like an excellent indicator of whether a company is headed in the right direction and is worthy of investor loyalty.

Where Can I Find Those Scores?

If you've come this far in this chapter, you may well be asking yourself, "So where can I get my hands on this NPS data so I can pick stocks that will beat the market?"

That's a very good question. Many firms have begun to report internally generated Net Promoter Scores—and I applaud their intentions. However, with no standard calculation process or auditing methodology, savvy investors are appropriately skeptical of the comparability of these self-reported NPS statistics. The *Wall Street Journal* spotlighted this problem in the summer of 2019, noting that

> Much of Corporate America is obsessed with its net promoter score, or NPS, a measure of customer satisfaction that has developed a cult-like following among CEOs in recent years. Unlike profits or sales, which are measured and audited, NPS is usually calculated from a one-question survey that companies often administer themselves. Last year, "net promoter" or "NPS" was cited more than 150 times in earnings conference calls by 50 S&P 500 companies, according to a *Wall Street Journal* analysis of transcripts. That's more than four times as many mentions, and nearly three times as many companies, compared with five years earlier.[11]

I agree with the *Wall Street Journal* that *any* unaudited numbers need to be taken with a grain of salt—actually, a pound or two. For example, I've been appalled to see NPS results reported in annual reports and initial public offering (IPO) securities registrations, often with no explanation of the process used to generate the statistic. Does that result represent a legitimate relationship benchmark score, derived through rigorous double-blind research?[12] Or is it merely a compilation of the scores generated by a self-administered survey, triggered in the wake of some episode or trans-

FIGURE 5-7

Wide gap between Chewy's self-reported NPS and Bain benchmark

Overall NPS, pet category, 2019
How likely are you to recommend shopping for pet items at [retailer] to a friend or colleague?

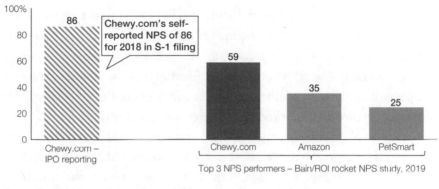

Source: Bain/ROI Rocket General Retail NPS Study 2019; Chewy 2018 S-1 filing

action? Without getting too far down into the weeds, there are a half dozen different "flavors" of NPS out in the world today (product NPS, relationship NPS, post-transaction NPS, . . .), and company pronouncements rarely bother to specify which score they are reporting. From the investor's perspective, there's really only one of these scores that should be relied on: the double-blind relationship score relative to competitors'. I suspect that more than 90 percent of the scores being reported today result from unmasked self-administered surveys triggered by specific transactions, which may be very useful for internal management purposes but have little relevance to competitive relationship benchmark scores.[13]

Online eyeglass retailer Warby Parker understands the nuances of these issues. For example, Warby Parker's self-administered Net Promoter Scores consistently run in the 80s. Meanwhile, the company's double-blind research yields scores about 10 points lower, which, I should point out, is still extraordinarily high for their industry.

Figure 5-7 illustrates an even more serious discrepancy, in this case between the Net Promoter Score reported by Chewy in its IPO document and Bain's double-blind relationship score. This is one of those happy instances where Chewy still comes out as its industry leader, but we clearly have some work to do before investors can rely on the scores they see reported.

Back when we were developing *The Ultimate Question 2.0*, we had much to learn about the right way to measure. The data we used to identify NPS leaders relied on some pretty rudimentary and low-budget market research techniques. Yes, the data were developed through a double-blind research process, but that process failed to distinguish between important customer segments (say, prepaid mobile phone versus postpaid) and was based on minimally acceptable sample sizes—as small as one hundred responses for each brand.[14] The NPS data that I've used in this chapter are far more accurate, based on carefully segmented samples that often exceed ten thousand responses per brand. We have come a long way.

How to explain this improvement? These unique and proprietary data are now being generated by NPS Prism, a data business that Bain launched in 2019 to fill the gaping market need for reliable NPS benchmark data. NPS Prism generates data each quarter, thereby making trends quickly visible. This reporting frequency is vital in order for NPS results to balance the attention now being paid to quarterly earnings reports. To support learning at a granular level, NPS Prism gathers Net Promoter feedback for every episode, enabling its subscribers in, for example, the credit card industry to compare not only their relationship scores but also how they stack up for both digital and human interactions at every episode along the customer journey.

For example, NPS Prism data revealed that the Discover card wins top brand ranking and delivers the best experience for customers applying for a new credit card, while American Express still delivers the best experience when customers request an increase in their credit line. You can imagine how useful this data is for company execs responsible for improving customer experience—and for the investor trying to get a bead on a company's current reality and future prospects. You can understand why demand for NPS Prism data is growing at more than 100 percent per year.

You might well ask why it took so long for Bain to invest in developing NPS Prism. Well, originally I thought we could convince the large accounting firms to develop an audit-worthy methodology for reporting NPS by offering to share Bain's expertise, including refinements we were then making to our measurement methodology. I'm sorry to report that this turned out to be a quixotic effort that quickly fizzled. The companies that were paying the auditors simply weren't interested in paying more for audited NPS numbers. Nor were audited NPS results being demanded by regulators or investors. In fact, the only players willing to pay for reliable NPS data turned out to be private equity firms—and, not surprisingly, they preferred to pay Bain teams to help them create proprietary data and insights.

Nevertheless, we went on refining the NPS tool kit. Bain was doing (and still does) far more customer-love–related consulting work than any other firm in the world, including a great deal of work for our private equity clients and their portfolio firms. As a result, we developed a deep appreciation for the challenges of measuring NPS ratings correctly and also developed an ever-clearer picture of how to do it right. For example, we learned that seemingly small changes in survey technique can drive large changes in scores—things such as the timing of the survey request, the wording of the email's subject line, the choice to embed the survey in the body of the email versus requiring a click-through, the implication that the score will have a direct impact on an individual employee, the decision as to whether to run the score from 0 to 10 or 10 to 0, and so on. All of these factors can have a substantial impact on who bothers to respond to the survey and how they score it.[15] And finally, it matters who's executing the surveys and doing the analysis behind the scoring. If you want reliable benchmark scores, you must engage a third party that has the deep expertise to do it right and do it consistently.

After hitting that dead end with the accounting firms, we began to notice that the market research firms that had once been critics of NPS—including J.D. Power and Gallup—were changing their tune because their clients demanded NPS feedback. Today, several of these companies publish NPS rankings for key competitors in a variety of industries. But in a sense, we're back where we started. Because these companies use various measurement techniques and often rely on rudimentary segmentation and small sample sizes, their results tend to be all over the map. Some firms do no measurement of their own; they simply accept self-reported NPS information from companies and then republish it, hoping this will serve as clickbait and bring eyeballs to their website. Even apparently credible sources publish NPS benchmarks that seem dubious. For example, one respected website recently published its rankings, and its top-ranked industry sector, the one with the *very highest* average NPS rating, is—and I wish I could cue a drumroll here—*auto dealers*!

Again, this creates all kinds of confusion. I received an email from Zeynep Ton—the MIT professor who put me in touch with Costco's Jim Sinegal—expressing concern that the casual dining chain I had told her topped Bain's NPS ranking in that sector (Texas Roadhouse, mentioned earlier) showed up with the *worst* NPS rating on a list one of her students came across while searching the web. Obviously, this kind of chaos isn't good for anyone. It frustrates executives, misleads investors, and diminishes the credibility of our NPS framework.

So, Bain resolved to make the investment required to do it right by building a separate data business that became NPS Prism. Since then, the company has been marching through the economy, industry by industry, investing millions of dollars to develop a flow of timely and reliable data. Today, we can provide quarterly NPS ratings (and supporting detail) to stack-rank competitors within their industry and for each major episode (which some call "subjourneys"). By the time this book is published, NPS Prism will cover these US markets: retail banking (including credit cards, wealth management, and mortgage lenders), grocery retailing, insurance (home, auto, and life), utilities (electric and gas), airlines, autos, telecommunications, and commercial banking (including cards and merchant lending). In addition, a sprinkling of these industries is now being covered in Canada, Mexico, Brazil, the United Kingdom, Turkey, Hong Kong, and Australia.

Despite this impressive progress, the truth is that most industries and most parts of the world will have to wait years before relevant NPS Prism data will be available. To compound this problem, the NPS Prism research process relies on assembling panels of representative customers. This approach doesn't work in many business-to-business sectors, in which decision makers are hard to identify, and recruiting them to spend time filling out surveys is nearly impossible. NPS Prism even struggles to assemble panels in some consumer businesses when the core customers are hard to find or difficult to recruit.

A good example is the challenge faced by First Republic Bank. As I've described in earlier chapters, this is where I do my personal banking. As I got to know First Republic, I became convinced that its true NPS rating was likely the highest in the banking industry. At the same time, I wondered if the NPS Prism method might deliver more reliable benchmark scores. Even though First Republic's NPS surveying process was conducted by a third-party research group, customers knew that First Republic was sponsoring the research, and Promoters are typically more willing to spend time responding to survey questions. I was convinced that NPS Prism could provide First Republic with much better data.

But to my dismay, the NPS Prism solution didn't work. Why? Although First Republic Bank is a substantial company—among the twenty largest US banks, more than $110 billion in assets, and a member of the S&P 500—the number of customers it serves is relatively concentrated, and NPS Prism couldn't recruit enough of its core customers to join a panel without invoking the "First Republic" brand name. This may sound like a small point, but it most certainly is not: assembling your panels by invoking the company name almost always leads to an oversampling of Promoters and, by extension, inflated NPS ratings. In general, survey response rates for Promoters are 50–100 percent higher than for other customers. You don't have to be a statistics major to appreciate how hard it is to estimate the true Net Promoter Score of a customer population with this kind of response bias.

So, despite the impressive progress of NPS Prism, there is still a broad swath of companies that need an additional solution. This is one of the central challenges I have been wrestling with in recent years: how to create reliable audit-worthy data for *all* companies, big and small, for any industry in every geography. How can we create a complementary sister metric for NPS that relieves the pressure to make a survey-based score into a target, which corrupts its accuracy and effectiveness? Executives and investors alike need a simple metric that gauges the health of the company's growth engine. Clearly, we needed to buttress survey-based scores with an objective *outcome* statistic: measurable by accountants and based on observable behaviors.

Discovering Earned Growth Rate

After more than a decade of searching, I believe I have finally found the answer—and have First Republic to thank for pointing the way. First, some history on how we met. First Republic had adopted NPS and invited me to keynote at its management conference in San Francisco. I had to decline because I had just started my cancer treatments. Radiation and chemotherapy don't mix well with cross-country travel.

Like all good companies, First Republic was persistent. After I had sufficiently recovered the following year, First Republic flew me out to deliver the keynote address at its annual leadership conference. I did some research on the company in advance and interviewed several key executives. I was so impressed that I thought perhaps I had discovered another Vanguard or Enterprise Rent-A-Car—a loyalty leader, but this time in the banking industry.

Of course I had no way to *prove* that First Republic's NPS rating was truly superior to competitors such as JPMorgan Chase, Citibank, and Bank of America. When we found that the NPS Prism approach would not work for First Republic—for the reasons described above—I went back to the drawing board.[16] I dug through my old files and reviewed some of the original materials First Republic had shared in preparation for my keynote. I noticed I had yellow-highlighted a bar chart from one of its investor presentations and also added a couple of stars for emphasis. I pondered these charts, trying to recall why they merited so much yellow marker on my first pass—and eureka! I hit on the answer. The slide that created that "aha" moment is reproduced in figure 5-8.

What had struck me as being so interesting about this chart? First Republic effectively quantified how much of its growth resulted from existing customers coming back for more (the bank's deposit balances expanded by 50 percent) and bringing their friends (referrals accounted for 32 percent). In other words, *82 percent* of the bank's deposit growth was earned by delivering great experiences to existing customers. For loans, it was even higher: 88 percent. I asked First Republic's chief operating officer, Jason Bender, how the bank managed to quantify these numbers. He explained that First Republic's systems consolidate accounts based on households, so deposit and loan balance growth can easily be tracked for existing customers. In other words, First Republic has built the capacity to do customer-based accounting.

Jason also noted that as new customers join First Republic, they are queried as to whether they are joining due to a referral or recommenda-

FIGURE 5-8

First Republic Bank investor presentation slide—the "aha" moment

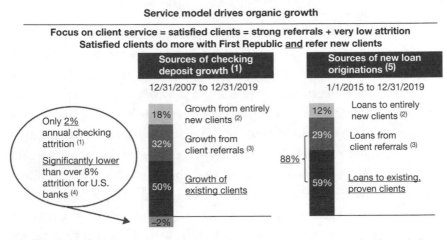

Service model drives organic growth

Focus on client service = satisfied clients = strong referrals + very low attrition
Satisfied clients do more with First Republic <u>and</u> refer new clients

(1) As measured by change in balances. Checking defined as all business and consumer checking, excluding money market checking.
(2) New clients defined as new relationships that joined FRC within the calendar year. The balances represent the combined accounts within the calendar year.
(3) Referrals as identified by KYC referral information for the first customer of new relationships in 2015–2019.
(4) Source: Harland Clarke. Represents US banking industry client attrition data from 2014–October 2017.
(5) Based on principal balance at origination, for loans originated during 2015–2019, excluding overdraft lines of credit and refinanced FRC loans. Includes all loan originations whether on balance sheet, sold, or currently held for sale.

Reproduced by permission from First Republic Bank.

tion. When I asked Jason why they tracked this data, he explained that the primary reason was to demonstrate that the bank's growth was safe and high quality. He explained that First Republic has been growing loans at approximately 15 percent per year in an industry that typically grows at 2–3 percent. What the data in figure 5-8 demonstrated, though, was that First Republic was *growing without adding risk*. Most of its growth came from customers they already knew well and from individuals referred by those long-term customers. It was not a result of lowering credit standards, which is a tactic frequently employed by banks that are hungry to grow their loan portfolios.

The name I coined for the statistic that First Republic Bank inspired me to create is *Earned Growth Rate* (EGR). It measures the underlying revenue growth generated by existing customers coming back for more and bringing their friends. The related statistic, the earned growth ratio, is simply the ratio of earned growth to total growth. That is what First Republic presented (see figure 5-8): 82 percent for deposits and 88 percent for loans. First Republic's total loan growth has been approximately 15 percent per year, so its EGR is 13.2 percent.

I described my Earned Growth Rate concept to Bain alum Kent Bennett, now a partner at Bessemer Ventures, who was very enthusiastic. He had been thinking along a similar path because so many of Bessemer's most successful investments had been in new ventures with outstanding earned growth (he called it "resting growth rate" because it indicated revenue growth that would occur with no additional customer acquisition cost). Kent cautioned us that in the venture world, investors and executives alike mistakenly presume that they understand the implications of earned growth because they already measure payback on customer acquisition cost or measure customer acquisition cost as a percent of customer lifetime value. This mindset, he warned, focuses managers on improving the efficiency of marketing spend rather than on the real root cause of profitable growth, which is the core offering's ability to generate such enthusiasm that Promoters grow the business without the need for marketing.

We have much to learn about how best to use and communicate earned growth, but for a primer on calculating this new metric, please see appendix B.

Customer-Based Accounting

In order to calculate earned growth, most companies will need to upgrade their basic accounting capabilities. This is long overdue. First Republic Bank was able to report earned growth to investors with the chart in figure 5-8, but even First Republic required some custom analysis to create that chart. In my view, every modern accounting system should be able to generate these numbers automatically. Until that happens, executives will be pressured to gauge progress based on traditional financial metrics that have no regard for customer love. In fact, accountability to current-period profits is the root cause of most of today's unloving bad-profit tactics (roaming fees, late fees, understaffed customer service centers, and so on).

This misplaced pressure hurts customers and also hurts investors, as demonstrated earlier in this chapter.

Obsession with quarterly accounting numbers makes it more difficult for executive teams who *want* to focus on loving their customers. They must deal with the carnival sideshow distractions of activist hedge funds pushing short-term gambits to boost quarterly earnings. They must spend inordinate time educating inexperienced portfolio managers about how their business actually works, then field the same old questions related to quarterly accounting results. Daily volatility in their share price unleashes questions and opinions from journalists and stock-picking "experts" who proffer interpretations and advice (which rarely have anything to do with loving customers better).

One possible solution is to shift to private ownership or convince someone like Warren Buffett to buy a large enough chunk of your stock to provide air cover. Of course, private equity partners (and the Buffetts of the world) are not softies about delivering quarterly results—in fact, just the opposite, in my experience. But the results over which they obsess are not reported accounting numbers, which often don't reflect true economics. Instead, they concentrate on more relevant metrics that reflect true customer economics. The founder of one of the world's leading private equity firms recently explained to a group of Bain partners that the reason he hired dozens of MBAs each year was to tear apart the accounting numbers for portfolio firms (and prospective acquisitions) and convert them into useful economic data. He told us what we already knew: accounting numbers have drifted further and further away from measuring economic reality and no longer illuminate the vital drivers of a business's health. For example, generally accepted accounting principles are mum on the subject of how many customers are buying more each year or how many new customers are coming through the doors, let alone how many join as the result of enthusiastic recommendations from existing customers.

The art of accounting needs a serious upgrade to support the movement toward customer capitalism. My colleague and coauthor on *The Ultimate Question 2.0*, Rob Markey, makes a compelling argument for customer accounting in his recent *Harvard Business Review* article.[17] Think about it: current accounting standards were graven in stone back when enormous amounts of financial capital were needed to build railroads, erect manufacturing plants, and acquire machinery to outfit factory floors. In-fluenced by the old-school paradigm that all excess value goes to inves-tors, accounting "profits" never take into account the cost of capital, which has led to very sloppy use of this resource.

Yes, accountants perfected techniques for capitalizing fixed assets and depreciating them over time. But we've embarked upon a new era in which manufacturing and capital goods represent only a small slice of the econ-omy. The service sector now accounts for more than 80 percent of the US economy, and that sector includes an even greater proportion of the start-ups that are likely to dominate the economy of the future. Those startups don't need capital to install steel rails and blast furnaces. They don't even need capital to buy their racks of computer servers, since computing can now be rented via cloud technology. Today far less capital is needed, and if it *is* required, that money goes to fund investments in intangible assets such as R&D, software code, supply chains, company reputation (and ratings), and—most especially—acquiring new customers and earn-ing their loyalty. These customer assets are not effectively valued by old-fashioned accounting techniques. Many firms can't even tell you with confidence how many customers they have! And those same firms are re-ceiving unqualified audits from their accountants—in other words, ac-counting today is so customer uncentric that it doesn't even care how many customers a firm has, let alone how many are coming back for more and bringing their friends.

Do we require our young entrepreneurs to drive Model Ts? No, but if they take their companies public, we require them to conform to Model T–vintage accounting.

The Two Components of Earned Growth

Customer-based accounting is already being practiced at firms such as Amazon, Costco, and Chewy, and most of these firms can already calcu-late the most important component of earned growth. For example, Chewy reported in its IPO document that its customer base from the previous year grew purchases by 120 percent. This comprises the first component of earned growth, which already has a name: net revenue retention (NRR).

FIGURE 5-9

Net revenue retention is a key driver of SaaS valuations

Valuation multiple (enterprise value/ARR)

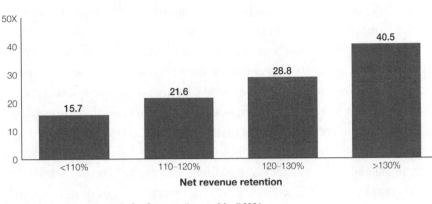

Net revenue retention

Note: Based on fifty-two public SaaS companies as of April 2021.

This battle-tested statistic is used today in several industries, most notably software as a service (SaaS). SaaS is that burgeoning sector of the economy that includes firms such as Salesforce, ServiceNow, Workday, Dropbox, and Zoom. The importance of NRR as a gauge for the quality (and sustainability) of growth is apparent from its impact on SaaS company valuations. SaaS Capital found that for each 1 percent increase in NRR, company value increases by a total of 15 percent over the subsequent five years.[18]

SaaS firms are typically valued based on a multiple of their annualized recurring revenues. As you can see in figure 5-9, NRR drives big changes in valuation multiples. Publicly traded SaaS companies with NRR above 130 percent are valued at more than twice the revenue multiple of firms with NRR below 110 percent. Evidently, SaaS investors understand that there is no more profitable and sustainable growth driver than a well-tuned loyalty-based engine.

Despite its widespread usage throughout the SaaS industry, individual firms report NRR based a variety of methodologies. Some use samples of customers, some exclude new customers who also defect within the same period and customers with multiyear contracts, and so on. My strong recommendation is to make this a formal generally accepted accounting principles (GAAP) metric with precise reporting rules, including footnotes detailing any variations from standard measurement guidelines.

The second (and typically much smaller) component of earned growth is Earned New Customer Revenue (ENCR), which quantifies revenues from the subset of new customers who were *earned* through recommendations and referrals from existing customers. NPS Prism began quantifying this component and found substantial variation across competitors. For example, among the top twelve credit card issuers, the portion of new customers who joined primarily due to recommendation or referral ranged from a low of 8 percent to a high of 31 percent. In checking and savings, the top US bank earns 53 percent of its new customers. We found one high-growth firm achieving a remarkable 90 percent ENCR. This wide variation in earned new customers indicates how important it is for executives to begin quantifying (and managing) this component of quality growth. This will require some elbow grease and innovation. But it is high time that we get serious about tracking it. Otherwise, firms will never be able to learn the full value of loving customers and will persist in their overinvestment in buying growth through promotions and aggressive sales tactics and underinvestment in delighting current customers.

Today few firms can parse new customers into earned versus bought, so we at Bain (in partnership with a team at Medallia) pioneered a practical solution to begin meeting this challenge. We provide more details on that solution at our website, NetPromoterSystem.com, but stated briefly, we tested out the best structure for a question to be integrated into the new-customer onboarding process. It is important to clarify the primary reason that customer decided to come aboard right at the beginning of the relationship, when the decision process is fresh in the customer's mind. I expect other solutions for parsing new customers into earned versus bought will evolve, but now that one proven solution exists (one simple question integrated into setting up the customer's account), there is no excuse for failing to track this vital statistic.

As customer-based accounting matures, I expect it will eventually generate the steady stream of information required to run the firm based on the full set of customer lifetime economics (which I detailed in *The Loyalty Effect* along with the process for calculating customer lifetime value). But in the meantime, every company should get started by tracking these

basic statistics: customer onboarding date and primary reason for joining, purchase frequency, volumes and pricing, costs of products/services,
changes in these items over time, and the date when customers become
inactive or defect. This data will enable you to compute earned growth.[19]
Viewing customers as a company's most important assets is just talk until
each customer's value is tracked and quantified.

Remember Truett Cathy's Bible-derived wisdom about the importance
of a good reputation, *a good name is more valuable than silver or gold*?
Well, leaders no longer must take this on faith. With customer-based accounting, they can start measuring the basic components of earned growth
and managing their loyalty-growth engine with real-time data. I think they
will come to the same conclusion as Truett. With customer-based accounting facts to support ongoing investment and budgeting decisions and to
buttress reporting to investors, this new focus of accountability will enable executives to stop tap dancing to the tune of outdated accounting metrics and start moving to the beat of customer love.

Implications for Executives, Investors, and Board Members

Maybe you're wondering why in a book primarily focused on enriching the
lives of customers I've included a relatively substantial chapter written
mainly from the investor's point of view. Well, investors still have a lot of
clout in the era of customer capitalism. I hope this chapter gives more confidence to CEOs, CFOs, and board members to make tough decisions in
favor of doing the right thing for customers, secure in the knowledge that
there is no inconsistency between customer love and investor respect. Wise
investors will support this priority. I hope more of my fellow investors become knowledgeable ambassadors for Net Promoter, not just the score but
also the system that supports learning and progress toward loving customers. Why? Once again, *the interests of long-term investors are best
served when executives inspire their teams to embrace loving customers
as their primary purpose.*

I hope more boards hold corporate leaders accountable for acting in the
best interests of customers and reward them generously when they deliver

TSR above the market average.[20] Directors now feel an explicit duty to protect investor interests. The evidence in this book demonstrates that to fulfill this duty, they must help eradicate bad profits, which are just as hateful for investors as they are for customers.

To reward executives for loving customers and to gauge progress toward this purpose, both investors and boards should insist on reviewing EGRs along with reliable NPS results compared to key competitors'—measured according to audit-worthy standards and generated (or verified) by a trusted third party. Finally, investors and board members alike should insist on reviewing customer-based accounting results. Today's narrow focus on current profits is destructive, because current profits are too easily boosted by abusing or exploiting customers rather than by loving them.

CHAPTER 6

Honor the Golden Rule

But First, Understand It

The Golden Rule—embraced in one form or another by most of the world's great religious traditions and stated succinctly in the Christian tradition as *love thy neighbor as thyself*—is one of the most profound ideas in the history of human civilization.[1]

I am not what most people would consider a very religious person, but I deeply believe that living the right life (or being a great leader) requires a profound understanding of the Golden Rule. This bedrock principle should help inform our standards for treating our fellow human beings, deciphering our own life's purpose, and determining how to measure progress toward achieving that mission. While the notion of living the right life may seem a bit philosophical, rest assured that this chapter also contains plenty of practical advice about building a great business and how the two things go hand in hand.

A number of years ago, I got to thinking about the Golden Rule and how it might pertain to the distinctly secular world of business. Wrestling with this notion, I decided to call on an old friend of mine who became a parish minister and continued to hone his scholarly skills by teaching at a nearby divinity school.

We had talked about the Golden Rule many years earlier; in fact, it was this friend who opened my eyes to the Golden Rule's long and nuanced history. The ancient precursors to today's Golden Rule, he said, date back to the time of Confucius who—more than twenty-five hundred years ago—told his followers, "Do not impose on others what you do not wish for yourself."[2] This negative formulation (don't do bad things to others) remained dominant through the time of the writing of the Torah and the rest of what came to be called the Old Testament. But then, according to Matthew 7:12, Jesus raised the stakes: *Do unto others as you would have them do unto you*. Then, in Matthew 22:39, they were restated in language that raises them even higher: *Love thy neighbor as thyself.*

This new gold standard certainly kicks it up a notch and sets the bar for moral behavior very high indeed. The new standard tells us not merely to avoid doing bad things to others but also to actively search out ways to do *good things* for others, to enrich their lives.

My friend and I agreed to meet at a local restaurant for lunch. After we placed our orders, I explained that I intended to write a business book centering on the Golden Rule. My friend was not enthusiastic. He told me that he didn't see how that could possibly work, given that—as he saw it—business is fundamentally built on selfishness and a zero-sum mentality. (In other words, for me to gain, you have to lose and vice versa.) And he went further. It was a stretch, he said, to imagine how the Golden Rule could serve as a practical tool for guiding daily life in *any* setting. "Why?" I asked. "Because it's simply too hard to know how that other person feels," he explained. He used himself and our server to illustrate his point. She was young, female, extroverted, multiply pierced, and—judging from one of her prominent tattoos—possibly an atheist. He was a senior citizen, male, introverted, and a fervent believer in God. How could either of them begin to understand the other? And absent that understanding, absent that empathy, how could the Golden Rule be followed?

I pushed back. I explained that I had observed exemplary business organizations that, as I saw it, had developed the leadership culture, structure, governance, and feedback systems needed to live by at least an approximation of the Golden Rule. I further asserted that even in the harshly competitive context of the free market, these firms were winning out because living the Golden Rule provided an unbeatable economic strategy. I shared some of the evidence that companies with superior Net Promoter Scores—which I equated to superior adherence to Golden Rule treatment of customers—were winning their respective competitive battles.

The look on my luncheon partner's face made it clear that he wasn't convinced. He offered me a caution: Might my invoking of the Golden Rule alienate business audiences and even push them in the wrong direction? In his own experience with congregations and seminary students, he knew that various members of our society have widely different (and firmly entrenched) ideas about what the Golden Rule actually means. Furthermore, most consumers and employees today seek the truth through their favorite web search engine, not in ancient texts or religious principles.

"Proceed carefully, Fred," he concluded.

• • •

And yet, the more I study companies that generate loyalty among customers and employees, the more leaders I find who preach and practice the Golden Rule. And these companies are winning—and winning big! Most NPS leading firms are Golden Rule exemplars, earning customer relationship Net Promoter Scores ranging from 50 to 70, sometimes even higher. Their employee Net Promoter Scores range between 40 and 60. These firms outgrow their competitors by delivering sustainable good profits, and their investor returns over the long run have been, well, heavenly.[3] It doesn't overstate the case to say that members of those company-centered communities are feeling a lot of, well, *love.*

When I learned that Four Seasons Hotels and Resorts had adopted NPS, I flew to Toronto to interview founder Issy Sharp, also the company's CEO at the time. To my surprise, he explained that he considered the Golden Rule to be the foundation of the Four Seasons culture, which helped him understand why the Four Seasons formula has worked so well in the many local cultures around the world where his hotels operate. He proudly pointed to his wife's research on this topic, which found that every one of the world's major religions incorporates the Golden Rule in one form or another. While its pedigree is ancient, I discovered, the term "Golden Rule" itself is relatively new. Nobody called it the Golden Rule until the seventeenth century, when Anglican preachers began using the term. This may explain why so many people assume that the rule is solely a religious idea, and why they presume that it has little relevance for commerce.

In my view, reinforced by Sharp and so many others, the core notion transcends religion. In fact, that notion provides the universal foundation for good relationships and healthy communities. But if that's right, and if the Golden Rule is such a winning strategy, why is it so hard to find in action? Consider the distracted, rude, pushy, and obnoxious drivers you encounter on your commute to work. Recall those shoppers at the grocery store who completely ignore fellow shoppers and even the checkout clerk as they blather on their cell phones. Visit your car dealer or call the customer service number for your cable TV provider and see if the Golden Rule is the first thing that comes to mind. Think about the lack of civility among leaders at all levels of government. Consider the armies of social media trolls. All of this selfishness and rudeness might seem to indicate that the Golden Rule is obsolete, so my putting it forward as the foundation of all good relationships and good communities may strike you as being a bit out of touch with reality. Many more people in your company surely feel this way, so be prepared to face a major challenge in changing your colleagues' mindset and convincing them that the best path to success is to treat their customers (and each other) with loving care.

I'm convinced that business leaders need to recognize six basic barriers that they must overcome to fulfill their duty to unleash the power of Golden Rule behavior across their corporate communities. Let's examine each of these challenges and practical solutions that have been embraced by loyalty-leading firms to conquer them.

Challenge #1: Superficial Understanding of the Golden Rule

Despite its apparent simplicity, there seems to be a great deal of confusion out there regarding how the Golden Rule should be interpreted. Many people were introduced to the rule in childhood, but many (even most) have never recognized its nuances and its potential applications to adult challenges. This shallowness of understanding is evidenced by criticisms such as "Treating someone the way you'd want to be treated means giving them Belgian chocolates because that is *your* favorite treat—but wait! They might prefer caramel. Or maybe they have diabetes, and *all* sweets are risky for them."

So maybe we should follow what some people call the Platinum Rule: *Treat others the way* they *want to be treated*. But of course, this creates its own problems. If a bully pushes his way to the front of a line at a restaurant, should the hostess seat him first because that's (obviously) how *he* wants to be treated? What about the patient who wants the doctor to prescribe a drug based on a persuasive TV advertisement or presidential endorsement? If the doctor knows that the drug could be harmful to this patient, she shouldn't simply follow the patient's wishes, right? The doctor must rise to a higher standard of dutiful care: the standard of love. She must find a way to treat the patient as she would a well-loved member of her own family.

The layers of complexity increase when you consider the interconnected web of relationships comprising the community. *Love thy neighbor as thyself* sounds as if there are only two people involved—you and your neighbor. But every relationship exists in the context of the community or the nested set of communities that support it. Effective solutions must bolster the health and vitality of the surrounding communities as well as the individual relationship. This is where issues such as protecting the environment, supporting diversity, and defending social justice come into the picture. While the primary purpose of a great business is making customers' lives better, this can't be accomplished by short-changing those broader responsibilities. A true Golden Rule solution has to satisfy requirements across multiple dimensions. It has to (1) enhance your neighbor's happiness and well-being; (2) maintain or, preferably, enhance your dignity and well-being; and (3) strengthen the web of communities supporting that relationship.

Think about it. If you were on the receiving end, would you be comfortable if a neighbor went so far overboard to make you happy that he sacrificed his life's savings and thereby shortchanged his family's future? Of course not; nobody wants the generosity that is directed at them to hurt others, just as no good person wants to become a parasite in relation to her or his neighbor or community. So, we need to discover ways to delight our neighbor without hurting ourselves (through workaholic hours or sacrificing our principles). We also have to protect our corporate community. For example, unprincipled cronyism or preferential treatment may boost the short-term happiness of two relationship partners but will diminish their dignity and reputation and also weaken the community, which is the foundation for our future happiness and well-being.

On the individual level, if you coach your daughter's basketball team, you shouldn't make her a starter just because that would make her happier. Similarly, in a business setting, propping up (enabling) customers or employees who are unprofitable, unproductive, or abusive to the community's values is incompatible with the Golden Rule standard. And this is a very high standard indeed, much higher and tougher to hit than, for example, "the customer is always right." Employees must innovate solutions that do not just serve to delight customers at the moment of purchase. These solutions must also enhance the long-term well-being and reputation of that customer, along with the dignity/self-respect of the server and, of course, the economic health of the business, while at the same time reinforcing the values, vitality, and sustainability of the hosting communities. The proponents of Environmental, Social, and Corporate Governance (ESG) reporting are simply making explicit this basic Golden Rule standard that defines a truly good relationship as one that enriches the lives of individuals and strengthens the surrounding communities.

As I said, a tough standard!

Solutions That Deepen Understanding

- For business teams to act in the best interest of the community, they need to understand their core economics to ensure that their decisions don't make one customer or one employee happy at the expense of the long-term health and sustainability of the company. Similarly, business teams need to be able to calculate, at least in rough terms, how much a proposed delightful innovation might cost—along with its likely benefits—to be sure the proposed investment is affordable. Extensive training in the economics of the business, including the share of profits provided by the most loyal customers, is therefore a substantial part of the employee-training curriculum at JetBlue and Southwest (NPS leaders in

US airlines) and at Qantas (a customer experience leader in Australia). Employees at Qantas learn that the lifetime value of business frequent flyers exceeds $10,000 and that their continued loyalty is vital to the firm's financial health. This knowledge helps employees make better judgments about whether it is worth a couple of dollars of fancy chocolates to make those customers feel special.

- Qantas also takes special care to ensure that its frequent flyers feel special but not at the expense of offending their fellow travelers (thus harming the community). So, when a flight attendant notices that a frequent flyer is seated in the back of the plane, the attendant looks for ways to make that passenger feel special. For example, if there are chocolates left over from first class, the flight attendant might bring some back for that frequent flyer. But the best practice here is to also offer chocolates to the people sitting next to that frequent flyer, which makes everyone happy. Instead of resenting the special status accorded that frequent flyer, her or his neighbors feel lucky they are seated next to the frequent flyer.

- USAA strives to serve its customers (primarily current and former military and their families) with empathy and compassion. So, the firm hires as many veterans and military family members as possible. Then to further build empathy—a foundational component of the Golden Rule—all new employees participate in the New Employee Orientation event. Newly hired senior executives attend alongside frontline employees. Employee volunteers get to wear battle gear and carry a full backpack. Other activities include eating a Meal, Ready to Eat (nutritional paste in a pouch), responding to military orders for immediate deployment, or roleplaying the experience of a military death notification.[4] The result is that when a phone rep hears from a customer, he or she can more easily imagine what that service person has been going through. Empathy training doesn't stop with the orientation. Senior executives and board members get a regular refresher course via the annual member day, during which 120 members spend time with 70 or so top USAA executives and board members who participate in exercises and small group sessions that enable the execs to more deeply understand current members' needs and concerns.

- Intuit has long appreciated the importance of building deeper empathy with its customers—a particular challenge for software firms, which rarely interact face-to-face with customers (and an increasingly common challenge for all firms as digital frontlines replace human interactions). Long ago, Intuit developed its Follow Me Home technique, which focuses on customers willing to allow Intuit employees to observe them at their home (or office) as they use the Intuit product. This firsthand experience with customers ensures that Intuit's software coders, product developers, marketers, and senior execs stay grounded in what customers need. With Covid-19 risks, the process has shifted to webcam solutions that still enable employees to see the world through the eyes of the customer. A related lesson that Intuit has learned through closing the loop with Detractors is that while there is clearly a benefit to customers—who feel that someone cares about solving their problem—the company benefits through increased empathy for customers that Intuit staffers build through these conversations. Staffers get a deeper appreciation for the struggles facing customers and how Intuit can help solve them. Closing the loop with customers might be the best empathy training program ever invented.

- Chick-fil-A franchisees face a particularly difficult challenge in building empathy in their team members. Many of their new hires are teenagers, who may have learned their social skills on TikTok or Snapchat. Looking the customer in the eye, talking in full sentences that don't begin with "like" or "so," and generally making customers feel welcome and special are learned skills. To address this challenge, the firm created a training video that operators could use to help their young hires recognize that the people on the other side of the counter are not just widgets to be processed quickly. Those people are *humans*, living their own lives with their own abundance of joys and concerns. In the video, each customer entering the store is accompanied by a thought balloon that reflects a challenge that customer is struggling with at the moment—a mother just diagnosed with dementia, a cancer recurrence for a daughter, a spouse just laid off from his job, and so on. The video helps these young employees imagine what it would be like to cope with these challenges and helps them begin to see the interaction with a customer as an opportunity for compassion and kindness rather than just an efficient delivery of an order of waffle fries. Perhaps this seems too scripted or overly mechanical, but operators teach their new crew members to avoid responding to a customer's thank-you with the popular but diffident-sounding "no problem." Instead, new employees are encouraged to respond with "My pleasure." Why? Well, all of us can do with a reminder that it is indeed a pleasure and a privilege to be of service to another human.

- Warby Parker executives (including its co-CEOs) foster empathy with customers and frontline teams by regularly doing side-by-sides with customer service reps. The executives also visit stores regularly, soliciting team and customer feedback in person. This direct experience serving customers ensures that headquarters execs stay close to current customers' concerns. And perhaps even more important, the executives experience the challenges—some of which are exacerbated by ever-changing systems or manual processes—faced by frontline employees in providing good customer service. Experiencing this frustration in person leads to more rapid solutions.

Challenge #2: Bad Incentive/Reward System

Engineer and efficiency expert W. Edwards Deming once observed that a bad system will beat a good person every time.

Let's apply that discouraging wisdom to this chapter's main themes. A good business system should make it easier for people to do the right thing and harder to do the wrong thing. It should recognize and reward individuals when they honor the Golden Rule and penalize them when they abuse it. Unfortunately, short-term profit incentives push many companies in the wrong direction. Instead of assets getting stewarded and built, they get milked. Salespeople overpromise benefits to customers because they earn the same commission regardless of whether the customer becomes a loyal Promoter or defects the following year as a vocal Detractor. Leaders burn out their teams in order to meet quarterly targets but don't have to bear the full cost of employee disengagement and turnover. Human resources departments meet recruiting targets by lowering hiring standards, knowing that the costs of poor customer service will show up in the budgets of other departments. Bonus plans reward executives for boosting short-term profits even if they embrace practices that abuse customers: late fees, understaffed customer service departments, complex returns policies, devalued frequent flyer miles, and all the other evils detailed in previous chapters.

The truth is, most governance systems today hold teams primarily accountable for meeting cost or revenue targets. Whenever profits are squeezed, departments get innovative with all manner of bad-profit policies. Walt Bettinger found that when he took on the leadership of the Schwab turnaround, one-quarter of company revenues resulted from bad profits. He asked his team to rank-order the offending policies—putting the worst at the top of the list—and committed the company to working its way down that list so that within several years they all would be eradicated. An important detail of this practice is that effective housecleaning, aimed at eliminating bad business practices, depends on an explicit and realistic time frame.

Inertia and bad habits can play a big role. One reason why the Golden Rule is so rarely considered in board rooms and operating plans is that it isn't a regular part of the decision-making discussion. If compliance with Golden Rule standards isn't measured—if it's not an explicit, measurable goal—it gets pushed to the back of the queue. Team members who deliver loving treatment of customers and colleagues get overlooked, while employees who deliver against cost or revenue targets get rewarded. Commission-based incentives can be particularly radioactive, motivating salespeople to oversell and to push inappropriate products.[5] Rewarding leaders for flouting the Golden Rule can make inherently good people do bad things. It can motivate them to exploit customers in order to pad their paycheck, often in the guise of maximizing shareholder value. When an organization not only tolerates such practices but also promotes those who employ them to positions of power and authority, the resulting system can overwhelm the good instincts of an awful lot of good people.

To sum up: bad business systems are powerful and almost never go away on their own. Leaders must take responsibility for shaping their company culture by modeling the right behaviors and, just as important, by shaping measurement and rewards systems to reinforce Golden Rule standards.

Solutions to Ensure Incentive/Reward Systems Reinforce the Golden Rule

- Beware of commissions. Too many firms assume that the only way to move products and services is to pay steep front-end commissions. As noted, this encourages salespeople to overpromise, push inappropriate products, and ignore shoppers who don't appear ready to buy today. It's worth remembering, though, that loyalty leaders such as Apple Retail generate an awful lot of revenues while completely avoiding commissions. The same is true for T-Mobile, Costco, and Discover. In fact, I can think of very few great firms that rely heavily on sales commissions. Maybe when your sales are sluggish, it's not because of a tepid economy or a weak sales team but instead because you have a weak product, your service is mediocre, or your pricing is out of line given the quality of the overall customer experience. Here's a clue: there are numerous industries that relied heavily on commission sales that have been turned on their heads by new entrants that got rid of commissions. Mattress retailing—with its tricks, traps, and commission-based salesforce—provided a dreadful experience until new digital entrants such as Casper, Tuft & Needle, and Purple arrived on the scene. Slick eyeglass purveyors were ambushed by Warby Parker. Old-school stock brokers have been displaced by Schwab, Vanguard, and Fidelity. The common thread? *No sales commissions.* If you as a leader feel you simply *must* use commissions, then make sure there are clawbacks if customers aren't happy long term, and make sure your company adopts generous returns and refund policies. Consider flattening commissions so that the effort invested to sell a new customer only pays off with repeated commission awards over the years as the customer makes repeat purchases. This approach ensures that the salesforce will target prospective long-term customers with an honest sales pitch that establishes realistic customer expectations.

- Again, if commissions absolutely can't be avoided, consider keeping an eye on NPS results for each sales team. California Closets had been using NPS for several years and was proud of the stellar feedback it was getting from customers. But the business leaders were worried: they suspected that prospects who came in for a design consultation and proposal but chose *not* to buy were less enthusiastic about their experience. Why? Commissions account for the bulk of a design consultant's earnings, and it seemed likely that if a consultant didn't think a purchase was imminent, he or she tended to become dismissive toward that prospective customer. Indeed, one rep had been overheard describing how she treated customers who chose not to buy on the spot. "Those people are *dead* to me," she declared. Well, that attitude was probably hard to disguise—if indeed she tried to disguise it!—and was completely inconsistent with the company's goal of delivering such an outstanding shopping experience that even if someone chose not to buy right away, that person would still tell friends and neighbors great things about California Closets and give the company another chance on the prospect's next project. So, the leadership team initiated a process to measure NPS for prospects who did not buy that was originally called *lost prospects* but thereafter referred to as *future customers*. When they began measuring it, future customer NPS was –23 percent, far lower than the +78 percent NPS for buyers. By publicizing results for all branches and highlighting the practices of star performers—one designer's NPS for "future customers" was an amazing

+67 percent!—the firm has made rapid progress. Moreover, most of the other companies across the FirstService Brands portfolio have now adopted this enlightened technique.

- Beware of paying for scores. In other words, paying a bonus based on survey-based scores usually works against the Golden Rule. (Think back to the auto dealer example in chapter 1, with all the pleading, manipulating, dissembling, and bribing.) When Bain launched its client NPS feedback process, we used feedback scores as part of the evaluation system for partners—a big mistake, as it turned out. Our Bain partners pushed back. They argued that the process smacked of bureaucratic overhead and provided little useful insight, in part because it made them reluctant to nominate survey recipients outside of their circle of friends and supporters at the client.[6] In response, we made two changes to make this process more Golden Rule friendly. First, we completely decoupled this feedback (positive or negative) from partner bonus evaluations, and second, we put frontline partners in charge of redesigning the system to make it useful to them. As a result, they now control when surveys are launched, which often means involving their entire case team in the choice of which individuals to survey. If you feel that you must include NPS ratings in employee bonuses, then follow the process used by T-Mobile in its customer service centers: link bonuses to team scores, never individual scores.

- Enterprise Rent-A-Car pays its people based on branch profits. This incentive seemed to work but led to some profit-centric behaviors that did not make the Taylor family proud. In response, they instituted a customer feedback scoring process—which they called the "Enterprise Service Quality index," or ESQi—that was the forefather of NPS. Simply measuring was not sufficient, so they experimented with ways to give this measure teeth without linking it directly to bonus arithmetic. (They had seen the appalling outcome at car dealerships, and they wanted no part of that.) The sweet spot for them, it turned out, was linking ESQi scores to promotion eligibility. Today, no one gets promoted—which is far more important to long-term career income than any single year's bonus—unless their unit ranks in the top half of comparable units, based on customer feedback scores.

- The milestones and achievements that a company honors speak volumes about what that company truly values. Many firms reward the top salespeople with trips and trinkets. At Bain, one of the most revered is the Bright-Dix Award (named for two consultants who were exemplary coaches whom we lost in the tragic Pan Am 103 terrorist attack over Lockerbie, Scotland). In each of the past thirty-plus years, we've conducted a nomination and voting process that recognizes managers at Bain for exceptional contributions to the development of consultants through training, coaching, and mentoring—a cornerstone of our team culture. It's not compensation exactly, but it's something that many people value far more than the marginal dollar.

Challenge #3: Inadequate Feedback/Measurement

Each person is unique; without a reliable feedback system, it's impossible to know when you are treating your neighbors in ways that they feel have enriched their lives. How does an introvert know what makes an extrovert happy? How can the vegan understand the omnivore? How does the pro-life partisan empathize with his or her pro-choice counterpart? In the business setting, if there is no reliable litmus test, how can an employee know whether his or her action has increased a customer's happiness and well-being?

This is where the Net Promoter System can play a vital role. The frontline server can review scores and comments and observe subsequent loyalty behaviors. Collectively, this information can help clarify the degree to which the customer felt loved and, by extension, how well the employee has lived up to the Golden Rule. This information also enables employees and whole teams to compare themselves with peers, spotlighting effective practices employed by others so they can be replicated.

Feedback must come frequently enough that customer happiness remains front and center in the employee's daily priorities. In addition, feedback needs to be delivered in a timely way so that the employee can recall the interaction clearly, including all the small but vital contextual elements. The feedback loop also has to reflect the reality of the specific transaction at hand. In some business settings, it's relatively easy to tell when you've succeeded at making a customer happy. The customer-group trainer at the Apple Store, for example, can observe the energy level and "student" reactions during their class experience and gauge firsthand how well he or she has managed to enrich lives at that class. But even that trainer can be surprised—such as when the student who is introverted in the store setting goes home and provides detailed commentary on the follow-up survey or when the satisfied student becomes much less happy when he gets home and finds out that he actually *doesn't* understand how to do overdubs using Garage Band.

The solution is twofold. First, you need to devise a way to gauge how your interaction with a customer made her or him feel through a feedback process that feels comfortable and frictionless. Again, this is where the Net Promoter System can play such a useful role. For this, all you need is a quick assessment of the experience—usually with a 0 to 10 rating—coupled with an opportunity for customers to explain in their own words their reasons for the score and how you might improve.

Second, surveys must be augmented with signals, real behavior, or operational data. Good systems track customer comments on ratings boards, how long customers spend on each screen, how many click streams go awry resulting in abandonment, how many callbacks are made to the service center representing failure to resolve customer issues, and so forth. Why this second data stream? Surveys can be bothersome, meaning that many (even most) customers don't respond to them. Over time, survey-based systems tend to deliver diminishing insights. Many older systems today have collapsed into entropy, yielding minimal response rates and top-box scores accounting for 80 percent of responses. This doesn't square with reality—it's still pretty rare and remarkable when a customer genuinely experiences Golden Rule treatment. If your system isn't identifying plenty of problems and opportunities for improvement, chances are good it is time for a major redesign.

Solutions That Measure Signals Accurately and Frequently

- Package delivery services now offer digital tools that enable customers to check on the status of their delivery. When the system detects that a customer has checked a delivery status multiple times, it is a safe bet that the company should prioritize that delivery. If a failure to meet the promised schedule appears inevitable, the system should signal a customer service rep to reach out to apologize and discuss alternative arrangements. Digital monitoring of the amount of advance notice customers receive about a changed delivery window combined with NPS feedback customers provide after the delivery is completed can help determine the right deadline for alerting customers to changes. For example, one firm noticed that NPS ratings drop precipitously when customers receive notification less than twelve hours prior to their originally scheduled delivery time, so the system sends alerts prior to this twelve-hour window whenever possible.

- One of our banking clients regularly polled its customer service reps to identify friction spots in the customer experience. The client learned, for example, that many customers were calling in with concerns about whether their automatic payment would be made on time—simply because this information was not prominently displayed on the web statements. This was quickly fixed once the design team understood the priority. Frontline feedback often provides highly reliable signals and avoids bothersome surveys to customers.

- **Warby Parker:** Warby carefully tracks NPS for all customer segments and monitors the relationship between customer NPS and the time between the moment a customer places an order for eyewear until its ultimate delivery. The company found a very direct relationship between the length of this fulfillment cycle and how many customers provide Promoter scores. Understanding what it takes to delight a customer helps determine evolving thresholds for achieving customer delight. This data drives decisions on how much the firm invests in expedited shipping. Warby's target is to ensure shipping times that drive NPS ratings above 80 percent.

- **Peloton:** When the Covid-19 pandemic closed gyms and in-person fitness classes, the demand for Peloton's already popular home exercise equipment exploded, while simultaneously disrupting the young firm's supply chain and manufacturing capacity. Peloton didn't wait to learn which customers were unhappy with delivery delays through NPS surveys; instead, the firm grabbed control of operational signals and proactively reached out to customers for whom delivery estimates were unrealistic and sent email apologies along with $200 credits and immediate (complimentary) access to the Peloton app.

- **Apple:** Apple has integrated all of its customer feedback—online, phone, and store—onto one platform, Medallia, which uses the NPS framework and taxonomy. This helps individual employees learn from customers in a timely way through an app on their iPhone and also allows the company to easily perform rankings and analysis at the store level by product line, customer segment, and so on. Apple can run quick tests on improvement ideas to see if they are appreciated by customers (from ideal shirt colors to a revised pickup process for phones that are bought online but picked up at a local store). Too many companies let separate departments run their favorite feedback process, using different technology platforms, questions, sampling techniques, and so forth. This makes no more sense than letting those departments choose their own process for reporting financial results. Signal and survey NPS should be integrated, calibrated to be sure feedback is accurately categorizing success and failure (Promoter, Passive, Detractor), and then provided to employees.

Challenge #4: No Safe Time and Place to Process Feedback

Today's workplace can often feel chaotic, moving at an ever faster pace. Given that reality, it's vital to stake out a time and place where employees can each review their results, consider feedback comments, recognize success, analyze failures, and ponder the right action implications. This needs to be done first *in private*, in preparation for subsequent discussions with one's coach or colleagues.

The need for safety extends to those discussions as well. People have to believe that it is safe to give and receive feedback. They have to believe that coaching and inspiration—rather than judgment, evaluation, or punishment—are the intent. Conversely, if team members feel that the feedback process is designed to rank-order them, shame low performers, or make their failures a part of their permanent record, they will focus their mental energy on reframing, excuse making, and blame-shifting. Unfortunately, most companies completely overlook the need for employee education in terms of both giving feedback and processing feedback effectively so they can learn and grow.

Intuit, the first company outside of Bain to adopt NPS, has been a member of our NPS Loyalty Forum since its early days. Like Apple, Intuit has put a great deal of thought into how best to use the framework to ensure that the company treats customers right. In Intuit's initial deployment of NPS, the company's phone center leader reported NPS ratings for each rep on public leaderboards, thinking that this approach would recognize the stars and put pressure on the laggards. The outcome, however, was far from what Intuit expected. Listening in on the phone calls of the rep with the highest score in an effort to discover best practices, managers instead heard the same opening line repeated to each customer: "I hope you are having a '10' kind of day!" This is all too similar to the car salesman reminding me that *in our dealership, only a 10 represents a passing grade!*

This embarrassing manipulation of scores led Intuit to reconsider its approach. When I visited the company's Tucson phone center about a decade later, I observed clear improvements. No leaderboards were posted on the walls. I asked a supervisor—they are called "coaches"—how he used NPS. He explained that scores and "verbatims" are forwarded to each rep for their own self-development. Then, each month the coach selects two calls handled by that rep (all calls are recorded for training purposes)— one that generated a Detractor score, the other a Promoter score. He and the rep sit and listen to both calls, and then the coach asks the rep which call went well and which one didn't, why this happened, and how the problem might have been handled differently. That process lets reps figure out in a safe, nonevaluative session what they want to work on, and they can self-grade their progress as they receive NPS feedback over the subsequent period. The reps like this process; it preserves their dignity, and they view the feedback as helpful to their personal progress. Meanwhile, Intuit continues to outperform its competitors.

Contrast this to the many stores and call centers run with a factory mindset, obsessed with logistical and operational efficiencies rather than customer delight. They refuse to grant time for daily huddles or coaching sessions, since that means there's less time available to staff the sales floor and the phones. There is little benefit implementing an expensive feedback platform full of the latest technology unless it feeds into a process that enables teams to ponder and process the feedback.

This factory mindset also leads to calls for narrower accountability metrics, based on satisfaction or effort, that relate only to a specific transaction. But unless service reps welcome and act upon feedback relevant beyond their narrow silo—and help drive improvements across the entire customer experience—their jobs will not be safe. Humans will be replaced by inexpensive bots if their roles don't incorporate judgment, interpretation, and creativity to deliver ever-better customer experiences.

Solutions to Provide a Safe Time and Place to Process Feedback

- **Apple:** As a successful Apple store manager once told me, "We share positive feedback for individuals in front of the entire team, but negative feedback gets handled in private." Customer feedback referencing specific team members goes right to their iPhone. Only their leaders get to see this detail so they can use it for coaching. Employees are never publicly ranked by their NPS results.

- **Bain:** As noted in chapter 3, the core feedback process at Bain is the team huddle. Performance pressures at Bain can be substantial, and unmanaged, these pressures could lead to a "Lord of the Flies" culture. With that in mind, everyone is trained to give and receive feedback in a frame of helpful coaching aimed at making the team a better place to work. Scores and feedback are designed to help our teams *win with clients,* and the rhythm of weekly huddles helps make feedback feel like a grade on a homework assignment, not a high-stakes test.

- Several of my clients—especially during the Covid-19 pandemic pressure cooker—redacted individual employee names and numerical scores from all feedback before sharing it with the team. While I was initially skeptical of this approach, it turned out to be quite effective. Negative feedback can be quite threatening to an individual employee, but when those employees are treated as part of a team, they can be less defensive and can better hear, process, and respond more constructively to customer feedback.

- Well-designed technology tools can help solve this challenge by skipping the boss and helping reps learn directly from customers. One popular tool uses artificial intelligence to select the most useful comments from customers recently served by a rep that deserve consideration and study. These self-help tools enable reps to learn to be more effective without any pressure from a supervisor or coach. This process helps reps assume responsibility for their own improvement programs, which often helps make them more receptive to feedback and open to discovering new approaches.

Challenge #5: Anonymity

Building a community of accountability requires that individual behavior—both bad and good—be visible and be noticed by leaders and the rest of the community. In other words, anonymity is often the enemy of Golden Rule behavior. It can enable bullies, slackers, and cheats to abuse community members—and the community itself—without incurring negative consequences. In the old days, shopkeepers in small towns had a pretty good idea which customers were reliable and would pay their bills. People knew one another and knew who they could trust; reputations were built on observable behaviors and actions. But in this day and age, it's impossible to always know what kind of person we are dealing with. Today, anonymity lets individual accountability get lost in the crowd. This problem gets magnified in digital communities of all types when they enable complete anonymity. People resort to inflammatory language they would never use face-to-face. Given the increasingly vital role these digital channels play in the world today, this anonymity *must* be mitigated if the Golden Rule is to prevail in the increasingly digital world.

Purely anonymous feedback and ratings can breed irresponsible, even reprehensible, behavior. But at the same time, full transparency—linking every piece of feedback to an individual—may diminish honesty and candor. The social pressure to be nice often mutes criticism and inflates scores. This circumstance is exacerbated when there is an imbalance of power. Patients might have a difficult time rating their dentist, for example, if they plan to be sitting in his chair anytime soon.

The upshot: while complete anonymity is inimical to living the Golden Rule, *structured anonymity* is often vital. "Structured" means that while individual identities are appropriately compartmentalized and hidden from the giver and receiver of feedback—say, the Uber driver and passenger—the system knows all. Responsible executives can access full details to make better decisions and to ensure system integrity. Amazon ratings don't reveal the identities of those raters, but Amazon knows who they are and can take steps to improve accountability to Golden Rule standards. The key is to design each feedback process with the optimal degree of anonymity—as little as possible, within the constraints of generating honest and constructive feedback.

Solutions for Optimizing Anonymity

- **Bain feedback:** Our internal process ensures that the right people are given a vote—and only one vote—and we guarantee anonymity, when requested, so people will say what they really think and feel. Similarly, when we gather feedback from our clients, we provide the option for individuals to mask their identity. Yes, this makes it far more difficult for teams to probe into root causes, since they can't reach out directly to respondents. But we have learned that some members of client teams (especially the most junior members) won't tell us what they really think if they fear that it might make them seem uncooperative or might reflect badly on the image they want to maintain with their boss.

- **Amazon:** Amazon's five-star reviews are anonymous to encourage candor. The firm has worked to improve credibility of reviews with its certified purchase program and by letting users rate the usefulness of reviews. But there remains plenty of room for improvement given that, according to experts, a substantial portion of Amazon's reviews are not genuine.

- **Airbnb:** Airbnb helps coax out all of the possible value from guest and host feedback with a two-way rating system that makes it possible to score honestly. Reviews remain blinded for a fixed time window, and then both sides are revealed simultaneously. Public ratings and commentary—visible to site visitors and to Airbnb headquarters staff—are supplemented with private channels. These enable guests to give friendly advice or coaching, such as noting a wobbly table leg, without hurting the guest's public reputation and without any fear of intervention from Big Brother at headquarters. Similarly, there is a private channel that lets a host report guest issues that may warrant Airbnb intervention.

- **Uber:** In order to avoid retribution and to keep things comfortable for passengers, both sides of Uber's ratings—of drivers by passengers and of passengers by drivers—are kept anonymous to those two players. However, those ratings are fully transparent to the executives at headquarters, who strive to design effective incentives for recognition and appropriate sanctions where necessary.

Challenge #6: Bad Behavior

The Golden Rule works best in communities composed of basically good people—that is, individuals striving to live the right kind of life, inspired by enriching the lives of others. But out there in the real world, some people care only about themselves. Organizational psychologist Adam Grant calls these people "takers."[7] Takers are not motivated by making the world (or their community) a better place; they simply want to take as much for themselves as possible.

I asked Adam for his current estimate as to what percentage of people out there are flat-out takers. His response: 19 percent. Ugh! I suspect and hope that the number of really bad people is less than that. Twitter estimates that all of the abusive, threatening, and hateful messages on its platform emanate from only 1–2 percent of its users.[8] Whatever the real number is, bad actors can't be tolerated. In order for the Golden Rule to work as a collective guiding principle, there must be a process for dealing with customers, colleagues, suppliers, partners, and investors who consistently exhibit bad behaviors. Tolerating these transgressions undermines the community and sucks away energy and resources from the people who deserve them. Special attention must be paid to ensure that our leaders practice the Golden Rule. If self-centered bullies, slackers, and cheats slither into leadership roles, the community is doomed to a lower standard of behavior, since members will imitate the moral standards exemplified by leadership.

One great strength of corporate communities is that they are voluntary associations within which customers, employees, vendors, and investors are free to choose and build relationships that are mutually beneficial. But those relationships must also serve to reinforce the vitality of the community. When individuals fail to make a valuable contribution or when they act in a manner that is hurtful to the general good, they should be held accountable. Leaders must be courageous enough to let values and principles drive their decisions and priorities and to protect all constituents from bad actors—whether they are customers or coworkers.

Solutions for Mitigating Bad Behavior

- **Uber drivers:** If a driver's customer scores drop into the bottom 10 percent versus their local peers' (4.6 percent or below in most markets), they receive a warning. They also receive suggestions for improving their performance based on passenger feedback comments. If drivers fail to make progress with this coaching from their local management team, they are encouraged to take an online course from a firm that specializes in helping them provide a better customer experience. If all this fails, drivers are dropped from the platform.

- **Uber customers:** Uber also scrutinizes driver ratings of its passengers. The system automatically penalizes low-rated customers, since drivers have access to this data, which can influence which rides they accept. In extreme cases, Uber bans customers from using its service. The regional manager for Australia and New Zealand revealed that his team takes this action with hundreds of customers each year. These are customers who are physically or verbally abusive to fellow passengers or to drivers. To ensure that there are no extenuating circumstances and that customers receive due process, banning a customer requires a phone conversation between a local Uber executive and the customer. In this way, the company can decide if this customer deserves another chance.

- **JetBlue:** Most of the airlines maintain no-fly lists comprising passengers barred from flying on their airline. Passengers can also be banished for abusive treatment of fellow passengers or crew, which typically requires the direct intervention of a flight captain. JetBlue was in the news recently when it discovered that a passenger who knew he had been exposed to Covid-19 chose to fly on a JetBlue flight, thereby exposing fellow passengers and crewmembers to the virus. That passenger was banned from the airline—for life.

- **Airbnb:** Low-rated hosts and guests are punished through free-market mechanisms. Hosts with bad ratings struggle to achieve competitive pricing, and their occupancy falls. Customers with bad ratings have difficulty renting desirable properties. If those bad behaviors continue, the offending parties are dropped from the platform. In the aftermath of the 2021 storming of the US Capitol, Airbnb worked closely with law enforcement agencies to identify individuals with criminal involvement and blocked them from using the platform.

- **Apple:** I asked a group of Apple store employees what changes could improve their work experience. A popular suggestion was to find a way to sanction the handful of customers who ruin the employee experience (as well as that of fellow customers). These are abusive customers who take advantage of Apple's customer-friendly system and regularly bend the rules. One employee described how a customer threatened to score him a zero on the next survey unless he gave in to the customer's demand for a free screen replacement for his phone, which was well beyond its warranty period. One Genius Bar employee was actually head-butted by an unruly customer who lost his cool upon learning that his erased data could not be recovered. Abusive customers deserve to be placed on a "no-buy" list.

For a devotee of Apple products, that would be punishment indeed!

● ● ●

Five simple words helped transform our world: *Love thy neighbor as thyself.* Or, if you'd prefer a secular version for use in the marketplace, *enrich the lives you touch.*

Great business organizations must pursue this purpose by creating the right culture and environment and using NPS to measure and manage progress. Which firms stand as exemplars? I'll resort to biblical language: *By their fruits you shall know them.* Rock-star Net Promoter Scores, supported with glowing verbatim comments, provide compelling evidence as to which firms' customers are feeling the love.

One of the great advantages of a business organization is that its leaders have an enormous degree of freedom to design their community to enable and reinforce Golden Rule standards of behavior and protect customers, employees, and investors against bad actors. The innovative approaches summarized in this chapter illustrate practical ways to make the Golden Rule the centerpiece of an organization.

Maybe you've come to the conclusion that this challenge is formidable and that overcoming the inherent barriers requires an awful lot of work. If so, then you've understood this chapter correctly.

Is living up to Golden Rule standards worth all the effort? Yes, indeed. Based on the evidence presented in this and earlier chapters, only firms with stellar track records of enriching customer lives sustainably grow and prosper. Treating people right should be the responsibility of all good companies and of all the good people who make up those companies. In fact, business organizations operating responsibly in a free-market system offer our greatest hope for building sustainable communities of accountability to Golden Rule standards of behavior.

Some readers may be asking what about governments, churches, charities, and other nonprofits? Of course they play an essential role. But the miracle of a great business is that it is self-funding. And it funds these other organizations, either directly through taxes or donations or indirectly through value created for employees, suppliers, and investors. Governments can establish the rule of law, but regulatory and legal standards merely echo the Old Testament notion of not harming your neighbor. Winning businesses kick it up a notch and innovate ways to *love thy neighbor*. That is the kind of community in which I want to live.

CHAPTER 7

Be Remarkable

Not Merely Satisfactory

On a recent Christmas day, my wife Karen and I drove over to visit our son Bill and his wife Alicia—our Apple Store newlyweds, introduced in the preface—at their new house.

At one point while we were catching up, I asked Bill if he'd observed any remarkable customer experiences over the holiday season. I confess, I was hoping to pick up some fresh new Apple stories. Instead, Bill shared a recent experience he'd had with Amazon, a story that illustrates why many Amazon customers have come to love that company as much as its investors do.

Ironically, the story he told me is likely to make a traditional financial-capitalist investor wince.

Bill explained that he had purchased a going-away gift for a colleague who was transferring to Apple's operation in Dubai. The item, which was worth something north of $100, was supposed to be delivered by Amazon directly to that friend's house, but his departure to Dubai was approaching, and the package hadn't yet arrived. Bill called Amazon to investigate and learned from the service rep that according to their records, the package had already been delivered. At this point, Bill noticed to his chagrin that he had entered the wrong address for his friend's house. He apologized, admitted his mistake to the rep, and offered to pay for the replacement order if she could help him by speeding a second delivery along. She determined that the address he had mistakenly entered didn't exist, and therefore Amazon should have caught the mistake. She took the correct address from Bill and rushed a replacement to his friend at Amazon's expense. Remarkable!

This reminded me of a more prosaic but still gratifying experience I had with Amazon a year earlier. I didn't recognize the title of a movie rental on my bill, nor could any of my family members recall ever watching that film. I called Amazon and told the service rep that the charge must be in error. The service rep was very polite and agreed right away to remove the charge but mentioned in passing that Amazon's billing system could tell me the type of TV on which the movie supposedly had been viewed if I was interested.

I jotted down the information and did some investigating. As it turned out, we did indeed own that model of TV in our guest room. After some further exploration, I found that a guest had viewed that movie intending to reimburse us but had forgotten to close the loop. So, I called Amazon back, apologized, and told the service rep that Amazon should reinstate the charge. The service rep replied politely that there was no easy way to do that. Then she said that it was obvious from my records I had been a very good customer and asked if I would please accept that movie rental as a gift, with the compliments of Amazon.

Again, remarkable!

Two epilogues to that story: the next day, I received a very brief survey asking about my experience. After I responded, I received a digital follow-up message from Amazon: *Thank you for helping us become the earth's most customer-centric company.*

As you might imagine, this caught my eye. *Quite a lofty ambition*, I remember thinking to myself. I was reminded of this episode later that year when we faced a household emergency. Something was eating all the koi fish in our garden pond. Where we live there are plenty of suspects when it comes to this kind of crime, including herons, otters, minks, foxes, raccoons, and coyotes. Before I could take any countermeasures, I had to identify the culprit. Since we saw no signs of poaching during the day, we figured that the thieves must be operating by night. So, I visited the Amazon website and bought the highest-rated night-vision wildlife camera I could find.

Sadly, when the camera arrived, the instructions were truly unintelligible, and I couldn't figure out how to make the thing work. (More on unintelligible instructions later in the chapter.) Defeated, I revisited the Amazon website to initiate a return. I had been in such a rush to get the camera mounted—determined to rescue the remaining koi before it was too late—that I damaged its shipping carton beyond repair. Now I was mentally prepping myself for a multistage hassle: finding an appropriate box, sealing it up tight, printing out a label, driving the package to the UPS store, standing in line, filling out a form, and so on. But I learned on the Amazon website that the company had invented a slick new return process. In real time, the company emailed me an authorization code. Now all I had to do was take the camera and my iPhone to the closest UPS Store (or Kohl's or Whole Foods), hand the camera over to the counter attendant, and the staff would take care of packing it in an appropriate carton with the right labeling.

So I went to a nearby UPS store. The young man at the counter scanned the authorization code on my iPhone, and my account was instantly credited—no need to wait for the shipment to be received and processed at the warehouse for funds to be transferred back to me. Once inside the store, the whole transaction took less than sixty seconds. Amazing, Amazon!

Not long after that, I read some of our Bain research on Amazon that forecasted it would soon account for over *50 percent* of all online retailing. That research concluded that one important reason for Amazon's success was its customer-friendly pricing. Maybe this surprises you; I know it surprised me. Over the years, I had certainly read those articles accusing Amazon of using sophisticated dynamic-pricing algorithms to charge customers the highest possible price—claiming, in other words, that Amazon used its big-data analytics expertise to extract the most money from customers based on their zip code, prior purchase behavior, computer model, type of internet browser, and so on.

Those accusations seemed entirely plausible, given the broad appeal of seemingly scientific dynamic-pricing algorithms that were already at work in the marketplace, covertly maximizing revenue from each transaction. These tools are widely used in such industries as entertainment and travel. You have probably experienced this in purchasing an airplane ticket. The price can fluctuate wildly for the exact same seat on a specific flight, depending on the time of day you are searching, your location, and even the day of the week. Third-party cookies are spying on your click patterns, informing stealthy algorithms designed to extract maximum dollars from you.

This infuriates me. So I interviewed several acquaintances who've spent time working for Amazon and asked flat-out if the firm does indeed use its deep data and technical wizardry to charge customers the highest possible price. They were uniformly skeptical, since this would run counter to Amazon's core principles.[1]

Bain's research confirms their skepticism. We shopped a variety of items across all major retail categories and discovered that Amazon was walking its talk. The company had the lowest (or was tied for the lowest) price on the web more than 80 percent of the time. Most of the items in which Amazon's price was not among the lowest cost less than $25. Like most things Amazon does, this is no accident. It turns out that on a Saturday morning in the spring of 2001, Jeff Bezos met with Jim Sinegal in a local Starbucks and learned about Costco's pricing philosophy. The following Monday, Bezos announced to his leadership team that Amazon's incoherent pricing strategy was about to change. "There are two kinds of retailers," he said. "There are those folks who work to figure how to charge more, and there are companies that work to figure how to charge less, and we are going to be the second, full-stop."[2]

I witnessed the transition firsthand. In the old days, I had to waste lots of time searching various websites to find the best deal, since prices—including Amazon's—were all over the map. But gradually, it became clear to me that if Amazon's posted price wasn't the best, it was pretty darn close. I also appreciated Amazon's practice of pricing its shipping fees honestly. Other retailers offered loss-leader pricing on the item itself, then clawed back their profit margins by gouging on the price they charged for shipping the item. Sometimes they hid these exorbitant shipping fees until the order was almost complete on the safe assumption that some people wouldn't notice and that others—while unhappy about being snookered—would choose to swallow the inflated shipping fee rather than starting all over again at another site.

This situation opened the door for Amazon to create something truly remarkable for its customers: Amazon Prime.

Prime Time

In February 2005, Amazon changed the rules of e-commerce in favor of the customer by creating Amazon Prime, a $79 annual membership program that offered unlimited free two-day shipping. It seemed obvious that this radical proposition would be a hit with customers, but no one could accurately predict the impact on profits. One very crude estimation: up to that point, Amazon had been charging $9.48 for two-day delivery, so any customer ordering more than eight times a year would benefit at the firm's expense. Some within the company were concerned that frequent purchasers would abuse the system and thereby hurt Amazon's already razor-thin margins.

Nevertheless, Bezos pushed ahead. As he explained to his team, "I want to draw a moat around our best customers. We're not going to take our best customers for granted."[3] He knew that regularly wowing those customers with innovative solutions would create loyal brand evangelists who not only would increase their spending with Amazon but also talk up the company. He explained his thinking in the letter he published on Amazon's website announcing the Prime launch, reproduced below.[4] Note especially the final paragraph:

> Dear Customers,
>
> I am very excited to announce _Amazon Prime_, our first ever membership program, which provides *all-you-can-eat* express shipping. It's simple: for a flat annual membership fee, you get unlimited two-day shipping for free on over a million in-stock items. Members also get overnight shipping for only $3.99 per item—order as late as 6:30PM ET.
>
> Amazon Prime takes the effort out of ordering: no minimum purchase and no consolidating orders. Two-day shipping becomes an every day experience rather than an occasional indulgence.

We are offering Amazon Prime membership at the introductory price of $79 per year, which includes sharing the benefits with up to four family members in your household.

Considering that we normally charge $9.48 for two-day shipping on a single book and $16.48 for overnight, many of our customers will find the program very rewarding. It works across books, DVDs, music, electronics, kitchen, tools, health, personal care, etc. etc.

We expect Amazon Prime to be expensive for Amazon.com in the short term. In the long term, we hope to earn even more of your business, which will make it good for us too. We hope you enjoy our latest innovation.

You can <u>sign up for membership</u> with 1-Click.

Sincerely,
Jeff Bezos, Founder & CEO

This courageous customer-centric innovation reminds me of Discover's CEO David Nelms's decision to risk $200 million in late fee revenues by sending customers an email alert the day before the fee would be levied, as described in an earlier chapter. Amazon's innovation also reminds me of Costco deciding to sell Calvin Klein jeans at the company's standard 14 percent markup when there was clearly more money on the table just waiting to be scooped up. It can't hurt to say it again, in this context: *If your company works hard at being remarkable*—at always acting in the customers' best interest by providing products and services that really enrich their lives and finding ways to make them affordable—*your customers will gladly pay for those innovations, and will tell their friends.*

Keep in mind that back when Amazon launched Prime, it was not at all clear who the real winners in e-commerce would turn out to be. The titan at the top of the mountain in those days was eBay, with a market cap of $33 billion. In 2004, Amazon still sold primarily books and music, and its market cap was $18 billion. The CEO of one of the world's leading customer research firms proclaimed that by expanding into additional business lines, Amazon.com (as the company was known back then) would soon become "Amazon.Toast."[5] Fifteen years later, Amazon's market cap had pushed past $900 billion, while eBay's had declined slightly to $30 billion. The reason, in my view, is that Amazon not only relentlessly expanded its product lines but also relentlessly upgraded the experience of its customers.

Here's a summary of key upgrades to the Amazon Prime customer experience:

- **2005**: Prime is launched (unlimited free two-day shipping for an annual $79 membership fee).

- **2006**: Third-party merchants are fulfilled by Amazon (and are eligible for Prime's free two-day shipping).

- **2011**: Instant streaming of videos included for free.

- **2014**: Thirty-minute early access to lightning deals on Amazon .com.

- **2014**: Prime Pantry (online shopping for everyday household goods in "everyday sizes") is launched, with free delivery to Prime members on orders over $35. Streaming music and unlimited photo storage are also made available.

- **2014**: Prime Now is initiated whereby members in large cities can receive commonly ordered items on the same day—often within two hours.

- **2017**: A flurry of innovations takes place, including Whole Foods discounts, Prime Wardrobe, Prime member-exclusive brands (such as Goodthreads), and the Prime Rewards Visa card from Chase, offering 5 percent cash back on all purchases from Amazon and Whole Foods.

- **2019**: Amazon implements free grocery delivery and pickup from Whole Foods, with expansion of free same-day delivery to more than ten thousand cities and towns, including delivery inside the homes of Prime members.

Customer-obsessed innovation, with new milestones every other year or so, has turned Amazon Prime into an extraordinary success. In a decade and a half, it has grown to comprise two hundred million members worldwide. Prime members spend 2.3 times as much as non-Prime customers ($1,400 per year vs. $600 per year), and Bain research shows that Net Promoter Scores for Amazon's Prime customers are consistently higher across all retail categories—in some cases by as much as 30 points. The price of a Prime membership recently increased to $119 a year, but it still represents an astonishing bargain. For example, Prime's free video-streaming feature offers three times as many movies as Netflix at no extra cost beyond the annual Prime membership, while Netflix's standard membership costs $168 per year for an infinitely smaller basket of services.

Remarkable!

Satisfaction Is Not Remarkable

Writer and consultant Peter Drucker—often referred to as the father of modern management—once wrote, "To satisfy the customer is the mission and purpose of every business."[6]

I respectfully disagree.

Of course, I completely support the idea that the company's purpose should center on customers, but simply satisfying them sets too low a hurdle. Consider the word "satisfy." The dictionary tells us that it means "to meet someone's expectations." One of its synonyms is "adequate."

Are we feeling inspired yet?

NPS kicks it up a notch—that is, from meeting expectations to exceeding them and from satisfying customers to delighting them. As I have emphasized throughout these chapters, the primary purpose of a great business is to enrich customers' lives. This requires doing much more than satisfying people, which implicitly sets a standard of no complaints. Instead, enriching customers' lives means delivering experiences so remarkable that they feel loved; so much so that they tell others about it. You have to *wow* customers. You have to move them from merely sated to truly elated. By clearing this high hurdle and *only* by clearing it will you convert customers into Promoters: precious assets who come back for more and refer their friends.

NPS exemplars regularly achieve the remarkable, and they do so in systematic and ever-changing ways. Costco's Jim Sinegal told me that in his view, simply providing the best everyday low price in his Costco warehouse stores wasn't enough for the company to thrive in the long term. The human brain is a bit perverse in this regard: as soon as it discerns a pattern, it starts to get bored with that pattern. We start out justifiably excited about something new—let's say, some *very good* thing—and over time we lose interest even though that thing remains very good.[7] We need some unexpected surprise to wow us and to inspire us to talk about that experience with friends and colleagues. That's why Costco strives to turn every visit into a treasure hunt, with fresh inventory and incredible bargains. The company rewards your need to *discover*. It amps up your adrenaline levels by (truthfully) suggesting that you had better *grab this great deal now* because it's likely to be sold out well before your next visit. And again, that's pretty much true, which is why you don't end up feeling stampeded or manipulated. Indeed, Costco makes it easy to return any item, removing the risk of buyer's remorse.

Consider the long list of innovations that initially wowed us but soon became part of our take-it-for-granted expectations. In 2009, for example, USAA became the first bank to enable mobile check deposits through its smartphone app. Let's remind ourselves that at the time, this was truly incredible. No need to visit the branch for deposits! Near-instant availability of funds! It seemed like magic. But now all major financial institutions and most small ones offer this feature, which transitioned from *wow* to table stakes in just a few short years.[8]

The same thing happened with automatic callback technology for customer service centers. My first encounter with this feature came during a blizzard when I tried to reach Southwest Airlines to rebook my flight. I had been on hold with another airline for thirty-five minutes just before calling Southwest. Instead of making me wait on hold (and miss another family dinner), an interactive voice response system offered to call me back as soon as an agent became available and assured me it would hold my place in line. I could even request a time slot for the callback. That was a memorable *wow* for me back then. Today, of course, I'm no longer wowed by this capability; in fact, I am sorely irritated when it's *not* available and

I am forced to wait in some company's seemingly endless phone queue, periodically annoyed by recorded messages that are either manifestly untrue ("Your call is important to us!") or cynically patronizing ("Did you know that you can get your questions answered on our website, easily, with no wait, at www.malair.com?").

So again, the need for innovation is constant. Yesterday's wow is today's yawn and tomorrow's minimum acceptable standard. How is an organization supposed to feed your and my insatiable desires and deliver a steady stream of remarkable innovations, repeatedly? For most firms, the answer requires tapping into that cognitive superresource that is a repository of near-infinite creative talent: the brains of your frontline employees and their customers.

The Jenny Question

I have long preached to my daughter Jenny and her three brothers the gospel of E. B. White, the legendary *New Yorker* writer and coauthor (with William Strunk Jr.) of the timeless *The Elements of Style,* a truly great guide to good writing.

One central message of Strunk and White's gospel is that *simplicity releases power.* You can see that philosophy reflected in the classic Net Promoter System survey, which included only two questions: (1) *How likely would you be to recommend?* (0–10), and (2) *What's the reason for your score?* (open-text explanation). When *Fortune* senior editor Geoff Colvin analyzed why NPS had risen to become the preeminent metric for customer success, he concluded that much of the system's success resulted from the "blasphemous" and radical simplicity of basing the system on "the world's shortest customer survey."[9]

Here's where Jenny came in. At the time, she was working for a large wine and spirits retail chain. Among other things, she was responsible for managing the company's NPS feedback, and that's what she wanted to talk to me about. "Dad, you are not going to like this," she began, "but we went from two questions to three."

Uh oh. "And what is that third question?"

She smiled gamely, knowing that she was swimming upstream. "We ask, *'Is there anything we could have done to make your experience more exceptional?'*"

I was incredulous. My own daughter, undermining my life's work!

My personal battle against "question creep" dated back to the very birth of NPS. Rookie practitioners too often conclude that they see a way to improve the system by slipping in an extra question, often in the name of tailoring the process to a company's specific circumstances. That one extra question becomes two and then three or four, and before you know it you have a survey that's become a chore for customers to fill out, resembling every other bloated market research instrument that presumes that consumers' time isn't very valuable and irritates them into punching the *delete* key, which ends the dialogue before it can begin.

I told Jenny that if customers had something important to say about that, they could put it in their answer to my second (open-text) question. Tongue mostly in cheek, I admonished her. "Jenny, you have introduced complexity: the dark force that absorbs power and sucks up energy. E. B. White would be mortified."

But my wife Karen and I didn't raise any pushovers; we taught our children to practice respect and kindness but with a backbone. Jenny backed up her decision by showing me her evidence, and it turned out that she was *right*. When answering question 2, her promoters typically responded with comments such as "We love shopping at your Fairfax store because Angela at the checkout always makes us feel welcome. She does a fantastic job." And yes, that's really important feedback. It gave the store manager the opportunity to praise Angela at the next storewide huddle, publicly recognizing a job well done and illustrating the value of strong customer service.

But what that feedback *didn't* give Jenny was clear and consistent insight into what her team could be doing better. And that's where her third question—*Is there anything we could have done to make your experience more exceptional?*—came in. She directs question 3 to two sets of customers: those who answered question 1 with a 9 or 10, or Promoters, and those who gave the company a 7 or 8, or Passives, who are satisfied for now but if a competitor caught their eye, watch out.

In his response to question 3, one Promoter noted that on recent visits, he hadn't been able to find his favorite craft beer. This created the opportunity for the store manager to call that customer and thank him for taking the time to fill out the survey. She let him know she had stashed some of that craft beer he loved behind the service desk and promised it would be there the next time he visited. This is what we at Bain refer to in our NPS work as "closing the loop," and Jenny's question had turned it into a chance to truly delight this valuable customer.

This third question, which I now call the Jenny Question, has proven useful in a wide range of circumstances. It helps companies learn from the customers who know them best and who want them to succeed. It's true: Promoters know your business—better than you do, in some ways—and asking the Jenny Question lets you tap into their goodwill and creative brainpower.

That said, I have warned Jenny and her three siblings (Chris, Bill, and Jim) that it is *really hard* for me to imagine adding any more questions. We don't want to defeat the simplicity of NPS. We surely don't want E. B. White, eloquent advocate of simplicity, spinning in his grave.

Chick-fil-A Aims for the Remarkable

During the years that I worked most closely with Chick-fil-A, I was privileged to attend some of its annual store-operator gatherings. One memorable meeting featured a video that re-created a scene from the Bible. Roman law required local Jews to act as a sort of combined guide and porter for Roman soldiers, carrying their heavy packs for a Roman mile—slightly shorter than today's mile—as the legions passed through their town. When asked about this burdensome duty, Jesus advised the locals not to shirk or even resent it but instead to gladly accept the packs and carry them not just the requisite distance but also a second mile (yes, that's where "go the extra mile" comes from).[10]

This vignette served as the introduction to Chick-fil-A's Second Mile Service program, which encouraged operators and their teams to think creatively about how they could go beyond merely satisfying customers to delighting them. Over the next few years, Chick-fil-A execs began calling this the "Be Remarkable" initiative and for a time referred to each store's NPS rating as its "Be Remarkable Score." Irrespective of the name or the score, what *was* important was unleashing the creative minds of Chick-fil-A's frontline teams to delight their customers and convert them into true Promoters, raving fans who came back more frequently and brought their friends and family.

And it *worked*. What ensued was a steady stream of remarkable innovations, mostly from local store operators and their teams. It was someone on the local level, for example, who came up with the peppermint milkshake that has become so popular around the holidays. It was another local store that pioneered chicken nuggets (a blockbuster success). Another suggested handing out dog biscuits to pet owners in the drive-through lane. I could go on and on—this list never ends.

Sometimes the central headquarters team helps an operator test out a promising idea and later refines it to make it easy to share with other stores. In the case of success stories, headquarters certainly spotlights them and shares the relevant statistics. But headquarters rarely mandates that these homegrown innovations be adopted by the stores. Individual franchisees make their own choices, adopting those innovations that seem to fit their particular location, their clientele, and their team's capabilities.

I remember taking my youngest son, Jim, to a Chick-fil-A on Florida's Gulf Coast after we finished a round of golf nearby. There were no Chick-fil-A restaurants near our home in Massachusetts at the time, and I wanted Jim to see for himself what made the chain so special. I ordered the spicy chicken sandwich, which was new at the time. Shortly after we sat down with our trays, a friendly employee stopped by to see how we liked our food and asked if she could refresh our drinks. (Jim had never experienced this complimentary service in a quick-serve restaurant before.) She asked me if I'd like to try some blue cheese dressing—normally reserved for salads—with my sandwich. I nodded enthusiastically—"Yes, please!"—so she went back behind the counter and fetched me a packet of salad dressing. She was breaking the rules, she told us somewhat conspiratorially, but she figured I might really like the combination—and she was right.

I mentioned to her that I occasionally write about Chick-fil-A and use the company as an example in some of my keynotes and seminars. I asked if she knew of any cool new ideas that might qualify as remarkable innovations. "Oh, for sure," she said with obvious enthusiasm. "Our store operator comes up with all kinds of great ideas!" She started listing one innovation after another, many of them quite creative. When Jim and I got back to the car a half-hour later, I had to take a few minutes to jot them down so I wouldn't forget them.

One in particular still sticks in my mind. She explained that the operator knew the manager of the local Home Depot and convinced him to provide the material and expertise for a Saturday morning craft project for parents and their youngsters. The first project, a birdhouse, proved to be so popular that the store repeated the event many times, adding new projects such as window boxes, race tracks, and so on. Saturday breakfasts, I learned, were regularly sold out.

I told this story to a group of partners in Bain's Dallas office, and one of them volunteered that Chick-fil-A had become his family's favorite restaurant. More accurately, it was his three-year-old son's favorite, which meant it was a must-visit-every-week family attraction. But the *why* was the most interesting part of the story. My colleague told me that on the family's first visit, a staff member was particularly kind to the youngster. The staff member's name, according to the badge on his chest, was Jose, and he was then in the process of mopping the floor, using one of those big wringer buckets on wheels. The toddler was fascinated by the rig. Jose asked the parents if the boy could help him mop the floor and, after receiving their approval, proceeded to give him a ride around the restaurant on the mop. (He explained to the boy that he needed the toddler's extra weight to get the floor *completely* clean.) Every time the family returned after that, Jose welcomed the son by name and recruited him to help with whatever his current task happened to be: filling the napkin holders, adding straws, handing out umbrellas during rainy days, you get the idea. My Bain partner concluded his story by saying that while the whole family liked the food, the service, and the overall ambience of the place, what made it truly remarkable was Jose.

Then there was the restaurant operator who dressed in a tuxedo for a special reservations-only dinner service on Valentine's Day. He laid out tablecloths, put vases with red carnations on each table, and serenaded each couple with his violin to help them celebrate their special night—at truly bargain prices. Another operator created a monthly event: Daddy-

Daughter Date Night. Dads made reservations to bring their daughters to a specially decorated restaurant for quality time together. To head off any awkwardness—maybe some of these dads hadn't spent all that much time alone with their daughters—the restaurant provided the fathers with a crib sheet of thoughtful conversation starters, such as "So tell me who you sat next to at the cafeteria today."

My niece and her husband take their two children to their local Chick-fil-A for its Tuesday Family Night. Activities vary but have included clowns, magicians, scavenger hunts, and backroom kitchen tours. Meals come with little kid-friendly craft projects on the side—for example, a kit for assembling a paper cow face.[11] But the biggest reason my niece's son loves that restaurant is Duane, a store employee who greets him by name on each visit and is always ready to engage in a friendly (but spirited) lightsaber duel. This recognition by an adult proved so special to their son that he insisted Duane be included on the family's Christmas card list.

I called Mark Moraitakis, the executive who produced that movie about Jesus's advice to go the second mile. By that time, Mark was responsible for designing the *career path of the future* for crew members. I asked him if there were any updates on remarkable experiences that I could include in this book. He recounted an unusually effective initiative that one store operator launched early on in the Covid-19 crisis when no customers were allowed in restaurants and most stores were experiencing major revenue declines. This operator was enjoying 20 percent growth in revenues. How? He got creative and reconfigured his parking lot to accommodate four drive-through lanes with an iPad mounted on a jury-rigged stand in each lane. This enabled customers in their cars to FaceTime directly with the employees inside the restaurant who would wave hello through the window.

Another cool innovation by a creative operator—temporarily put on hold during the pandemic—was the Teddy Bear Overnight Experience. That store faced low traffic on certain weeknights and decided to offer a storybook reading hour on one of them. By design, it was both enjoyable and educational, providing a social event for families and an opportunity for young children to practice their reading skills. Parents came to the store in the early evening to participate in the reading hour, and at the end of the story youngsters tucked in their teddy bears for the bears' first sleepover and then headed home with their parents. In the morning, they all returned to have breakfast with their teddy bears. Not just remarkable but brilliant!

Finally, Mark encouraged me to check out a podcast series created by Shawn York, one of the company's California store operators. In the podcasts, Shawn shares the leadership philosophy he developed at his Chick-fil-A restaurant, including the insights and actions that inspire his team members to treat each other, and especially their customers, right. It was a remarkable act of generosity in the sense that Shawn and his restaurant wouldn't benefit in any direct way from that significant investment of time, and the resulting product provides a guide that almost anyone who runs a small business should find useful.

The name of the podcast is *Love Works Here*.

The Power of Digital Innovation

Now let's revisit some companies introduced in earlier chapters and see how digital solutions provide myriad opportunities to upgrade—indeed fully reimagine—customers' experience.

Few companies have done a better job of this than Warby Parker, which over the past decade has revolutionized the purchasing process for glasses and contact lenses. Warby's founding team of four Wharton MBA students (two of whom are Bain alums) put the Net Promoter philosophy of aiming for *remarkable* at the heart of a new business model. The founders saw an industry locked into the old-school mentality of charging the highest possible price and marketing aggressively through a commission salesforce while providing mediocre service. Inventory was locked away in glass cases so the frames could only be inspected with the help of a commission-driven salesperson (have I mentioned how rarely this leads to happy outcomes for customers?). Warby figured out that by eliminating commissions and marketing overhead, they could profitably offer a pair of custom prescription glasses for $95, while the industry was selling that same product for $400–$500. However, Warby's goal was not to compete on price; it was to create enthusiastic Promoters by delivering wows throughout the customer experience. To do this, the company completely reimagined every step in the customer journey.

When I ordered my first pair of eyeglasses from Warby Parker, I was delighted to find an easy-to-navigate website that helped me find a handful of frames that looked promising. Then for no charge or obligation, Warby sent me a box of my five top choices, which arrived in a couple of days. I was able to try these on in the privacy and comfort of my own home, check them out in the mirror, and gather opinions from family members about which ones looked good. I ordered the frame that worked best (with just a few clicks on the Warby app on my phone) and then returned the sample frames in a prepaid shipping box, and my new frames with custom lenses arrived a few days later. In the box, there was a reminder that because of my purchase Warby was distributing a new pair of glasses to someone in need. Incredible!

No surprise that I recommended Warby to lots of people, including my daughter Jenny, who has also become a loyal Promoter. Warby's co-CEO Dave Gilboa told me we are not alone—most of Warby's new customers come through recommendations from existing customers. Many of them, moreover, decide to buy multiple frames from their free box of samples.

I have also been impressed with how closely Peloton listens carefully to its customers (whom they call "members") and to its support reps to identify "wow" opportunities. For example, when support teams reported numerous requests from members seeking details for a song used during their workout, the firm introduced the Track Love feature that enabled members to love a track with one touch of their screen and sync it to their personal Apple Music or Spotify playlist.

Then the company noticed that rather than inputting their geographic location in that field of the member profile quite a few members were inserting hashtags such as #BlackGirlMagic and #RN in order to self-organize group rides or give high fives on the leaderboard. So, Peloton designed a new software feature called Tags that enabled members to add up to ten unique hashtags to their profile. This helps them connect with various communities of common interest such as college alumni, hometown pride, employees of specific firms or industries, favorite hobbies, and training styles. The platform shows trending classes for members' tags, helps them find new communities, and allows member communities to scale smoothly. Over 325,000 Tags have been added since the feature's launch.

#BlackGirlMagic has grown to become one of the largest Tags groups, with over twenty-nine thousand members. In addition to facilitating group rides, Peloton hosts virtual community events by reaching out to members of specific Tags and inviting them to join conversations with Peloton's leadership team, instructors, and other members. The first virtual community event was with #BlackGirlMagic and John Foley, Peloton's CEO, held during the summer of 2020. Feedback from the hundreds of attendees was overwhelmingly positive; the event earned a Net Promoter Score of 94! Here is one member's comment: "It was a great opportunity to hear from the CEO. Being part of the BGM group has really helped me in my Peloton journey. Knowing that others are there riding with you and rooting for you really makes a difference. Thanks to Peloton for giving this group an opportunity to be seen and heard." Pretty remarkable.

Chewy offers one more example of a digital innovator that wows customers repeatedly. Chewy declares that the company is obsessed with "exceeding expectations through every interaction." Approximately 70 percent of net sales come through automatic order refills (which makes life easier for customers and for Chewy). Many firms, including Amazon, offer a similar feature, but Chewy made it much better.[12] Chewy sends a friendly email reminder alert shortly before each automatic shipment. Directly in response to that alert, customers can modify or delay the shipment. Chewy ensures that there are plenty of items to add to that order. The company stocks sixty-five thousand different products, from food to toys and crates—a 30 percent increase over the past two years. Chewy offers services too, including the recently launched Connect with a Vet, which provides initial veterinarian consultations online.

Chewy customers have the ability to set up a profile for pets in their account, documenting breed, weight, diet, and birth date, which enables Chewy's recommendation engine to highlight items your pet would likely enjoy (just like Netflix recommends movie titles based on ratings by similar customers). This data also helps Chewy's knowledgeable customer service staff, who are available around the clock 365 days a year to provide the kind of customized advice you might expect to find only at your local pet store.

Chewy also has a Wow team, staffed with over a hundred people, who dream up and implement innovative ways to delight customers. Tapping into the special emotional tie between owner and pet, the Wow team some-times sends flowers or a note after an owner cancels a standing order fol-lowing a pet's death. The hand-painted pet portraits that the Wow team mails as surprise thank-yous so delight customers that they often post them, along with glowing testimonials, across social media, giving Chewy authentic and powerful endorsements.

Defeating the Enemies of Innovation

In part to control costs, large organizations typically structure themselves into functional silos such as finance, operations, and marketing. Within those silos, they define processes carefully and strive for perfection by re-lentlessly stamping out deviations from the norm.

This approach can indeed lead to standardized quality and lower costs, and for some products—the proverbial widget, for example—it can make good sense. But when it comes to more complex products and services, the relentless pursuit of perfection within silos can be counterproductive because it can stifle innovation and creativity. Most meaningful innova-tions must transcend these kinds of functional boundaries.

This isn't just a theoretical concern. In the early years of NPS, many large bureaucracies focused their NPS programs on "fixing" (i.e., prevent-ing or converting) Detractors, and as a result they linked the NPS pro-gram tightly with quality initiatives that were aimed at reducing defects. There was certainly a logic to this: reducing defects and relationship *ows* will help keep customers satisfied. But here we're back to that troublesome word "satisfy." What if you want to do more than merely satisfy? What if you must create a remarkable experience that *wows* customers into be-coming Promoters?

Most siloed bureaucracies struggled with this. Initial efforts to create more Promoters often focus on identifying existing Promoters, ferreting out good practices by studying the verbatim comments generated by ques-tion 2, and then trying to reinforce and replicate these practices. But that isn't enough. To repeatedly wow customers, winners find that they—and especially their frontline teams—need to encourage variation and exper-imentation. They must maintain the advantages of reliable process—

product quality was still very important—but also overlay what might be called the "wow factory" to come up with a steady stream of innovations.

This challenge is most acute in highly regulated industries with extensive compliance requirements. When you add process standardization and bureaucratic management to these already stifling siloed organizations, you have a recipe for undifferentiated commodity offerings—which delight neither customers, employees, nor investors.

And where might you find this recipe in regular use? Well, look no further than traditional banking, which seems mired in a risk-averse mindset and complex operating models that slow decision making and progress.

This helps explain why my first visit to a First Republic Bank branch was so delightfully remarkable. First, my account manager—the same person who answered the phone when I called the main phone number, thus sparing me being trapped in voicemail jail—was knowledgeable and worked hard to find a way to say "yes." She offered me fresh-baked cookies to sample (and take home), and my thank-you gift for opening a new account with First Republic was a cool new umbrella that supposedly would not drip on my car seat. (It doesn't.) There were plenty of pens at the signature table—no chains—and there was a wooden display case full of reading glasses of various magnifications to help customers read the fine print. As I soon learned, the branches hold receptions every few months to help customers meet the entire staff and one another. They celebrate major anniversaries and not-so-major ones. I just received an email from the bank's CEO celebrating the bank's thirty-fifth anniversary. Two sentences in that email really caught my attention: "Our growth over the years has never been our goal. It is rather the direct result of taking exceptional care of our clients, one client at a time, consistently for decades."

First Republic's investment in up-front "wow" shows that the company understands how important it is for new customers to feel like they made a wise choice. It's true: One of the most potent episodes in any customer experience is the initial welcome. If your brand can generate delight at this critical moment—so that your customers feel welcome, believe that they will be cared for, and conclude that this is a community where they belong— you will not only get the relationship off on the right foot but also increase your chances of keeping it there. Yes, this sets a high standard for all of the episodes that will follow. But that big win up front tends to earn you the benefit of the doubt. Malcolm Gladwell wrote an entire book about the vital role of the first impression: both setting the stage and influencing the rest of the relationship.[13]

BILT to Wow!

It is true; you only get one chance to make a first impression. With the rapid shift to e-commerce, firms are finding this increasingly difficult as they struggle to provide new customers with an engaging, warm, and personalized welcome. This is why I was so pleased to hear from Bill Wade, a partner in Bain's Dallas office, about his discovery of BILT, a top-rated app that transforms the customer welcome, assembly, and instructions episode into digital delight.

My mind went back to all those horrible indecipherable instruction booklets that were supposed to help me assemble those products I had purchased over the years—booklets infused with bad English printed in a tiny font to allow for the inclusion of half a dozen other languages, interlaced with inscrutable diagrams and illustrations. BILT sidesteps all that, using 3D animations with voice and text prompts to demonstrate the ideal sequence of setup or installation steps, along with hints about common pitfalls to avoid.[14] BILT automatically communicates in the language you've already selected for your smartphone.

The boom in e-commerce has increased the need to flat-pack disassembled products for efficient shipping, increasing the challenge of delivering that all-important good first impression. Every day, there's more stuff out there that needs assembling by nonexperts. I wondered if BILT might transform instructions and assembly the way Google Maps revolutionized driving directions.

I downloaded the free app for a test-drive and pretended I had just bought a new grill. My wife and I still shake our heads about an earlier attempt at assembling a grill using traditional paper instructions. That episode—along with using paper instructions to assemble a children's playset—stand out as two of the worst experiences in our forty-plus years of marriage. The BILT tool made the assembly experience a dream. After a quick product overview, BILT pictured the tools required and listed the parts included in the package. The app gave me the expected time required for completion, and then—using intelligent animations directed by voice and text—guided me through the assembly procedure step by step, at my own pace. On my smartphone I could zoom in to enlarge the images, drag my finger across the screen to rotate them, or tap on a part for more information.

BILT also includes a virtual filing cabinet to manage receipts as well as warranty and registration information. I predict that the app will substantially reduce returns and customer support calls, which will save money for retailers and manufacturers. The app measures user time spent on each step, which will illuminate friction points to address with improved instructions and product design. Updates to instructions happen in real time. Imagine the substantial savings from avoiding reprinting and distributing instructions related to product recalls. Last but not least, BILT makes paper instructions superfluous, which will eventually minimize paper waste.

Way cool, I was thinking. But the feature that really grabbed my attention was the last screen that popped up at the end of an instruction set: a two-question NPS survey asking customers to rate the product or service and explain their rating. What a treasure trove of customer feedback linked to a specific SKU and product registration!

This led me to schedule a conversation with BILT's CEO, Nate Henderson, who surprised me by saying that he built the firm on the principles I laid out in *The Ultimate Question 2.0*. Nate asks applicants to read my book prior to the interview so they can discuss what they learned. "If the applicant's eyes don't light up when we talk about *The Ultimate Question*," Nate explained, "they are not the right fit for BILT." The firm's mission is to "create an experience so enabling and empowering [that] it transforms users into promoters of the brands we serve." What an amazing find: a company founded on NPS principles that is entirely devoted to helping *other* companies do better at NPS—an NPS booster rocket!

Whenever I encounter a company committed to the NPS philosophy of making the world better for customers, I try to help it succeed (thank you, Bob Herres). In this case I made a substantial investment in BILT, joined its board of directors, and recommended it to my friends. I should also note that this investment decision was one of my first practical applications of the new statistical tool that I described in chapter 5, the Earned Growth Rate. Yes, BILT's revenues had been growing at more than 175 percent per year, but like most software-as-a-service startups, the business was eating up cash. What really got my attention was that BILT's net revenue retention was running at 150 percent, and most of its new customers resulted from recommendation and referral, resulting in Earned Growth Rate of 160 percent. That evidence persuaded me that the company's growth was sustainable, so I doubled down on my intended investment. So yes, this is just one more example proving that by loving your customers, you treat investors with respect. And the best way to demonstrate your love to customers is delivering truly remarkable experiences—repeatedly.

CHAPTER 8

Be Persistent

Build Culture-Reinforcing Systems

One of my favorite places, anywhere in the world, is my garden at our house on Cape Cod.

To say that gardening has become an obsession for me is surely an understatement. The computer I am using to write this book is propped up on a stack of *Gardens Illustrated* magazines, carefully balanced on top of my dog-eared copy of *Dirr's Hardy Trees and Shrubs*. My printer is piled high with old seed, bulb, and rare plant catalogs, which rest atop my recent editions of *The English Garden*.

Let me say quickly that I still have much to learn about gardening, but lack of enthusiasm is not holding me back. We were thrilled when our neighbors (and dear friends) agreed to sell us the vacant lot between our houses almost twenty years ago. The land plunges steeply down from our houses into a so-called kettle hole, formed tens of thousands of years ago when a glacier shoved its massive weight over a giant block of ice, which was ground ever deeper into the earth. Eventually the glacier receded and the ice block melted, leaving behind a bowl-shaped hollow. By the time we acquired it, the hollow was an almost impenetrable tangle of weeds and brambles.

Why do I so love gardens? First, there's all the art, science, and natural history that converge in the garden. Gardening gets you much closer to nature's wondrous systems. For example, the forces of cooperation and competition are embodied in the delicate lichens that grace our stone walls. Lichens are actually two organisms—a green alga or cyanobacterium and a fungus—coupled in a symbiotic relationship so resilient that it can survive for centuries and even cope with the hostile environment of outer space. Or consider the slime mold I noticed the other day, which turns out to be an aggregation of single-cell organisms that demonstrate something akin to community intelligence when they work in concert to find and move toward their next meal. I am regularly humbled by these wondrously persistent natural systems that remind me how much more there is to learn.

Second, gardening provides a constant reminder that every living thing depends on being in a harmonious relationship with its surrounding community. And finally, there is the patience required—it is the ultimate exercise in delayed gratification. What looks beautiful today is most likely the result of many years of persistent attention. Gardens are not for seekers of immediate gratification; shortcuts such as chemical fertilizers may yield fleeting advantage but end up weakening the garden's health and vitality. Meanwhile, nature is often working against you—in the form of aphids, leaf borers, fungal blights, hungry critters, hurricane winds, and disease—requiring you to push back, year after year.

And there is another influence at work each time I venture out into my garden. Bear with me—because I'm at risk of sounding a little moralistic here—but one of my core life principles is to leave things at least a little better than they were when I found them. This is an impulse that I inherited from my parents. Whether it was their neighborhood, the church choir, the Society for the Blind, or the Kiwanis Club, my parents were always givers rather than takers—always making things better.

So, when this unruly bowl of a weed patch became the responsibility of me and my family two decades ago, we got to work. It was a slow transformation but a successful one—well worth the investment we put into it. Today that overgrown kettle hole is a magical setting for family gatherings, including the weddings of our children, as well as musical performances for our neighborhood and annual reunions of my Harvard Krokodiloes college singing friends. My fervent hope is that it becomes a favorite playground and retreat for our grandchildren.

A centerpiece of the garden—and the most-loved feature for all visiting children—is our koi pond, mentioned in an earlier chapter when I was describing the elusive critter that was sneaking down to the water by dark of night and grabbing a fish for dinner. Why create a fish pond? First and foremost, the koi are beautiful, adding color and motion to the landscape. But I was also pleased to discover that in traditional Chinese art, they represent the symbol for *persistence*. Koi evolved in brackish river mouths in Asia, where freshwater flows out into the saltwater of the sea. The koi's body requires freshwater—slightly brackish for optimal kidney and immune system functioning—to survive. Since the freshwater river current flows incessantly out toward the ocean, koi must constantly swim against that current or be swept to their death in the salty sea.

• • •

Why such an obsession with persistence? Persistence provides a foundation for building loyalty. You have to *keep at it*. You have to expend energy, constantly, to fight against counterproductive currents and temptations for short-term solutions. In today's business organizations, the predominant currents are generated by financially oriented metrics and governance systems. In addition, as noted earlier, most organizations experience a steady influx of newcomers who aren't adequately focused on the challenge of building customer loyalty. This puts even more pressure on the organization's stalwart culture carriers to resist unprincipled shortcuts and persist in the pursuit of customer loyalty.

And this brings me to a second feature in my garden: the Loyalty Bell.

As phase one of our gardening project was nearing completion, my wife Karen and I decided to add a personal and symbolic touch. We commissioned a custom-cast bell with the same dimensions as Philadelphia's celebrated Liberty Bell. But whereas the Liberty Bell is inscribed with scripture—"Proclaim liberty throughout all the land"—our bell is engraved with one word, LOYALTY, with our family name (in a much smaller font) just below.[1]

Today, that bell sits on a knoll just up the hill from the koi pond. It is mounted on matching granite pillars, with one representing freedom and the other wisdom. Our idea was that freedom is indeed a precious gift but shouldn't serve as an end in itself, because once freedom is achieved, one then must decide what to *do* with it. Using freedom to act selfishly or irresponsibly—to pursue personal profits above all else, what might be called an unprincipled existence—wastes that precious gift. But bringing wisdom to bear on freedom lets us choose what we want our lives to stand for and, by extension, what principles, organizations, and people are worthy of our loyalty.

By now, you can discern the outlines of the case I'm building here. Succeeding at the difficult task of building and maintaining customer loyalty in the face of countervailing pressures requires incredible persistence. But persistence implies an unyielding adherence to a specific principle or set of principles: *What do we stand for?* Why are those principles worthy of our loyalty? Does our understanding of those principles (and their implications) need refinement as we incorporate challenging lessons throughout our life?

And there's still one more ingredient. The only hope for organizations that seek to embody, persistently, the broader principles of customer capitalism—loving customers, honoring teams, respecting investors, honoring the Golden Rule, and striving for remarkable innovation—is to embrace systems and processes that help teams battle and succeed against all those prevailing currents that are pushing in the wrong direction. Without such systems, employee energies will be swept downstream by the torrent of budget meetings, weekly sales targets, capital allocation models, and similar systems, all reinforcing the drift toward maximizing short-term profits.

This speaks to the very evident flaw in my koi metaphor: time frame. Leaders can't wait patiently for evolution to imbue each of their charges with the genetic urge to swim against the harmful prevailing currents. Instead, effective leaders have to create systems to reinforce the right tendencies in their teams. Of course, they should hire as many like-minded employees as possible. But as organizations grow and incorporate large numbers of new employees, leaders have to be creative and develop systems to embed and reinforce a Golden Rule culture focused squarely on the purpose of loving customers. Only the most senior executives have the power and perspective to build and nurture such systems. They must become the head gardeners of their corporate community.

This is a key point, so let me say it again in slightly different language: *Great organizations are built on great principles.* But these principles will not effectively govern daily decisions and priorities unless the organization's leaders clearly understand the natural currents pushing their teams downstream so they can develop practical systems that help make it easy for teams to do the right thing and hard for them to do the wrong thing—systems that will help them swim upstream to make the world better.

So, how is this done? One of the most effective (and ancient) systems for promulgating guiding principles involves infusing them with symbolism and then disseminating them through routines and rituals. Consider the powerful and emotional impact generated by symbols such as religious talismans, the flag, and the Liberty Bell. Symbols illuminate and inspire. Systems—such as those described throughout this chapter—inculcate and reinforce. Together they make *persistence possible.*

The Power of Words Reinforced by Deeds

Let's dig deeper by looking at a very concrete example from a seemingly prosaic sector: the insurance industry.

You might recall my mention of PURE Insurance in chapter 3. At one point fairly early in the company's evolution, its executives realized that traditional "insurance thinking" ultimately could lead to a bad outcome: the company's pricing teams might be tempted to follow the industry practice of overcharging loyal long-term customers in order to subsidize below-market prices that would bring in new business. To head off this outcome, PURE published its pricing philosophy online, which reminded *all* constituents of the company's overarching goal of caring for existing members (such as me). The effort continues today, with the company sending annual reports and other communications to members, intended to hammer this point home with regularity. Finally, the company provides a cost reduction once members reach their fifth renewal and offers cash distributions (further reducing net coverage costs) after ten years of membership.

Obviously, that message—although aimed at the outside world—is not lost on internal constituencies, including those pricing teams that otherwise might be tempted to stray off the path.

Similarly, I receive annual reports from First Republic Bank highlighting the bank's core values, along with plenty of stories from customers about how First Republic has impacted their lives.[2] "The stories of our clients are the story of our bank," as the headline on the bank's email to me read, which by the way strikes me as a pretty compelling way to talk about true customer centricity. In a recent report, those stories were followed by a section labeled "Who We Are and What We Value." As the name implies, the ensuing text consists of biographies of First Republic's senior executives and board members. These in turn were followed by an illustrated list of corporate values (figure 8-1).

Take a moment to read the short paragraph of text under each value. Also take a look at the implied priorities signaled by the sequence in which those values are presented. I think it's not accidental that "do the right thing" and "provide extraordinary service" are top-line values, while priorities such as "grow" and "have fun" come later down the list. Be sure to notice the clever illustrations—symbols that help make these values memorable. In the early 2000s founder, chairman, and CEO Jim Herbert felt that it would be vital to clarify these values so the organization could maintain its service-oriented culture as it continued to grow.

First Republic's chief operating officer, Jason Bender, explained to me that this project was one of his first assignments after joining the bank out of Stanford Business School. "I was tasked with joining our CMO, Dianne Snedaker, on a road trip to visit with over one hundred employees around the country," he said. "We weren't looking for aspirational principles; we just asked people what it is that really makes us us?" The resulting list represents their distillation, what they heard from the organization explaining what made their culture special.

It isn't such a different list at FirstService Residential—which you'll recall is the nation's leader in condominium and homeowner association management—but in that context, the task of clarifying values and getting people to rally behind them presented a much greater challenge. Rather than being built around the values of an individual founder—such as Jim Herbert at First Republic—FirstService Residential was created through the acquisition of a number of independent regional competitors around the country, each with its own distinct culture and values.

That was the challenge faced by Chuck Fallon in 2013 when he took the reins as CEO of FirstService Residential. One of his first priorities was to create across these separate companies a single culture that was bound together by common values and systems. With strong encouragement from Chuck, the regional teams came together and hashed out the list illustrated

FIGURE 8-1

First Republic Bank core values

Maintaining our culture: core values

Do the right thing

We strive to do things right at First Republic. We also recognize that we're a business of humans; mistakes will happen. Therefore, our mandate is to do the right thing: act with integrity, own your actions, correct mistakes, learn from experience.

Respect the team

Everyone at First Republic makes a difference and everyone at First Republic deserves to feel that his or her contribution is valued. We place high value on collaboration because we know that the power of many is greater than the power of one.

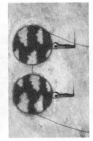

Think positively

We operate in an environment of trust and encourage openness and flexibility. We hire positive people who act positively. Our goal is to "manage toward yes."

Grow

We've evolved greatly since our inception, expanding ourselves and our business purpose. At First Republic, we embrace change and every person has the opportunity to grow and contribute. We want our people to soar.

Provide extraordinary service

We always aim to exceed expectations and serve our clients in unexpected ways. We'll take on only what we can do right. Our business may be about wealth management and banking, but our success is all about service—exceptional customer service.

Move forward, move fast

There are two types of organizations— organizations that spend time checking and organizations that spend time doing. We're doers. We value action and decisiveness and recognize that the best opportunities come to those that act quickly.

Take responsibility

At First Republic, it's not enough to do our own jobs well. Making sure our clients are satisfied is everyone's job. So if something needs fixing, we step up to the plate, "own" the problem and make things right.

Have fun

We know that if everyone enjoys their work they'll do a better job—and our clients will feel the difference. It's really that simple.

⌄ FIRST REPUBLIC BANK / *It's a privilege to serve you*®

Reproduced by permission from First Republic Bank.

FIGURE 8-2

FirstService Residential: our values

Be genuinely helpful. We take pride in serving each and every one of our communities. Whether it's opening a door with a friendly smile or tackling a problem, being genuinely helpful is what defines us.

Aim high. We are passionate about being the best at what we do. By attracting, training, and retaining great people, we set the standard for service and professionalism in our industry.

Do what's right. Our clients trust us to do what's best for their community. We are guided by our ethics and clients' interests in everything we do.

Own it. Each of us is accountable. When facing any challenge, we see it through to resolution with perseverance, integrity, and open communication.

Improve it. We learn from our experiences. We are open-minded, collaborative, and continuously looking for ways to improve.

Build great relationships. Relationships based on respect, trust, and effective communication are the cornerstone of our success.

in figure 8-2, which was broadly published and promoted in literature and now adorns the entry wall in every regional office:

Note, again, the power of simple declarative value statements, reinforced by symbolic illustration. (I for one am pleased that "be genuinely helpful" tops the list.) In your mind's eye, picture these statements up on the wall, larger than life—collectively a powerful symbol—in the entryways of all the company's major workplaces.

Chuck reconvened the leadership team and asked its members to define the behaviors that would indicate teams were living these values. They came up with fifteen service standards that helped define what Chuck describes as "what good looks like." For example, the team decided that to "be genuinely helpful" required nonemergency email requests to be answered quickly—certainly within twelve hours. Fallon's next move was to create a system of daily huddles known as FirstCall. In these small-group meetings, team members recounted their own experiences (or challenges) in acting on one or more of these values and service standards. This is essentially the same system originated at the Ritz-Carlton hotels by cofounder Horst Schulze. He built these daily stand-ups on one central insight: *values don't really come to life unless teams talk about them regularly in a structured way*, and the best process involves team members telling their own stories about how a given principle affected them personally.

Another routine that Chuck is experimenting with allocates at least one huddle each quarter to a somewhat different approach. Team members are each asked to select the value they feel the team is doing the best job at embodying and to give an example that illustrates why they feel this way. Next, they identify the value in most need of improvement—again with an illustration. Through this process, each team (and each unit within the larger hierarchy) focuses on values well lived and on areas where improvement is called for. This helps make those values both *personal* and *shared*. And the fact that this happens repeatedly, over time, reflects the core prescription of this chapter: *be persistent*.

One of my favorite examples of the power of publishing core principles is Discover's so-called Culture Book.[3] You'll recall my description of Discover from previous chapters: a notably customer-focused credit card issuer and payment network. The Culture Book was one of the first things I was handed when I made my initial visit to Discover's headquarters north of Chicago several years back to interview the company's senior executives. It's a bright orange 140-page booklet made available to all Discover employees that declares the firm's core principles. Those principles are worded and sequenced so that they spell out the word "DISCOVER":

- *D*oing the right thing

- *I*nnovation

- *S*implicity

- *C*ollaboration

- *O*penness

- *V*olunteerism

- *E*nthusiasm

- *R*espect

Each value is illustrated with stories told by employees explaining how they have attempted to live by those principles at work.

As I soon learned in my interviews, the Culture Book was seen as only a first step. The company's leaders next developed systems and rituals to reinforce those principles, such as the ritual by headquarters staff welcoming Pinnacle of Excellence Award winners with a standing ovation from employees looking down from every floor of a four-story atrium. These customer-facing reps were nominated and voted on by their peers using the following criteria:

- Are the employee's behavior and results consistent examples for others?

- Does the employee have a strong reputation in our culture?

- Will peers be excited for the employee?

- Does the employee have a strong sense of pride or gratitude for Discover?

This ovation shows respect for the winners and for the values-based process by which they were chosen. The ritual demonstrates Discover's high esteem for the role of customer service representatives. So too does the process whereby all executives listen in on a couple of hours of customer service representative calls every month, then meet with their colleagues to discuss what they learned and what process or technology changes would help make the work of the customer service representatives easier—and thereby help them delight customers.

Discover's principles are also reinforced by the executive bonus system. The senior execs in charge of marketing and operations have a joint bonus target that's based on reducing the number of customer complaints by 10 percent every year. Again, this calls for creating practical systems that keep values such as innovation and respect at the forefront of every team's priorities.

Amazon's Fourteen Principles

Amazon too is built on the rock of core principles.[4] In an interesting twist, the company has chosen to be explicit about how *leaders* should embody those principles, as expressed in this list on the company's website:

Customer Obsession
Leaders start with the customer and work backwards. They work vigorously to earn and keep customer trust. Although leaders pay attention to competitors, they obsess over customers.

Ownership
Leaders are owners. They think long term and don't sacrifice long-term value for short-term results. They act on behalf of the entire company, beyond just their own team. They never say "that's not my job."

Invent and Simplify
Leaders expect and require innovation and invention from their teams and always find ways to simplify. They are externally aware, look for new ideas from everywhere, and are not limited by "not invented here." As we do new things, we accept that we may be misunderstood for long periods of time.

Are Right, A Lot

Leaders are right a lot. They have strong judgment and good instincts. They seek diverse perspectives and work to disconfirm their beliefs.

Learn and Be Curious

Leaders are never done learning and always seek to improve themselves. They are curious about new possibilities and act to explore them.

Hire and Develop the Best

Leaders raise the performance bar with every hire and promotion. They recognize exceptional talent, and willingly move them throughout the organization. Leaders develop leaders and take seriously their role in coaching others. We work on behalf of our people to invent mechanisms for development like Career Choice.

Insist on the Highest Standards

Leaders have relentlessly high standards—many people may think these standards are unreasonably high. Leaders are continually raising the bar and drive their teams to deliver high quality products, services, and processes. Leaders ensure that defects do not get sent down the line and that problems are fixed so they stay fixed.

Think Big

Thinking small is a self-fulfilling prophecy. Leaders create and communicate a bold direction that inspires results. They think differently and look around corners for ways to serve customers.

Bias for Action

Speed matters in business. Many decisions and actions are reversible and do not need extensive study. We value calculated risk taking.

Frugality

Accomplish more with less. Constraints breed resourcefulness, self-sufficiency, and invention. There are no extra points for growing headcount, budget size, or fixed expense.

Earn Trust

Leaders listen attentively, speak candidly, and treat others respectfully. They are vocally self-critical, even when doing so is awkward or embarrassing. Leaders do not believe their or their team's body odor smells of perfume. They benchmark themselves and their teams against the best.

Dive Deep

Leaders operate at all levels, stay connected to the details, audit frequently, and are skeptical when metrics and anecdote differ. No task is beneath them.

Have Backbone; Disagree and Commit

Leaders are obligated to respectfully challenge decisions when they disagree, even when doing so is uncomfortable or exhausting. Leaders have conviction and are tenacious. They do not compromise for the sake of social cohesion. Once a decision is determined, they commit wholly.

Deliver Results

Leaders focus on the key inputs for their business and deliver them with the right quality and in a timely fashion. Despite setbacks, they rise to the occasion and never settle.

"We use our Leadership Principles every day," the preamble to the preceding list says, "whether we're discussing ideas for new projects or deciding on the best approach to solving a problem. It is just one of the things that makes Amazon peculiar."

I do like that use of the word "peculiar." I wish it weren't true—I wish that adhering to leadership values such as these didn't make a company an outlier—but I think it is. May more companies go this route and thereby make Amazon less peculiar!

I believe that the larger idea stated above is also true. My interviews with current and former Amazon executives have convinced me that these principles *do* get discussed every day and are thoughtfully embedded into every management process—from hiring to training to promotions and, of course, to how the company treats customers. Note that *not a single word* of these fairly comprehensive principles has to do with revenue growth or profit targets. That is refreshing in a world all too often dominated by financial-capitalist thinking. Note too that several ideas recur in different words. For example, leaders "never say 'that's not my job,'" and no task is beneath a leader. Leaders "look for new ideas from everywhere," "are never done learning," "are curious about new possibilities," and "look around corners." When it comes to inculcating values, a purposeful reiteration can be a powerful aid.

Despite the firm's extraordinary performance, though, there is something troubling about Amazon's fourteen principles: the Golden Rule is not apparent. No principle refers to treating employees with loving kindness or caring deeply for their safety and well-being. And there is nothing about "treating people right." So, if there's one part of the Amazon model that makes me wonder if its success is sustainable, it's the firm's failure to dedicate itself to becoming a truly great place to work where employees can lead great lives.[5]

In his 2020 annual report's letter to shareholders—his last as CEO— Jeff Bezos seemed to share this concern.[6] The company had just beaten back a unionization drive at its Bessemer, Alabama, facility, winning 71 percent of the vote. Even so, the experience clearly affected Bezos, who noted in his letter, "We need to do a better job for our employees." He went on to make this commitment: "We have always wanted to be Earth's Most Customer-Centric Company. We won't change that. It's what got us here. But I am committing us to an addition. We are going to be Earth's Best Employer and Earth's Safest Place to Work."

Only time will tell if Amazon will be able to adjust its culture in this direction. Any company as large as Amazon has regular opportunities for executives to make poor decisions—decisions that are pro-profits but anti-love. One such policy recently uncovered by the *Wall Street Journal* is Amazon's throttling of competitors in smart speakers and video doorbells by refusing to sell them key ads on its website, which could boost their search results.[7] The *Wall Street Journal* also published accusations by sellers on Amazon Marketplace that Amazon employees were gleaning data from the marketplace platform to compete unfairly. How quickly these transgressions get resolved in favor of the Golden Rule—assuming they do!—will indicate how well Amazon's principles are holding up under the constant financial pressures of a public company.

Even without missteps, any giant company—whose success was accelerated by a pandemic that brought suffering to so many—can easily become viewed as hateful and exploitive. There are indications that Bezos recognized this long ago. For example, when the firm surpassed $100 billion in sales, he composed and distributed a memo titled "Amazon.love" in which he declared that he wanted the company to be loved rather than feared. "Defeating Tiny Guys is not cool," he wrote. "Capturing all the value only for the company is not cool."[8] Now that Bezos has passed the CEO mantle to Andy Jassy, the world will get a chance to see how committed this new generation of leaders feels to living Golden Rule principles.

With these serious cautions and caveats in mind, any company striving to become more *customer*-centric should study Amazon's example of putting principles into practice explicitly, systematically, and persistently. The company's overarching precept—the principle at the very top of its list—is "customer obsession." Note that many of the subsequent principles serve to support and reinforce the concept of customer obsession: for example, "invent and simplify" and "insist on the highest standards."

"Persistence" also comes to bear on the arc of an Amazon manager's career. Here are some excerpts from a conversation I had with a former Amazon executive who described the way the company embeds its leadership principles in its system of management:

- As a job applicant, you are interviewed based on those principles.

- Starting on day one, you are trained in them.

- When you interview others, you have to vote "yes" or "no" strictly on whether they passed on the leadership principles, which are more important than their experience or skillset.

- The feedback you provide your peers is based on the leadership principles.

- The all-hands meetings are themed around the leadership principles.

- Your promotion documents are written based on how you perform against these leadership principles.

- You get "managed out" if you don't demonstrate that you can deliver against the leadership principles.

- Working within these principles isn't a choice at Amazon, not just a recommendation or a nice-to-have—it's the foundation of what it means to be an Amazonian. It's a relentless commitment to excellence. You're either in it 100 percent or you're out.

Amazon's management systems also interlock in ways that reinforce customer focus. For example, to earn promotion to a senior role, leaders must be able to point to a string of innovations that have made life better for customers. But *delivering* those kinds of innovations requires funding, of course, and the system that controls the funding of new initiatives requires the sponsor to write up a simulated press release that explains the novel features and benefits of the innovation, which must be remarkable enough to be considered newsworthy by journalists. The package must also include expected questions (with answers) about how the service will be delivered, what resources are required, and what the schedule is. In other words, the sponsor must demonstrate that he or she understands how this innovation will wow customers and what it will take to deliver the innovation on time and within budget. Only *after* someone has cleared these rather high hurdles repeatedly is that person considered for a senior management role.

I will be watching Amazon carefully as its new generation of leaders begins the next chapter in the company's history. Hopefully the transition will work as effectively as it did at Apple, where Tim Cook took the baton from founder Steve Jobs and demonstrated even greater commitment to treating customers and employees right. Apple's success is evidenced by its continued growth but also by its stellar Net Promoter Scores. But the truth today is that NPS results for Amazon point to a dark cloud on the horizon: Amazon's relative customer NPS rankings have been slipping in most of its retail categories. Bain's Retail Practice, which examines ten sectors each year, reported that in 2020 Amazon held the leading Net Promoter Score in only one sector: home furniture. Since 2017 Amazon's competitors have led in most categories and by a different competitor in each sector. I conclude that Jassy and his team have their work cut out for them. I hope they respond by aligning their core principles with the Golden Rule and follow them with even greater persistence.

More Than Words

At the risk of stating the obvious, simply publishing a list of inspiring values is insufficient. Persistence and symbols must be undergirded by both principles and systems and, most important, *by the example set by the company's leaders.* How persistently do they embody those principles?

Remember the implosion of Enron, which sent senior execs to jail for their unprincipled pursuit of profits? That once high-flying company turned out to be a clear example of talking the talk without *walking* the talk. For example, here are the four corporate values Enron celebrated in one of its annual reports:

- Communication—We have an obligation to communicate.

- Respect—We treat others as we would like to be treated.

- Integrity—We work with customers and prospects openly, honestly and sincerely.

- Excellence—We are satisfied with nothing less than the very best in everything we do.[9]

In retrospect, this is kind of depressing to read, right? But it is no more so than the case of Arthur Andersen LLP. That huge accounting firm, which employed some eighty-five thousand people, collapsed almost overnight thanks to its ties to Enron (as well as Waste Management, Sunbeam, and WorldCom). And this disaster happened despite Arthur Andersen LLP's very public embrace of a set of seemingly robust values that had been passed down through several business "generations" from the firm's founder:

- Integrity and Honesty

- One Firm, One Voice Partnership Model

- Training to a Shared Method[10]

So no, it's clearly not value statements, however eloquent and lofty, that set great firms apart from the rest. Instead, it is leadership's ability to build reinforcing systems to ensure that these principles live and breathe throughout the organization. And it's the leadership team's willingness to act as exemplars in living those principles, especially when the chips are down. Will leaders put principles and team success ahead of their own personal interests when things get rough?

The problem is that *you never know until the moment actually arrives.* I was impressed at how quickly the FirstService board elected to slash board member and senior executive compensation when the Covid-19 crisis hit the company's frontline teams. I think this will be critical as we move forward through this crisis and into the next one—whenever that comes. All employees will be watching to see how hard leaders work to avoid crisis-driven layoffs and how generously they compensate themselves if they decide they must cut frontline jobs. At the risk of stating the obvious, there is no better way for leaders to drive home their commitment to principles than to make meaningful sacrifices themselves in the service of those principles.

Steve Grimshaw understood this, which is why he and his senior team slashed their compensation when Caliber Collision entered the pandemic-driven downturn. Pay was reduced for everyone with an annual salary of over $100,000. Caliber committed to keeping all its locations open (while competitors shuttered up to 50 percent). Then Grimshaw guaranteed body techs a healthy base rate of pay even if their weekly shop volumes failed to cover that base through their standard volume incentives. My guess is that when the collision industry returns to pre-pandemic levels, Caliber's rate of share gain earned during the pandemic will further accelerate. The reason? Leaders demonstrated to everyone (employees, vendors, insurance companies, and customers) that Caliber lives its principles.

Pathways to Persistence

I've already described a number of the systems Bain has implemented over the years to ensure that the firm's client-focused mission—*to help our clients create such high levels of value that together we set new standards of excellence*—remains front and center and also to make sure that mission is presented powerfully and persistently. Let me reiterate just a few. Weekly huddles, for example, ask team members to evaluate how well their work is delivering client value. In parallel, the "annual results" challenge motivates teams in every office worldwide to vie for recognition for delivering the best client results.

Another core principle supporting our mission is *making Bain a great place to work*. In support of that principle, we ask team members every week how likely they would be to recommend their team to colleagues in the larger organization. Those responses drive huddle discussions so that teams can fix most of their own issues, but in addition, aggregated results roll up to the monthly office meeting, where teams are rank-ordered. These scores inform key office management decisions ranging from coaching to team resourcing. The scores are also shared across the office with all consultants and associate consultants, which focuses even more attention on the challenge of *making teams fun and productive*. And in what is perhaps the most powerful system of all, teams vote on the quality of their leadership every six months, and leaders who do not earn the support of their teams cannot be promoted to a position of greater power and authority.

My point again is that values—even powerful values—need help. Yes, as I've just emphasized, leaders must behave as exemplars and live the values. But they must also reinforce cultural values by building effective systems.

Those systems yield *persistence*. They just keep humming in the background, 24/7/365, even when people aren't consciously aware of their impact or cumulative power.

You don't have to take my word for it. The following is an excerpt from a story in the *Boston Business Journal* that was based on an interview with Tamar Dor-Ner conducted shortly after she was appointed the new head of Bain's Boston office:

> When Tamar Dor-Ner joined Bain & Co. in 1999 after studying European intellectual history at Northwestern, her plan was to stay for six months. "I thought I would do an anthropological expedition," she said. "I would observe businesspeople in their natural habitat, and I would leave to write the Great American Novel of the workplace."
>
> She never left. Two decades later, Dor-Ner is running Bain's Boston office—at just under 1,000 employees, the consulting giant's largest location—and leading the brand positioning and strategy group that she co-founded. It's Bain's culture, she said, that convinced her to turn her expedition into a long-term encampment. . . .
>
> Far from corporate drones, she found her co-workers smart, funny and hard-working. "I got here and felt pretty immediately an alignment of values, insofar as the people I liked were the people everybody respected and admired and they were the people that got promoted," Dor-Ner said. "The people that I thought were (jerks), they were flushed pretty quickly out of the system like toxins."[11]

The "alignment of values" to which Tamar refers is, on the face of it, an unexpected congruence between her own values and those of her new colleagues. But on a deeper level, I think, Tamar was picking up on the cumulative impact of Bain's persistent systems. Why did the people she admired get promoted and the jerks get flushed out? This was because of values, published explicitly and reinforced systematically and persistently. I believe that the reason Bain recovered from its near-death experience thirty years ago was not because of a new set of brilliant strategic initiatives; it happened because we returned to our core mission of helping clients achieve great results through servant leadership. And we designed systems that persistently reinforced the principles that underpinned that mission. That's why people such as Tamar decide to stay at Bain and make it an even greater place to work.

Perhaps you're inclined to dismiss Bain as a special case—an exclusive club with so many high earners with multiple degrees from fancy-pants schools. But the same principles and reinforcing systems drive success across the entire business spectrum. For example, consider the experience at one of FirstService Brands subsidiaries, CertaPro Painters, the largest franchised residential and commercial painting company in North America. The leaders of CertaPro recently presented their business strategy update to their board of directors, on which I serve. They explained to us that the reason they chose gold as the company's color—prominently featured in all advertising and signage—is to communicate that the company tries to live by the Golden Rule.

This is part of a bigger picture. In fact, all the FirstService Brand companies strive to live by these values:

- Deliver what you promise.

- Respect the individual.

- Have pride in what you do.

- Practice continuous improvement.

When I asked Charlie Chase, CEO of FirstService Brands, to explain how these were chosen, he replied that these values simply reflect "different dimensions of the Golden Rule, which work equally well in our painting business, home inspections, restorations, floor coverings, and California Closets."

I think Charlie is right. Every list of core values at successful firms simply parses the Golden Rule into components that make it more practical and understandable for its employees in that particular business setting. When I asked Charlie to describe how FirstService Brands developed systems and rituals to reinforce these values and make them persistent, he said that first the company turned those values into the following "Service Basics" to help teams know when they were living these values:

- Ensure your words and actions align with our Brand Promise.

- Display our Brand with pride.

- Create Brand loyalty with everything we do.

- Practice immediacy.

- Engage customers to tell their story only once.

- Educate, communicate and collaborate with the customer.

- Solicit feedback from customers throughout their journey.

- Be prepared, present and personal.

- Respect the customer's property and preferences.

- Celebrate and confirm completion of the project with the customer.

Charlie also explained the ritual that FirstService Brands holds each year to identify the people in its organization who are doing the best job of living these ideals. The ritual is called the Golden Rule Awards, a peer-nominated process that culminates in the selection of four winners from each brand: one customer-facing sales team member, one customer-facing production team member, one franchise general manager, and one headquarters staffer. Winners attend the annual FirstService Brand Experience Summit and are brought onstage to tell their own stories, reflecting on the core values and brand-serving basics. These stories come to define what it means to live by the Golden Rule and set the standard of excellence for employees and executives throughout North America.

When financial analysts ask Charlie or his boss Scott Patterson to explain why FirstService can continue to outgrow and outperform many of its competitors across its business lines or how it can continue its remarkable track record of total shareholder return—imagine, a company composed of mature business lines such as residential property management, painting, home restoration, and custom closets delivering returns over the decade on par with Amazon and Apple—they notice that those analysts are not usually looking for answers such as *ensuring that our teams are ever more diligent and persistent in living the Golden Rule*. But in fact, that is a big part of the answer.

Love and Persistence

Wise leaders recognize that currents with the force of Niagara will try to sweep your favorite koi back downstream. The vast majority of employees, customers, investors, and society presume that the primary purpose of business is profits. No matter what business fad or pop philosophy is being preached, people believe what leaders do much more than what they say. They observe bosses continuing to set budgets, allocate capital, measure success, and pay bonuses based primarily on financials. So, if you want your message to love customers to be taken seriously, you had better back up those words with carefully designed culture, ritual, and systems that reinforce the Golden Rule.

Let me remind you of the famous passage about love read at many wedding ceremonies. It is taken from St. Paul's first letter to the Corinthians:

> Love is patient, love is kind. It does not envy, it does not boast, it is not proud. It does not dishonor others, it is not self-seeking, it is not easily angered, it keeps no record of wrongs. Love does not delight in evil but rejoices with the truth. It always protects, always trusts, always hopes, always perseveres.

In the case of love for customers, I think the case is clear that love can only persevere with plenty of systematic help from committed leaders.

CHAPTER 9

Be Humble

Net Promoter 3.0 and Beyond

A t Bain, we teach that in every communication you should *give the answer first* and always *finish high*—with a call to action.

I will try to follow that advice in this final chapter. The answer first: you will be humbled by the distance you must travel in order to become truly customer-centric. This chapter will help clarify that distance by providing a checklist of requisite components comprising a state-of-the-art Net Promoter System 3.0. Here, I have attempted to distill twenty years of learnings gained through working with and observing leaders at the vanguard of the movement toward customer capitalism.

First, though, I want to return to what I consider the central idea in this book: that an enlightened understanding of the Golden Rule provides the bedrock principle underpinning customer capitalism and serves as the foundation for generating good and sustainable profits. You may recall that I opened chapter 6, "Honor the Golden Rule," by recalling a luncheon with an old friend who was a pastor and divinity school instructor. Two vital lessons stuck with me from that lunch discussion. I've already shared one of them: that my friend—who is a very bright and thoughtful man—expressed his deep skepticism that "love thy neighbor as thyself" might have any relevance for business.

I hope he reads this book and comes to a different conclusion, but at the very least, he should know that I took his caution to heart. I reluctantly conceded that most folks would share his skepticism that making the world a better place for customers might represent a successful business strategy, let alone be the primary purpose of a winning organization. My proposition probably strikes many people—who believe that business runs on selfishness rather than service to others—as either hopelessly naive or half-baked. The notion that enriching customer lives should rise above all other stakeholder duties as the company's primary purpose must seem utterly preposterous to the traditional Wall Street crowd.

But if you've stuck with this book this far—almost to the end—maybe you're ready to join that small hardy band who believe that the future belongs to customer capitalists. If so, welcome aboard—and be aware that you are part of a very select group. Remember, only 10 percent of executives today believe that the primary purpose of their business is to enrich customer lives.

Let me return once more to that luncheon with my minister friend and to the second lesson that stuck with me from our discussion. As we were walking out of the restaurant, I shared a biblical conundrum that had long vexed me. One of the beatitudes from the otherwise compelling Sermon on the Mount never made very much sense to me: "Blessed are the meek, for they shall inherit the earth."[1]

Meek? Really? Meekness as a winning life strategy? In my experience, loyal, principled people shouldn't meekly fold in the face of challenge. If they want to make this world a better place, they must stand up courageously for their beliefs.

Looking back, I believe that my friend must have been amused by my consternation. He told me to stop fretting, because biblical scholars today pretty much agree that "meek" was not a very precise translation. The scribes of the King James Bible settled on that word simply because its single syllable suited the cadence of their very poetic interpretation. The accurate translation, he reassured me, is not *meek* but rather *humble*: Blessed are the humble, for they shall inherit the earth.

Slightly less poetic but surely more sensible. Without humility, there is little hope for true servant leadership, a prerequisite for earning loyalty. Without humility throughout the organization, selfish entitlement—which stalls learning and growth—blossoms. And to tie this into the main themes of this book, without humility, employees up and down the organization won't prioritize or process feedback, which is vital for innovation and upgrading the customer experience. Humility clarifies the need for constant learning in order to better serve others and is therefore a foundational ingredient for sustained success in a customer-centered world.

We've already looked at Jim Collins's *Good to Great* and its collection of putative exemplars. As we've seen, many of those companies soon fell on hard times. Collins, to his credit, then tried to figure out what had gone wrong. In his follow-up book, *How the Mighty Fall*, he concluded that their downfall began when executives became arrogant, intoxicated by success, and committed to the undisciplined pursuit of *more*.[2] I think Collins was largely correct, but I would also argue that aside from arrogance and greed, these executives were to some extent victims of our financial capitalist system, which has traditionally rewarded short-term quarterly performance and growth (irrespective of its quality or sustainability) versus a long-term focus on growing employee and customer assets by enriching their lives.

I'd add that the fragility of large-company success extends far beyond that handful of *Good to Great* companies. You might think that companies that are adept enough to elbow their way into the top tier of big business should be able to leverage the resulting advantages of scale, experience, financial strength, brand familiarity, and lobbying power to *stay* on top. Not so. Over a decade ago, I found that the half-life of *Fortune* 500 companies was only seventeen years. Today's accelerated pace of creative destruction will likely shorten this half-life even more. Do we remember Blackberry, Blockbuster, Compaq, and America Online? Just barely, right?

Back in October 1997, at my Loyalty Roundtable, I asked a group of loyalty-leader CEOs for their take on why so many successful companies stumble and fall. That gathering included the CEOs of Intuit, State Farm, USAA, Harley Davidson, Bain, Enterprise Rent-A-Car, both Dan and Truett Cathy of Chick-fil-A, and Tom Donahoe, former vice chairman of Price Waterhouse.[3] Their consensus was that the primary enemies of sustained success are not external threats, such as new competitors armed with breakthrough technologies. Instead, the real enemies often arise from within, the heinous four horsemen: greed, arrogance, complacency, and entitlement. These four deadly sins represent different facets of the same transgression: failure to be humble.

The longer a firm enjoys success and the more powerful it becomes, the greater the risk of greed, arrogance, complacency, and entitlement combining to derail progress. At the same time, it becomes easier for executives to focus internally—contesting political turf wars, revamping organizational charts, and so on—instead of listening to customers. Time gets wasted on internal squabbles rather than being spent on innovating ways to solve customers' problems and enrich their lives.

How do you avoid this trap? The best way I know is to embrace the mission of *enriching the life of every customer you touch* and to make sure you are listening to customers and scrutinizing their behavior so you know whether or not you are actually delivering on this mission. Asking for and acting on feedback from customers requires great humility, and this challenge increases as a company grows in power and stature. We have yet to discover a company with no detractors, so even the greatest firms have room to improve. Embracing this Golden Rule–inspired purpose of enriching every life you touch keeps you humble. Being humble helps you get to the top but plays an even more vital role in helping you stay there.[4]

It is good news that two-thirds of the *Fortune* 1000 companies now use NPS, with many reporting their NPS ratings to investors. The bad news is that so few have adopted the Net Promoter System mindset required to win in the era of customer capitalism. So let me declare here, in the form of a manifesto, the foundational mindset and core elements comprising NPS 3.0.[5]

The Net Promoter (Customer Capitalist) Manifesto

Great companies help people lead great lives—they are a force for good. Great leaders build and sustain such communities. They inspire team members to forge lives of meaning and purpose through service to others—service not merely satisfactory but so thoughtful, creative, and caring that it delights customers and enriches their lives.

The building blocks of great communities are relationships, founded on the principle *treat others the way you would want a loved one to be treated* or, in its purest form, *love thy neighbor as thyself.*

This Golden Rule establishes the highest standard of excellence in human affairs.

When companies create policies, procedures, cultures, and rules of membership to reinforce accountability to Golden Rule standards—across all community members—they provide the foundation for building relationships worthy of *loyalty*.

Companies earn loyalty from customers by treating them with loving care. That loyalty is apparent when customers come back for more, recruit their friends, and provide precious feedback on how to build an even better relationship. In this way, *love begets loyalty*, which powers sustainable, profitable growth, and illuminates the path to greatness for the organization, its teams, and for each individual team member. This system underpins the financial prosperity enjoyed by communities that hew most closely to Golden Rule standards.

Therefore, the primary mission of every organization striving for greatness should be *to build a community whose primary purpose is to sustainably enrich the lives of customers and where all members are treated in accordance with (and are held accountable to) the Golden Rule.*

This mission demands that leaders:

1. **Embrace an unbeatable purpose.** Leaders clarify that enriching customers' lives stands foremost as the organization's primary purpose. They teach team members how this philosophical North Star should guide priorities, decisions, and trade-offs, thus illuminating the path to personal and organizational success.

2. **Lead with love.** The primary duty of leaders is to care for their people. They must inspire teams to embrace this customer purpose and enable their success by allocating sufficient time, education, and resources to accomplish this mission. Leaders must be role models who practice, preach, and teach Golden Rule principles and values that systematically reinforce a loving culture through symbols, words, and deeds.

3. **Inspire teams.** Team members must feel energized by this mission to enrich customer lives and be empowered to root out policies, procedures, and behaviors that are contrary to the Golden Rule, confident that they will be supported in their efforts to always do the right thing.

4. **Unleash NPS-caliber feedback flows.** Systems and technology support timely and reliable feedback from customers and colleagues, augmenting surveys by incorporating the entire signal field of purchase behavior, usage, online commentary, ratings, and customer service interactions. Constant innovation is required for collecting, curating, and distributing the right feedback in a world overwhelmed with dataflow that has grown tired of surveys—a world that relies increasingly on digital bots, data science, and algorithms.

5. **Nurture relentless learning.** Leaders must create a culture of loving feedback, a prerequisite for honoring the Golden Rule. This includes training on the most effective techniques for giving, gathering, and receiving feedback and providing a safe space for processing it.

6. **Quantify earned growth economics.** Leaders and employees must understand and utilize customer-based accounting metrics (provided and endorsed by the CFO) to evaluate trade-offs and investment decisions.

7. **Regularly redefine the remarkable.** Leaders and teams must humbly recognize how much progress and innovation are required to make sure each customer feels loved. Leaders strive continuously to invent new ways to delight customers with remarkable products and experiences. Each individual, team, and group feels empowered and responsible for creating such remarkable experiences that customers come back for more and refer their friends.

Embracing the Movement

The elements of my manifesto may seem daunting, especially for leaders of well-established firms with an entrenched financial mindset. Almost every leader will feel humbled after reviewing our comprehensive checklist of NPS 3.0 requirements in appendix A. But failing to reorient your firm's mindset toward loving customers by incorporating the full checklist of best practices is probably the riskiest path of all, given the growing evidence—summarized in chapter 5—that *NPS laggards can't deliver true value to investors*. To help you make a clear-eyed assessment of where your organization stands versus customer-love winners, we have created an NPS 3.0 diagnostic that is freely available at the website: NetPromoterSystem.com.

I had once hoped that together with my colleagues at Bain and our clients we could drive the NPS revolution forward, but over the past decade I have acquired a bit more humility myself. To change the way the business world defines and measures success, we need additional courageous leaders to join the movement. We must build a stronger and broader community across all stakeholders to hasten the transition from financial to customer capitalism. We need:

- **Investors and CFOs to embrace earned growth economics.** Financial accounting—and the financial planning and analysis that accompanies it—must incorporate customer-based accounting, which reliably measures the health of the firm's customer relationships (the most valuable asset in most businesses). Customer-based accounting must track, among other things, the number of active customers and when they came aboard, increases and decreases in their purchases each period, defections by segment and tenure cohort, revenues per customer by tenure cohort, volume of new customers, cost of acquisition, split of new customers between earned (referral, recommendation, word-of-mouth, etc.) versus bought (advertising, promotional deals, commissions, sales, etc.)—in other words, all the key elements needed to estimate customer lifetime value for each customer.

- **Customer rating sites and e-commerce platforms to make ratings reliable.** Customer ratings sites must innovate solutions to provide ratings that are both honest and relevant and therefore more useful. As a frame of reference, Fakespot estimates that as of 2020, 42 percent of Amazon reviews are fake.[6] I predict that in many industries individual customer tastes will vary so much that for ratings to be relevant, they will have to be curated and organized to highlight the most relevant raters for each consumer.

- **Investors to challenge self-reported (uncertified) NPS scores.** As I mentioned previously, many companies report unaudited customer feedback scores. Investors who want to understand the value of a company's customer assets need to understand how these metrics are derived and demand consistent and reliable methodologies.

- **Boards to become true customer advocates.** Boards of directors must assume responsibility for ensuring that their organization's policies and practices treat customers right—a higher standard than simply not breaking the law. Boards should consider establishing a customer committee to serve along with existing nominating/governance, audit, and compensation committees. This oversight will become even more important as companies embrace the promise (and risk) of interactions with customers that are driven by artificial intelligence (AI). Companies must go beyond ethical AI and regulatory requirements and raise the bar to the Golden Rule standard of customer love. For this committee to have real accountability and clout, it will need reliable NPS data. This data will be available from third parties, such as Bain's NPS Prism, for some companies and from trusted internal processes for other companies. But for many firms, this will only happen when we have robust customer-based accounting that enables reporting metrics, such as earned growth, that gauge customers' love and are audit-worthy and therefore most appropriate for public reporting and for driving executive bonuses.

- **Boards to reward executives that play the long game.** Executives must be shielded from the distractions of short-term speculators if they are to make decisions in favor of treating customers right. Since the highest total shareholder return (TSR) accrues to firms with the highest NPS ratings, long-term investor interests are best served by encouraging leadership teams to love customers. Executive compensation plans should evolve so that generous bonuses accrue to leaders who deliver true value to long-term shareholders— that is, TSR exceeding the hurdle of average stock market returns. In addition to TSR, customer and employee outcomes should become part of compensation plans.

- **Employees to be more selective and insist that employers help them live the right life.** Employees are already demanding purposeful work, particularly as the workforce transitions to the Millennial and Gen Z generations. You've heard a lot about the employee loyalty earned by the companies in this book. The best employees—from call center agents in Phoenix, Arizona, to user experience designers in Shanghai to meal-delivery providers in Madrid—have a choice about where they will work. The work community they select will deeply affect their ability to live the right life, so they should make this choice wisely, which means, in part, using the right data.

I realize that the path I have just outlined requires much work. Perhaps your humility is kicking in and you're wondering if this effort might exceed your capabilities. My response is that *it's worth the effort*. Why? Making the effort to hasten the transition from financial to customer capitalism will provide the most rewarding path for you and your team and will help you *win*. Remember the spectacular TSR performance of customer-love winners? That didn't come easy, but I am sure the leaders in those companies would tell you it was well worth the effort.

Let's look at one example.

First Serve Others

I first met Scott Patterson, CEO of FirstService, when he attended Bain's NPS Loyalty Forum in the fall of 2011. We rode back to our hotel in the same car, and Scott explained that he was keenly interested in learning more about how NPS could help his business leaders build even stronger relationships with their customers. With a market cap over $7 billion and with twenty-five thousand employees, FirstService is North America's largest manager of residential communities—that is, condominiums and homeowners' associations—and also owns a portfolio of so-called essential property services, including CertaPro Painters, California Closets, Century Fire, and First Onsite Restorations. Over the years I have had the opportunity to learn much more about these businesses, including how they build superior customer loyalty and how the leadership philosophy guides FirstService, which is nicely summarized by its hashtag: #FirstServeOthers.

One day I received an invitation from FirstService founder and chairman Jay Hennick to have breakfast under a canopy of palm trees at a restaurant overlooking Miami's Biscayne Bay. I didn't know it at the time, but that breakfast was the beginning of a long process aimed at recruiting me to join his board. The more I learned about Jay and the company he founded, the more intrigued I became, mostly because he and his colleagues seemed to care about customer loyalty as much as I did.

FirstService began implementing the Net Promoter System across all its businesses in 2008. In truth, though, Jay had learned the importance of treating customers right and earning their loyalty many years earlier. When he was fifteen years old, he turned his first job as a lifeguard/pool attendant at a local apartment complex into a pool-servicing business that employed hundreds of employees while he was still in high school. A recent article about Jay titled "From Pool Boy to Billionaire" explains how Jay kept running the pool business on the side as he pursued a career as an attorney.[7] In 1989, he rolled his ownership stake into a property services company (FirstService) and left his law firm to concentrate on the business full-time.

As I learned more about FirstService through my regular board meeting visits to Toronto, I came to realize what a compelling customer-love example the company provided. Every executive I met cared deeply about building superior customer loyalty—and was enthusiastic to learn even better ways to implement NPS to its full potential in their business. Their results provide a wonderful case study on the economic benefits of earning superior customer loyalty. You've seen in figure 5-1 (chapter 5) that FirstService's TSR has been in the same league as that of Amazon and Apple over the past decade. But FirstService's remarkable run started long before that. Its stock was listed on the NASDAQ exchange in 1995. Of the approximately twenty-eight hundred public companies in North America at that time with revenues over $100 million, FirstService's TSR over the subsequent twenty-five years ranked number eight (99.7th percentile)— almost 22 percent per year. An investment of $100,000 in FirstService stock in 1995 would have grown to $13.6 million by 2019. In retrospect, I wish Jay had invited me to breakfast a few years earlier!

What accounts for this remarkable track record? You already know the answer. FirstService has been powered by a loyalty-fueled growth engine that generates superior cash flow. Jay and his team utilized that love-driven cash machine to acquire other firms over the years, including Colliers International, a substantial real estate professional services and investment management company. When Colliers grew to the point that it could sustain itself as an independent company, Jay proposed that we spin it off as an independent public company so it could get the appropriate level of attention from its own board and generate its own cadre of long-term investors who understand and value its global brokerage and management services.

Why is this spin-off story unusual? It is unusual because humility does not come naturally to many CEOs today. They strive to build empires large enough to get invited to attend the annual World Economic Forum in Davos, Switzerland, as well as the Augusta National Golf Club to watch the Masters Tournament, film openings, Academy Awards parties, and other high-visibility, ego-stroking events. And executive compensation consultants presume that the bigger the company, the bigger the CEO's paycheck should be.[8]

Wise (and humble) leaders such as Jay Hennick and Scott Patterson understand the importance of an owner's mentality. They ensure that the leader of each of their businesses has incentives aligned with those of their long-term investors.[9] This approach works best when that equity stake is not dissipated across lots of unrelated businesses that happen to be operating under the same corporate umbrella. For example, it is far better for the California Closets franchisee in Miami to own equity in that local franchise than to have a stake in the FirstService brand. A core philosophy at FirstService is therefore to ensure that business leaders have a substantial equity stake in the business they run. This same discipline runs throughout the organization, all the way up to CEO Scott Patterson and the rest of his senior leadership team, whose bonus plans pay out only when the company achieves ambitious growth in earning-per-share targets. This ensures that long-term investors as well as customers and employees are treated with respect.

Jay's ownership stake (beefed up with supervoting shares) provided air cover, enabling his business leaders to confidently play the long game and focus on the right measures of success.[10] This enables executives to build resilient strategies based on loving their customers. As evidence of this resilience, consider the shocking impact the Covid-19 pandemic wreaked on the real estate services sector, in which FirstService competes. Yet somehow the company kept motoring along.

Scott explains that "FirstService has lots of little engines of growth where every branch manager acts more like an owner than an employee because they are measured and compensated based on the success of their own little engine." This organizational structure, coupled with a customer-focused mindset founded on service and loyalty, has proven that loving customers provides a resilient winning strategy—even for public companies, if they are built like FirstService.

Humility

You might not expect much humility from leaders with such a remarkable track record, but Jay and Scott continue to learn and grow. When I described my plans to develop an earned growth statistic to Scott, he exclaimed, "That's a great idea, Fred. It perfectly reflects the way we think here at FirstService."

Scott attributes much of his firm's performance to nurturing a customer-service culture reinforced through local-equity ownership. Local managers can see the importance of generating what Scott calls *organic* growth. Each local business leader understands the enormous expense required to replace a customer lost through defection. They also know how much more efficient it is to earn new customers through referrals and word of mouth from existing customers. Scott estimates that half of all new customers in FirstService's community management business come through referral. In both California Closets and CertaPro, 70 percent of the quality leads come via this route. Local franchisees know that when a lead comes through referral, this represents a quality lead that is likely to result in good business.[11]

By tracking and publishing audit-worthy Earned Growth Rates, companies such as FirstService will be able to clarify the source of their advantage and thereby help investors understand the sustainability of their loyalty-growth engines. Scott admits that he struggles to convince investors about the sustainable advantage that FirstService's customer-centric culture delivers. "They hear my words," he says, "but their financial mindset just can't make sense of them. They keep asking for the real secret sauce behind our impressive track record so they can assess our future." For this reason, Scott views the development of a measurable science around earned growth as being very much to his advantage and looks forward to the day when, armed with credible and rigorous metrics, his investors can see with confidence what's driving FirstService's profitable growth.

FirstService also provides another reminder that really good things happen when you hang around with good people—including the fact that they introduce you to other good people. One reason chapter 1 of this book opens with Steve Grimshaw's Caliber Collision story is that Jay and Scott asked me to help them recruit Steve to join our board. I am pleased to report that Steve agreed to join us, but I recall thinking during our first phone call that given his remarkable accomplishments at Caliber and the fact that he had recently handed off his CEO duties and moved into the less time-demanding job of chairman, he would have many options for spending his time. So I asked him what made him consider investing his precious time serving as a director at FirstService. He replied, "You know, Jay Hennick and Scott Patterson have built such a great business and achieved such spectacular success, and yet they are such humble guys. Those are the kind of people I want to work with."

I agree with Steve—that is certainly a central reason why I had signed on as a director. Spending time with Jay, Scott, and their executive team has been another eye-opening experience that further clarified my understanding of customer capitalism. And of course, the benefits to investors (including me) have been remarkable. However, my continuing fascination with the company goes deeper. My overriding interest in FirstService stems from its impact on its customers and employees.

Now, it would be tempting to tell stories at this point demonstrating how FirstService employees behaved in dramatic fashion to save customers in crisis, such as after a hurricane, fire, or flood. And there are many such stories, given that disaster recovery and restoration represent a core business for the company, especially in its Paul Davis and First Onsite divisions. But every company has such stories. When human beings see their neighbors or even strangers in tragic or life-threatening situations, many will heroically step up. Luckily, there is something in our wiring that makes us help one another in a crisis. But most of us are less good at showing this same loving care throughout the humdrum of our daily routines. That's when it's easy to occasionally lapse into our lazy or selfish selves. And that is where great companies separate themselves from the rest. Their culture of loving care, reinforced by systems, processes, measurement, accountability, and leadership, helps team members become their best selves—consistently.

Let me share a few seemingly mundane examples to illustrate how FirstService helps its employees live the Golden Rule. First, a recent experience of my own as a customer: I hired California Closets to design and install new racks and shelves in the master bedroom closet of our Florida condo.[12] The installers arrived on time, clearly explained their process, built out the closets, and cleaned up afterward. They finished sooner than expected, and rather than dashing out the door for a long coffee break, they asked if there was anything they could help me with around the apartment.

It so happened that I had been struggling for weeks to find a handyman to fix the counter on our kitchen pass-through, which had sagged so badly that objects that could roll or slide downhill ultimately ended up on the living room floor. No repair person would touch the job because it was too small. So, I purchased a support bracket and started the repair myself but soon recognized I was out of my league. I had no idea how to find the metal support stud in the wall, push the counter up to level, and hold it there while simultaneously attaching the bracket without hitting any electrical or plumbing lines hidden within the wall. I was stuck (and frustrated)!

The California Closets installer said he and his helper would be happy to fix it, which took them about twenty minutes. When I offered to pay them something extra, he said that wasn't necessary. I could see his young associate raise his eyebrows in surprise.[13] The installer must have seen this as a teachable moment, because as the workers exited down the hallway toward the elevator, I heard him explaining to his assistant that doing favors for customers makes good business sense. They were speaking Spanish at that point, so I am guessing, but I think he told his associate that finding ways to delight a customer was a smart way to run a business— and the right way to live a life.

I mentioned this story to Charlie Chase, the CEO of FirstService's brand businesses, and he was not at all surprised. He explained that FirstService teaches crews to seek out ways to go the extra mile for customers whenever possible. He forwarded this recent YELP review about one of FirstService's installers as another example:

New Review for California Closets—Palm Desert

★★★★★ 2/5/2021

This is not related to California Closets work alone, but one of their AMAZING employees who happened to notice that my front passenger-side tire had popped in a parking lot. This occurred as I was leaving a convenience store and he grabbed my attention, suggested I pull over into a parking space and then proceeded to help me change the popped tire to the emergency spare in the back of my trunk. The person who helped me is named Matthew H. In such a moment of despair, I didn't know what to do and Matthew was there to help me when I needed it . . . and even after helping me with the tire, he [showed] me what to do etc. My horrible day became such a heart warming day. Thank you so very much to not only Matthew but to California Closets for hiring such an amazing young man. It is very rare to find people like Matthew! Amazing people!! You guys rock!

Charlie contacted Matthew's boss to ask him why he felt confident taking this extra time to help a stranger. After all, Matthew was a relatively new employee, only recently promoted to a lead installer role. His boss reported that "Matthew said he felt empowered because it was the right thing to do. Since we trust him as a lead installer, it means we trust him to make the right decisions. He knew that once he explained the scenario, we would be supportive."

FirstService tries to make it easy to do the right thing. CertaPro execs developed a list of potential wows to help keep them front-of-mind for their painting crews. Two examples: When painting a stairway atrium where a ceiling light is mounted high and out of reach, before the painters take away their ladders, they offer to replace the light bulbs. If there is a brass knocker on the front door, they offer to polish the brass. The list goes on.

These small acts of kindness cost very little but generate lots of smiling customers and smiling employees proud of a job well done, and so the economic flywheel begins to spin—customers tell their friends and request additional jobs. The result is that yes, investors love FirstService, but its primary beneficiaries are the thousands of employees and millions of customers who get to experience a life based on #FirstServeOthers—a life that makes the world a better place.

I couldn't resist including Charlie's message back to me after vetting this section of my book draft for accuracy:

> Fred, your book hits on the themes we live every day. Be humble, empower people to live the Golden Rule, and lead them in ways that inspire. But, you should be aware this creates a real problem. We earn more customers than we can handle. Living the Golden Rule creates promoters who grow your business faster than anyone thought possible. Staffing up to meet the demand presents a difficult challenge!

Looking Forward

I began this book by sharing some special days that shaped my understanding of what it means to win in business, how to measure success (in both business and life), and the relationship between love and loyalty. I hope I have been clear that my definition of winning in business is measured by how many lives have been enriched, net of those diminished. The best way to win is for leaders to inspire teams to love their customers. To gauge progress, you can tell that customers felt the love when they are loyal, as evidenced by repeat purchases, increased purchases, increased share of wallet (or category), respectful treatment of employees, constructive feedback, and, most especially, recommendations to friends, family, and colleagues. This worldview has evolved throughout my work at Bain over the past forty-four years and through my experiences as a customer, an investor, board member, father, and now grandfather. There have been lots of special days that opened my eyes to this new mindset of customer capitalism.

Over the past few years, it has become apparent that we are living in a special era—an inflection point, if you will—in which rapid change is generating so many "special days" that the cumulative effect can sometimes be bewildering. Cloud-based computing, technology giants, smartphone apps, digital innovations, big-data analytics, and AI are merging with pandemic-induced changes in lifestyle patterns and priorities for both customers and employees. These are driving tectonic shifts in how companies can better love (or abuse) customers. I don't have all the answers here by any means, but I'm confident they will emerge over time and morph into NPS 4.0 and beyond. But hopefully by viewing the changes of the past four decades through the lens of customer capitalism, we can provide some useful suggestions to help guide priorities in this brave new world.

In many industries, the vast majority of customer transactions will become digital. As I mentioned earlier, digital already accounts for 80 percent of all US banking interactions. This creates a new service workforce—the digital front line, consisting primarily of apps and self-service kiosks (ATMs, self-checkout) guided by AI, algorithms, and bots. Leaders must ask themselves a key question: How can we ensure that our bots love our customers? If bot learning models are based on optimizing financial accounting numbers—that is, selling more stuff at the highest possible price and lowest possible cost—then we are in for a rough ride. Somehow we must ensure that customer-based accounting as well as objectives such as the coefficient (or perhaps gradient) of NPS and earned growth predominate the objective function for each interaction, and that these metrics become fully integrated into our digital learning models. Net Promoter–style feedback loops must exist to enable bots to learn how to love customers and enrich their lives.

Several of the exemplar companies featured in this book are leading the way here. Thank goodness Amazon decided to follow a Costco-style pricing strategy or we might be having our electronic wallets emptied by computer scientists with access to way too much data about our personal lives, preferences, wallet status, and shopping habits! Thank goodness Apple decided to guard the privacy of customer data rather than exploiting that information to maximize profits.

Despite the best corporate intentions, the shift to a digital world brings new risks. Leaders must be clear that their organization exists to enrich customer lives and should exercise painstaking care to ensure that this mission becomes integrated into the digital front line. There will be far fewer humans on those front lines who can serve as cultural ambassadors and exercise the judgment required to ensure that decisions and trade-offs remain true to the Golden Rule.

Data and decision models ultimately power the digital front lines. If you have spent any time working with such models, you know two things. First, they are only as good as the data that goes into them. Second, a model needs clear constraints and an even clearer objective function—in other words, a single dimension that the model should optimize. Getting this wrong has massive risks. We have seen the emergence of the concept of ethical AI as leaders in technology and broader business begin to understand the risks. This is important and necessary. We need boundaries to ensure that our bots do no harm. We can't accept digital redlining in financial services, health care, or, frankly, *any* industry. Machines won't exercise judgment or care about treating people right; they won't have the ability to avoid treating some customers preferentially. They won't understand the cost of infringing on one's privacy and could easily expose customers to harmful actions by bad actors who buy or steal leaked customer data.

But ethical AI is too narrow an objective. We should strive for loving AI in which the ultimate objective of AI is—you guessed it—to enrich customers' lives. Consider what a challenging pivot this represents. Today most models run unchecked on objective functions aimed at maximizing accounting results. That is why airline ticket prices skyrocket in the path of a hurricane. That's why automated hospital billing systems charge the highest price possible (even to those least able to pay). Until we have perfected a way to incorporate the Golden Rule into the machine's decision matrix, how can a company ensure that customers will feel the love so they come back for more and bring their friends? And how can a firm deliver respectable returns to investors without this kind of customer loyalty? The challenge will grow as machine learning gets deployed at scale and executives hand over even more of the brains (and soul) of customer service to bots.

What is the solution, then?

Well, to me it's clear. In stark contrast to the pundits who claim that Net Promoter will become less relevant in the digital age, I believe that the Net Promoter philosophy and the digital tool kit to support its implementation are becoming even more vital. As physical locations get shuttered and employees are replaced by digital alternatives, the voice of the customer will drift further away from the decision makers. It is essential that companies leverage Net Promoter feedback tools (both digital signals and surveys) to ensure that employees and their AI models are learning from the voice of the customer. Net Promoter critics have suggested that some of its core tools—surveys, customer verbatim explanations, and customer callbacks—are obsolete because digital technology can give us all the data we need. I disagree. Technology can't tell us *why* customers feel and behave the way they do.

Yes, I am very excited about the possibilities of signal data, predictive NPS, voice sentiment analysis, session replay, and a host of other amazing innovations. But let's not pretend that click patterns and digital observations can understand how a customer is feeling or tell us why. The most sophisticated digital dashboard will never yield the same insight as a conversation with a customer. AI requires many more years of development to approach the genius of human intelligence. It will surely take much longer for artificial love to approximate real love. Machines can never understand or replace human love. The unbeatable strategy of loving customers will always depend on us humans.

Final Thoughts

As I finish writing this final chapter, I am preparing to visit my local cancer center for my annual screening exams. Few things reinforce my humility these days like these unavoidable reminders that my time on Earth is finite.[14] For two main reasons, I'm thankful that my health has held up. First, I've been able to see this book through to completion, distilling the lessons of my forty-four years at Bain into a set of principles—a framework based on Golden Rule standards of loving care persistently reinforced with metrics, processes, and systems.

Second and more important, I was blessed to be able to welcome two new grandchildren into this world, Adelaide and Clare.

My primary goal in writing this book was to help companies successfully transition toward and win in the customer capitalism era. But I hope it has broader relevance for Adelaide, Clare, and their hoped-for siblings and cousins along with extended family, friends, and neighbors young and old. No matter what path their lives take, the ideas in this book can make that path smoother and more successful.

Adelaide, Clare, and their cohorts will certainly be customers. I hope some of the lessons in this book will help them discover the very best suppliers—those that strive to love their customers.

At some point in their lives they're also likely to be employees, and the ideas in this book should help them figure out which companies would be worthy employers. In their roles serving customers they will benefit from a service mindset, embodying the goal of enriching the lives of their customers in truly remarkable ways.

Maybe they will be leaders. If so, they can experience the joy of helping team members lead lives of meaning and purpose through delighting customers. I hope they will innovate enhancements to internal systems to reinforce more persistently standards of accountability to the Golden Rule. And finally, as Adelaide and Clare become investors, this book should help guide them in placing winning bets.

When you add it all up—as more and more individuals realize their moral and economic power as customers, employees, and investors—the advantages of customer capitalist firms will accelerate. Smart leaders will get out in front of this wave. They will expedite the shift toward a customer-centered worldview and embrace the wisdom of building the right corporate culture in which all members hold one another accountable to Golden Rule standards of behavior and where success is gauged by the number of customer lives enriched.

Why is culture so important? It takes a community to make the Golden Rule work. Only strong and prosperous communities with strong cultures—such as the examples cited throughout this book—are capable of nurturing relationships that bring the Golden Rule to its full potential. Only when individual members can trust the community for protection from abusive takers—those bullies, slackers, and cheats who care little for enriching the lives they touch—can individual members safely concentrate on building relationships of service and devote their full energies to enriching the lives of their customers.

As noted, community turns out to be key. There is surely some truth to that old adage that one's life becomes the weighted average of the company you keep. Your relationships with the people with whom you spend the most time profoundly influence your goals, your norms, your hopes, your dreams, and the way you measure success. I hope this book will help all my readers seek out and nurture communities that enable relationships affirming Golden Rule standards of love and service. These organizations will enrich your life, and they will win—*on purpose*. They will attract and retain the people who heed this grandfatherly guidance: *Keep good company and choose your loyalties wisely. They will shape your life and define your legacy. Above all else, they will help you live the right life, a life that turns frowns into smiles and leaves things better than you found them.*

Net Promoter 3.0 Checklist

With thousands of firms now utilizing at least some core components of the Net Promoter System, our suite of organizational tools and processes comprising NPS continue to grow and evolve. We at Bain invented only some of the components of this system; we helped launch an open-source movement and integrated the best of what we observed working well at innovative practitioners.

Many of the leading innovators are members in Bain's NPS Loyalty Forum who regularly share best practices and seek help on their thorniest challenges.[1] This group deserves enormous credit for helping us at Bain understand the essential elements of today's state of the art.

So, what follows is a summary of the elements that comprise today's NPS management system, what I call Net Promoter 3.0. I have detailed most of these practices in the body of the book, but I bring them together here to serve as a sort of checklist. How many elements of NPS 3.0 has your organization already implemented? If you can check most of these boxes, then you should feel confident that you are on your way toward building a Golden Rule culture that persistently focuses on enriching customer lives.

I've distilled the system to seven main components, with their associated subsystems:

1. Embrace an unbeatable purpose

Leaders embrace enriching customers' lives
as the organization's primary purpose

Leaders clarify that enriching customers' lives stands as the organization's primary purpose. They teach team members how this philosophical North Star should guide priorities, decisions, and trade-offs, thus illuminating the path to personal and organizational success.

- Regularly declare the primacy of customer purpose and commitment to Golden Rule treatment of all stakeholders (through symbols, words, and deeds).

- Create and embrace strategies true to this purpose.

- Measure progress toward this purpose as your North Star.

2. Lead with love

Leaders practice (act as role models), preach, and
teach Golden Rule principles and values

The primary duty of leaders is to their people. Leaders must inspire teams to embrace this customer purpose and enable their success by allocating sufficient time, education, and resources to accomplish this mission. Leaders must practice (model), preach, and teach Golden Rule principles and values that systematically reinforce a loving culture through symbols, words, and deeds.

- Act as a role model for the right behaviors and explain major decisions and priorities in terms of core values.

- Foster a culture that embraces playing the long game, ensuring that short-term financial goals never trump principles.

- Make the customer the center of every decision—from product development to employee hiring to digitizing customer service and operations.

- Break down barriers (organizational and other) that impede progress.

3. Inspire teams

Team members should be fully engaged and supported in the mission to enrich customer lives

Team members must feel energized by this mission to enrich customer lives and be empowered to root out policies, procedures, and behaviors that are contrary to the Golden Rule, confident that they will be supported in their efforts to always do the right thing.

- Teams should be recruited, trained, structured, and organized to facilitate (and be inspired by) delighting customers.

  - Teams' ability to enrich customer lives should be constantly monitored; leaders listen/act on team feedback and identify and prioritize constraints/roadblocks requiring resolution.

  - Employees are trained how to give and receive feedback in a way that reinforces and nurtures a culture of loving feedback.

  - Teams provide upward feedback to leaders in a carefully designed process that provides useful coaching and is appropriately linked to leadership evaluation.

    - A safe feedback process should enable employees to signal how well principles are being followed and where improvements are required.

    - A system should be in place to protect teams from abusive customers (warnings, sanctions, and appropriate process for firing customers, including lifetime bans if necessary).

- Recognition/reward/promotion systems should reinforce principles.

  - Safeguards should be established to ensure that executives cannot prosper at the expense of customers, employees, or investors.

- Customer-based accounting results (including earned growth) and relationship NPS relative to competition should appropriately impact senior executive rewards.

- Survey scores for individual frontline employees should not be corrupted by being made into targets or linked to individual frontline compensation so that they can inspire and guide learning and improvement.

- Leaders at every level must embody (in the eyes of peers and teams) core principles to be considered for promotion to more senior roles.

4. Unleash NPS-caliber feedback flows

Real-time NPS, signal, and other customer feedback should be integrated with core systems to accelerate learning, innovation, and progress

Systems and technology support timely and reliable feedback from customers and colleagues, augmenting surveys by incorporating the entire signal field of purchase behavior, usage, online commentary, ratings, and customer service interactions. Constant innovation is required for collecting, curating, and distributing the right feedback in a world overwhelmed with dataflow that has grown tired of surveys, a world that relies increasingly on digital bots, data science, and algorithms.

- Timely, reliable flow of NPS feedback should be measured at the right places with the right methodology and objective.

  - Utilize the external NPS Prism–caliber competitive benchmark NPS to understand performance versus key competitors overall and at the product and journey level.

  - Use internal relationship, product, and journey NPS to identify specific themes and systematic opportunities.

- Use individual touchpoint NPS primarily for team and individual learning, coaching, and improvement.

- Map customer journeys, identify priority episodes and touchpoints, and utilize clear, sustainable strategies for fixing defects and creating wows (results tracked versus NPS Prism–caliber competitor benchmarks).

- Use the entire signal field (call centers, social media, ratings, chat, email, etc.) to augment/replace surveys. Calibrate Promoter/Passive/Detractor categorization to actual behavior and utilize continuous innovation (e.g., predictive NPS).

- Regularly upgrade the survey process to reduce friction for customers, evidenced by high response rates and rich verbatim.

- Continuously innovate to find reliable alternatives to traditional surveys.

5. Nurture relentless learning

Rhythms should be embedded to enable team members to listen, learn, and act on feedback

Leaders must create a culture of loving feedback, a prerequisite for honoring the Golden Rule. This includes training on the most effective techniques for giving and receiving feedback and providing a safe space for processing it.

- Team Learning and Improvement

  - Team Huddles

    - Teams should be trained in how to best utilize daily/weekly huddles, incorporating agile rhythms and best practices.

    - A portion of team huddles should focus on issues/solutions to ensure that team members are inspired and working together effectively. Safe space should be provided for contemplating feedback. Messages and structured anonymity should be utilized to enable candor.

- Inner Loop (loop closed with all Detractors and sampling of Passives/Promoters)

- Team members (or their supervisor) close the (inner) loop with every Detractor and an appropriate sample of Passives/Promoters.

  - Teams use feedback to set priorities and to solve problems within their control.

  - Issues that require elevation (outside a team's control) should be prioritized with clear accountability for resolutions.

- Outer Loop (identify and prioritize changes requiring policy/process changes, things outside the team's control)

  - Top Down (executive call-listening)

  - Accountability should be assigned for all priority issues (along with required resources/time frame).

- Executive Listening/Learning

  - Board members and senior executives receive continuous education on organizational purpose, principles, and primary challenges/obstacles.

  - Use empathy training for all leaders so that decision makers understand customers and their needs.

  - Executives should regularly listen in (or handle) customer calls/problems and should read customers verbatim and follow up when appropriate.

  - Cross-functional reviews of customer survey and signal feedback should drive priorities/actions.

- Resolve issues cited by frontline employees as priority constraints to delighting more customers.

- Fix policies/processes that teams cite as being inconsistent with principles (including work/life balance, sustainability, and impact on environment and social priorities).

- Periodic communication should update employees on actions taken based on their feedback ("you said, we did").

6. Quantify earned growth economics

Utilize CFO-certified customer-based accounting that guides decisions and that investors trust

Leaders and employees must understand and utilize customer-based accounting metrics (provided and endorsed by the CFO) to evaluate trade-offs and investment decisions.

- CFO-certified earned growth economics should be quantified and utilized to evaluate investment options.

- Earned growth economics should be integrated into strategy, customer acquisition/retention, and operations.

- Customer-based accounting enables the calculation of customer lifetime value and guides investment decisions.

- Referrals and word of mouth should be rigorously tracked and incorporated into customer lifetime value calculations.

- Audit-worthy customer-based accounting results should be reported to investors. There should be full transparency in how any publicly reported NPS ratings were derived. Publicly reported NPS scores are ideally derived through a double-blind research process (the same rigor as for standard financials), with a clear understanding of the valuable roles played by other NPS categories and how they relate to double-blind benchmarks.

7. Regularly redefine the remarkable

Leaders and teams must humbly *recognize* how much progress and innovation is still required to make sure each customer feels loved

Leaders and teams must humbly recognize how much progress and innovation are still required to make sure each customer feels loved. Leadership should strive continuously to invent new ways to delight customers through remarkable products and experiences. Each individual, team, and group feels empowered and responsible for creating such remarkable experiences that customers come back for more and refer their friends.

- Macro innovation

    - Every executive feels responsible for generating and championing new product and experience innovations that add more value for customers.

    - Regular competitor benchmarking (by episode and overall relationship) highlights opportunities and keeps a focus on "how high is up."

    - The elevation process enables frontline employees to escalate their best candidates for increasing customer "wows" and decreasing customer "ows."

    - The executive team prioritizes customer experience upgrades through capital and budget allocation processes (clear accountability and the time frame for deliverables).

    - There should be consistent focus on leveraging new technology to reinvent products and experiences.

- Micro innovation

    - Empathy training should be used so that every employee can relate to customers, utilizing their own personal perspectives and experiences as consumers in search for intelligent wows.

– The "Jenny Question" (what can we do better?) should be incorporated to augment employee idea generation.

– All employees should be encouraged to find innovations to delight their customers, confident that these efforts will be recognized appropriately.

– Frontline employees should understand how to analyze the cost/benefit of proposed innovations so they can demonstrate sustainable best practices.

Calculating Earned Growth

The illustrations on the following pages should help clarify the components of the earned growth calculation and their importance. Growth for every company results from the sum of its earned and bought revenues. By separating the two, we can better understand the quality and sustainability of the firm's growth, thus improving our understanding of its future prospects. We also provide further instructions at the website, NetPromoterSystem.com, as well as an online earned growth calculator tool that we built to help guide the application of the ideas contained in these illustrations.

In figure B-1, the standard accounting process would show that the firm grew by 30 percent from revenues of $100 to $130 (this could represent thousands of dollars or millions—the proportion is what counts, and using 100 for base-year revenues simplifies all calculations) over the period covered. The third bar (far right) illustrates how customer-based accounting illuminates the underlying changes in customer flows and purchases yielding the 30 percent revenue growth. The bar shows that this 30 percent is the result of net revenue retention (NRR) of 85 percent (some existing customers reduced purchases while others expanded, netting out to a 15 percent decline). New customer purchases generated an extra 45 percent of revenues, 20 percent of which was bought and 25 percent of which was earned. To calculate earned growth, we add NRR of 85 percent to the 25 percent new customer earned revenues of 25 percent for an earned growth factor of 110 percent (which means a 10 percent Earned Growth Rate). In this example, the earned growth ratio is 33 percent; in other words, one-third of the reported growth rate (using standard accounting) was earned growth. Net Promoter Score leaders don't need to buy new customers to grow, so you would expect them to have earned growth ratios much higher than 33 percent.

Shortcut

Some firms won't be able to calculate all the factors comprising NRR—for example, it may be impossible to quantify revenues lost through customer declines or defections—either through systems inadequacies or because their business has a long and unpredictable purchase cycle (such as automobiles and eyeglasses). No worries, because a simple shortcut will let you calculate your Earned Growth Rate. Simply quantify current period revenues from customers who had purchased from you previously and divide by total revenues (all customers) from the previous period. That will estimate your NRR.

Then, add your best estimate of earned new revenue (as a percent of total current period revenues) to derive your earned growth factor (and Earned Growth Rate, which is simply the factor minus 100 percent). As noted in chapter 5, earned new customer revenue (typically the much smaller component of earned growth) quantifies revenues from the subset of new customers who were earned through recommendations and referrals from existing customers. Today, few firms can parse new customers into earned versus bought, so we at Bain (in partnership with a team at Medallia) pioneered a practical solution to begin meeting this challenge. We provide more details on that solution at our website, NetPromoterSystem.com, but stated briefly, we tested out alternative structures for the question that can be integrated into the new-customer onboarding process.

Calculating the Earned Growth Rate (EGR)

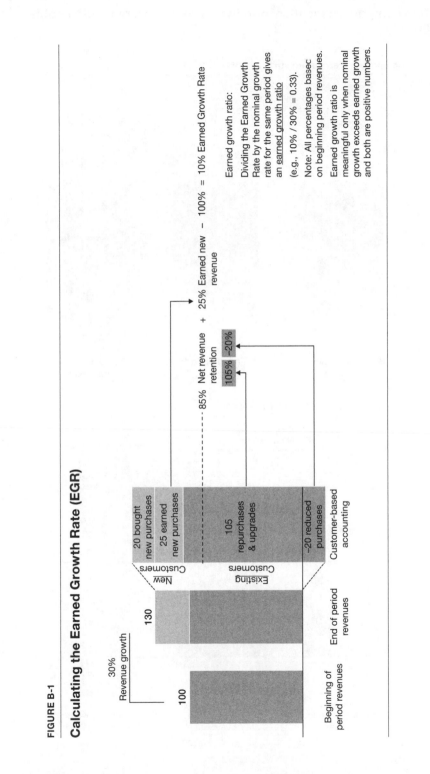

Two companies: identical nominal growth, different sustainable growth

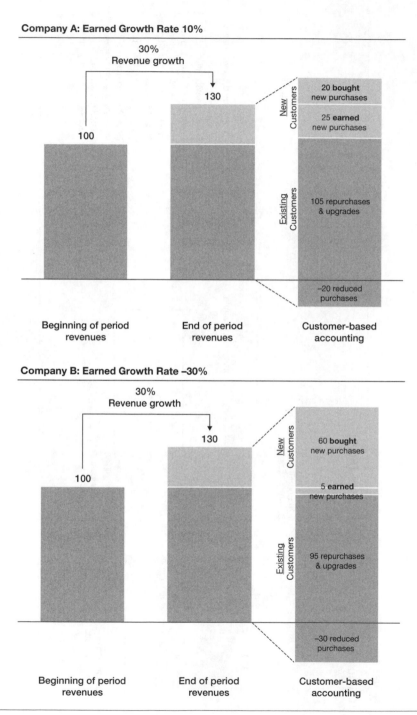

Company A: Earned Growth Rate 10%

30% Revenue growth

100 → 130

New Customers
- 20 **bought** new purchases
- 25 **earned** new purchases

Existing Customers
- 105 repurchases & upgrades
- −20 reduced purchases

Beginning of period revenues | End of period revenues | Customer-based accounting

Company B: Earned Growth Rate −30%

30% Revenue growth

100 → 130

New Customers
- 60 **bought** new purchases
- 5 **earned** new purchases

Existing Customers
- 95 repurchases & upgrades
- −30 reduced purchases

Beginning of period revenues | End of period revenues | Customer-based accounting

Digging Deeper

Figure B-2 illustrates two hypothetical firms (A and B) with the same reported revenue growth using standard accounting, 30 percent. With customer-based accounting, the very different paths these firms have followed to achieve that growth are revealed by their contrasting Earned Growth Rates. Company A has better NRR and is benefiting from a healthy flow of referral/recommendation-generated new customers, while company B must buy lots of growth to make up for its weak NRR and paltry flow of earned new customer revenues. We would expect that company A's NPS will be superior relative to B's (if relative scores are available) and that A will enjoy far superior economics over the years ahead if these patterns hold. If these were public companies priced at similar multiples to earnings or revenues, it would probably make sense to invest in company A and take a short position against company B.

Notes

Preface

1. Unless otherwise cited, the sources of all statements and quotations in this book are personal conversations or interviews with Fred Reichheld.

Introduction

1. Per a July 2021 Bain survey of business executives.

2. For readers unfamiliar with the business school case method, this is the term for a typical opening of a class session in which the professor calls on a hapless student to analyze the case that the students should have all studied the night before.

3. And the field of marketing in general had fallen out of the front ranks of academic concerns decades earlier.

4. Frank Newport, "Democrats More Positive About Socialism Than Capitalism," Gallup News, August 13, 2018, https://news.gallup.com/poll/240725/democrats-positive-socialism -capitalism.aspx.

5. In that address, Bloomberg emphasized (among other things) the importance of treating employees fairly—a "good act that makes sense," as he put it. See Clea Simon, "Former New York Mayor and Philanthropist Urges Grads toward Ethical Business Practices," *Harvard Gazette*, May 30, 2019, https://news.harvard.edu/gazette/story/2019/05/michael -bloomberg-extolls-moral-leadership-at-harvards-class-day/.

6. All the other dimensions must be treated as constraints with threshold requirements. Once these constraints are met, all of the energy and creativity can be focused on maximizing the one objective function.

7. For example, treating the cost of capital as a true cost (say 8 percent in the current interest environment) removes the confusion of trying to maximize shareholder value at the same time the organization is maximizing customer value (along with employee engagement, community contributions, innovation, human rights, sustainability, etc.). There will be more on this in subsequent chapters.

8. The first time I recall seeing this phrase in print was in Roger Martin's excellent article "The Age of Capitalism," *Harvard Business Review*, January/February 2010. In subsequent research, I discovered that a book titled *Customer Capitalism* was published in 1999 (London: John Murray Press) by Sandra Vandermerwe, a marketing professor at Imperial College in London who coauthored several articles with scholars, including HBS professors Christopher Lovelock and John Quelch.

9. This research is described in Fred Reichheld with Rob Markey, *The Ultimate Question 2.0: How Net Promoter Companies Thrive in a Customer-Driven World* (Boston: Harvard Business Review Press, 2011), 47–51.

10. See, for example, Siemens, "Sustainability Information 2020" (Berlin, 2020), 34, https://assets.new.siemens.com/siemens/assets/api/uuid:13f56263-0d96-421c-a6a4 -9c10bb9b9d28/sustainability2020-en.pdf.

11. Geoff Colvin, "The Simple Metric That's Taking Over Big Business," *Fortune*, May 18, 2020, https://fortune.com/longform/net-promoter-score-fortune-500-customer-satisfaction -metric/.

12. Fay Twersky and Fred Reichheld, "Why Customer Feedback Tools Are Vital for Non-profits," *Harvard Business Review*, February 2019.

13. Open-source means practitioners are free to use the theories, methods, and tools associated with the Net Promoter System to drive sustainable, profitable growth for their businesses. The NPS marks, including NPS, NET PROMOTER, and NET PROMOTER SYSTEM, may not be used for commercial purposes except under license from Bain. For example, licenses are required for feedback, analytics, and data firms that incorporate NPS into services and solutions they sell to their customers. All use of the NPS marks—whether by practitioners or commercial licensees—must comply with Bain's trademark attribution requirements. More information about NPS licensing and use is available here: https://www .netpromotersystem.com/resources/trademarks-and-licensing/.

Chapter 1

1. Per the July 2021 Bain survey of business executives (previously cited).

2. According to Chain Store Age, Apple registers a staggering $5,546 per square foot per year. In second place is Murphy USA, a gasoline and convenience store retailer ($3,721 per square foot), followed by Tiffany & Co. ($2,951 per square foot). For the 2017 numbers, see Marianne Wilson, "The Most Profitable Retailers in Sales per Square Foot Are . . . ," Chain Store Age, July 31, 2017, https://chainstoreage.com/news/most-profitable-retailers-sales -square-foot-are.

Chapter 2

1. For the video of this roundtable, visit https://www.netpromotersystem.com/insights /journey-to-greatness-nps-video/.

2. Collins's highly influential book, published by HarperBusiness in 2001, continues to be a bestseller today.

3. Jim Collins, *How the Mighty Fall, and Why Some Companies Never Give In* (New York: HarperCollins, 2009).

4. We examined all public firms over $500 million in revenue and took the median of all these firms—not cap-weighted, since cap weighting conflates size with greatness.

5. This also muted the skyrocketing performance of *The Ultimate Question 2.0* stars such as Amazon and Apple, thus providing a more conservative comparison.

6. See Christopher Mims, "Apple Pitches Values along with Credit Card, News and TV Plus—but Will People Buy It?," *Wall Street Journal*, March 27, 2019, https://www.wsj.com /articles/apple-bets-that-plugging-its-values-can-help-create-value-11553607751.

7. Subsequent to that book's publication, I recognized that anointing Facebook and Alphabet as NPS leaders was premature because we surveyed consumers (who loved free use of the social media platform and search engine) rather than advertisers (who were the actual paying customers). Luckily, the index results change very little whether these two stocks are included or excluded, so for now I have left them in.

8. The Total Stock Index is cap-weighted, however, so a more appropriate benchmark would be the nonweighted Invesco Index. During the past decade these two benchmarks yielded similar results, but that is not always the case.

9. Kaplan noted that a 26 percent return placed the FREDSI in the top quartile of net returns to private equity fund limited partners. And my investment in FREDSI companies didn't burden me with the risks of leverage and lack of liquidity inherent in private equity investing.

Chapter 3

1. Bain's NPS Loyalty Forum is a group of several dozen companies that are passionate about earning superior customer loyalty. The group gathers quarterly to help solve challenges and share best practices and has played a vital role in advancing the NPS mission.

2. See page 5 of Chewy's SEC S-1 filing, June 12, 2019, https://www.sec.gov/Archives /edgar/data/1766502/000119312519170917/d665122ds1a.htm.

3. As you will see in chapter 6, Bain estimates that Chewy's true relationship NPS is lower—just under 60—but still more than 25 points higher than those of Amazon and other leading competitors.

4. See Farhad Manjoo, "New $4,000 Treadmill May Illustrate the Future of Gadgets," *New York Times*, January 9, 2018, https://www.bendbulletin.com/nation/new-4-000-treadmill -may-illustrate-the-future-of-gadgets/article_46dec879-6eb7-5360-9e2f-d638771f20f4.html. The company has created a virtual community of bike riders who can compete with one an- other and anointed a cohort of fitness class leaders, some of whom achieve celebrity status.

5. Ibid.

6. "Airbnb Statistics," iProperty Management, https://ipropertymanagement.com/research /airbnb-statistics.

7. I later checked up on this claim, and sure enough, cumulative TSRs for Costco in the thirty-four years since its initial public offering exceeded the TSR of the Vanguard 500 Index Fund by a factor of five times over the same period.

8. *The Good Jobs Strategy* was published in 2014 by Amazon Publishing. Ton focuses on how investing wisely in employees lowers costs and boosts profits.

9. Sarah Nassauer, "Costco to Raise Minimum Hourly Wage to $16," *Wall Street Jour- nal*, February 25, 2021.

10. Brendan Byrnes, "An Interview with Jim Sinegal, Co-founder of Costco," The Motley Fool, July 31, 2013, https://www.fool.com/investing/general/2013/07/31/an-interview-with -jim-sinegal-of-costco.aspx.

11. More on this in the next chapter. It turns out that customer service reps find living the Golden Rule extremely motivating.

12. This only happens to customers who have opted in to email alerts.

13. A FICO score is a well-known brand of credit score created by the Fair Isaac Com- pany in 1989. The higher your score, the lower the risk that you will default on your loans.

14. It's more fun to deal with happy customers than cranky ones. *Fortune* now lists T-Mobile among its top one hundred great places to work.

15. This is her real name—and what a perfect middle name for a person in customer service.

16. Specifically, NPS jumps from 69 at the fourth-year renewal to 79 at the fifth year.

17. In insurance lingo, PURE has a loss ratio 10 points better than its less tenured peers'. In other words, even after the discount, profit margins are still 10 percentage points superior.

18. From a company press conference, quoted in Junko Fujita, "Tokio Marine to Buy U.S. Insurer Pure Group for About $3 Billion," *Insurance Journal*, October 3, 2019, https://www .reuters.com/article/us-pure-m-a-tokio-marine-idUKKBN1WI0BJ.

19. See, for example, Scott McCartney's excellent article "The Hotel Fees That Barely Even Make Sense," *Wall Street Journal*, January 1, 2019.

Chapter 4

1. Harry Strachan and Darrell Rigby deserve special thanks and credit for this.

2. I've already explained that I'm skeptical of these lists because they tend to focus on things that may make employees happy without making anyone else happy. But Bain shows up on a lot of them and, I'd say, mostly for the right reasons.

3. See "2021 Best Places to Work," Glassdoor, https://www.glassdoor.com/Award/Best -Places-to-Work-LST_KQ0%2c19.htm.

4. Times have changed: today, more than half of the members of Harvard College's grad- uating class apply for a slot to interview with the firm.

5. One advantage of asking teams for their best ideas anonymously—prior to the huddle— is that introverts and junior team members are more likely to give voice to their ideas.

6. Organizations with more stable teams may find that this question works better: *How likely is it that you'd recommend your team leader as a person to work for?*

7. In the spirit of full disclosure, I was a member of Bain's nominating committee that tapped Tierney and next joined the compensation and promotion committee.

8. Yes, we borrowed that name from Apple Retail, but the content is based primarily on the systems and processes we developed to make Bain a truly great place to work.

9. The inspiration may have come from nearby neighbor Amazon. Jeff Bezos had already declared that in order to deliver on Amazon's customer-obsessed mission, he would restructure into "two-pizza" teams (small enough to be fed with two pizza pies). See Brad Stone, *The Everything Store: Jeff Bezos and the Age of Amazon* (New York: Little, Brown & Company, October, 2013), 169.

10. The Second Mile Service program you will read about in chapter 7 has biblical roots and illustrates how serving others is the basis for a life with meaning and purpose.

11. Steve Robinson, *Covert Cows and Chick-fil-A: How Faith, Cows, and Chicken Built an Iconic Brand* (Nashville: Thomas Nelson, 2019), 6.

12. For comparison, Harvard College's acceptance rate hovers around 5 percent—about ten times higher than Chick-fil-A's. Even Bain & Company's acceptance rate for 60,000 or so recent college grads who applied for a job last year ran just under 2 percent, reinforcing just how picky Chick-fil-A is in selecting its store operators.

13. Matthew McCready, "5 Things You Need to Know before Investing in a Chick-fil-A Franchise," *Entrepreneur*, January 13, 2020, https://www.entrepreneur.com/slideshow /307000. The acceptance rate and foot traffic statistics are also from this very informative slide show.

14. Frederick Reichheld, *Loyalty Rules! How Leaders Build Lasting Relationships* (Boston: Harvard Business Review Press, 2001). See the Loyalty Acid Test, pp. 191–198.

15. Of course, public company CEOs visit with Wall Street analysts regularly, but most would never think to set foot in a call center.

16. Even if the balance rolled, the interest rate was typically much lower.

17. Officers and vice presidents are expected to attend two of these sessions, which are scheduled on Tuesdays and Fridays every week. Supervisors from those areas attend to help explain the circumstances of each call and to answer questions that arise.

Chapter 5

1. The lunch was an item up for bid at an auction supporting a San Francisco–based charity that Buffett's late wife Susan had supported.

2. Howard Gold, "Opinion: Jack Bogle Even Towered over Warren Buffett as the Most Influential Investor," MarketWatch, January 17, 2019, https://www.marketwatch.com /story/jack-bogle-even-towered-over-warren-buffett-as-the-most-influential-investor -2019-01-17.

3. John Melloy, "Warren Buffett Says Jack Bogle Did More for the Individual Investor Than Anyone He's Ever Known," CNBC, January 16, 2019, https://www.cnbc.com/2019/01 /16/warren-buffett-says-jack-bogle-did-more-for-the-individual-investor-than-anyone-hes -ever-known.html.

4. You will recall that my FREDSI index selects companies with superior customer love, as indicated by their superior NPS ratings.

5. Is it possible that in mature markets, *only* NPS leaders consistently beat the total stock market index?

6. We end the period of analysis in figure 5-2 with 2019 because T-Mobile acquired Sprint in 2020.

7. We specify our regression TSR versus NPS models using natural logs of TSR because that number is a compounding advantage, which implies a geometric relationship with NPS over time.

8. These percentages come from the companies' 2019 annual reports.

9. Note that Chrysler is missing from this auto industry analysis because the company was bankrupt at the beginning of this period, so calculating a meaningful (and comparable) TSR was impossible. Chrysler's NPS at 46 was the lowest in the industry.

10. The period of study for restaurants ends in 2019 rather than 2020 due to lack of data available for same-store sales at some restaurants as of the writing of this book.

11. Khadeeja Safdar and Inti Pacheco, "The Dubious Management Fad Sweeping Corporate America," *Wall Street Journal*, May 15, 2019, https://www.wsj.com/articles/the-dubious-management-fad-sweeping-corporate-america-11557932084.

12. Just to remind ourselves, a double-blind experiment is one in which the identities of both the tester and the tested are concealed from both parties until after the test is completed.

13. Visit NetPromoterSystem.com for further explanation of the various types of NPS ratings and their appropriate uses.

14. This was the sampling methodology utilized in the 2010 Satmetrix NPS study we used to identify industry leaders in *The Ultimate Question 2.0*.

15. In one recent case, simply changing the order in which the rating scale was presented—with the scale running from 0 to 10 (with 0 on the left) versus 10 to 0 (with 0 on the right)—changed the resulting score by more than 10 points!

16. Again, that approach wouldn't work because the only way PRISM could recruit a large enough sample of First Republic Bank customers was to invoke the bank's name, which results in a sample overpopulated with Promoters.

17. Rob Markey, "Are You Undervaluing Your Customers?," *Harvard Business Review*, January–February 2020, https://hbr.org/2020/01/are-you-undervaluing-your-customers.

18. For a deeper dive, see SaaS Capital's white paper "Essential SaaS Metrics: Revenue Retention Fundamentals," November 12, 2015, https://www.saas-capital.com/blog-posts/essential-saas-metrics-revenue-retention-fundamentals/.

19. And it turns out that you can get by with less, as detailed in appendix B.

20. Most private equity funds set a hurdle rate of 8 percent (approximately the returns from investing in Vanguard's total stock market index since inception), which they must exceed before earning substantial bonuses. A similar structure should be used for executive compensation in public firms.

Chapter 6

1. Jesus is quoted in the gospel of Matthew (7:12): "In everything, do to others what you would have them do to you." And in Matthew (22:39): "Love thy neighbor as thyself."

2. *Analects of Confucius*.

3. Sorry; I couldn't resist.

4. A Meal, Ready to Eat, or MRE, is nutritional paste in a pouch bag with a flavoring such as "Brisket & Sausage."

5. When regulators insisted that investment managers act in their customers' best interest—at least when handling retirement accounts—the political pushback was so intense that the rule was reversed.

6. The same phenomenon arises in poorly administered "360" reviews.

7. Adam Grant, *Give and Take: Why Helping Others Drives Our Success* (New York: Viking, 2013).

8. See Deepa Seetharaman, "Jack Dorsey's Push to Clean Up Twitter Stalls, Researchers Say," *Wall Street Journal*, March 15, 2020.

Chapter 7

1. This probably needs some airing out. Amazon doesn't discourage the independent vendors on its website from using dynamic pricing. In fact, Amazon encourages the practice but

in specific and limited ways. If you can raise the price of your sunglasses in the summer, says Amazon to the sunglass company, go for it. See the interesting "Amazon Pricing Policy," Feedvisor, https://feedvisor.com/university/amazon-pricing-policy/. "If [the seller] does not take into account seasonal changes, consumer demand, seasonality, and so forth," advises Amazon, "he could end up missing out on profits." But—and these are important qualifiers—*your Amazon price has to be equal to or lower than the price you charge in other virtual marketplaces, and every buyer has to get the same offer as any other customer at any given point in time.* As for Amazon's own vast inventory, in those vast and proliferating warehouses I've found no evidence that the company engages in the intrusive and predatory forms of dynamic pricing described in the text.

2. Brad Stone, *The Everything Store* (New York: Little, Brown, 2014), 125–126.

3. Robert D. Hof, "The Wild World of E Commerce," Bloomberg, December 14, 1998, https://www.bloomberg.com/news/articles/1998-12-13/amazon-dot-com-the-wild-world-of-e-commerce.

4. Christina Animashaun, "The Making of Amazon Prime, the Internet's Most Successful and Devastating Membership Program," Vox, May 3, 2019, https://www.vox.com/recode/2019/5/3/18511544/amazon-prime-oral-history-jeff-bezos-one-day-shipping.

5. Part of the reasoning behind this prediction was that Barnes & Noble was about to launch a website aimed in part at crushing the upstart Amazon. Experts warned Bezos to "play the hedgehog" by defending his core business, advice that Bezos wisely ignored.

6. "Principles Underlying the Drucker Institute's Company Rankings," Drucker Institute, https://www.drucker.institute/principles-underlying-the-drucker-institutes-company-rankings/.

7. Think of the fall lineup on TV, the new model year in the auto industry, the steady stream of brand refreshments and website relaunches across almost all industries, etc. It's a little embarrassing to admit, but we humans crave shiny new things.

8. Current patent litigation may yield additional income for USAA. See Penny Crosman, "USAA Won $200M from Wells Fargo in Patent Fight. Will Others Be on the Hook?," American Banker, November 18, 2019, https://www.americanbanker.com/news/usaa-won-200m-from-wells-fargo-for-patent-infringement-will-it-stop-there.

9. Geoff Colvin, "The Simple Metric That's Taking Over Big Business," *Fortune*, May 18, 2020, https://fortune.com/longform/net-promoter-score-fortune-500-customer-satisfaction-metric. "Blasphemous" was Colvin's dig at the designers of those massive hundred-question surveys that we all hate to fill out.

10. Matthew 5:41. To be honest, I was unaware that "going the extra mile" had biblical roots, but I wasn't surprised.

11. This is the cow that implores us to "EAT MOR CHIKIN."

12. It's no accident that Chewy's NPS rating tops Amazon's by 28 points.

13. Malcolm Gladwell, *Blink: The Power of Thinking without Thinking* (New York: Time Warner Book Group, 2005).

14. "Paper diagram, step aside," says the BILT website (https://biltapp.com/). For the technical among us, BILT converts manufacturers' CAD into interactive cloud-based 3D instructions. I got a kick out of learning that the company grew out of an evening of frustration experienced by a software sales executive and his wife who were trying to assemble an IKEA nightstand. Enough said about IKEA.

Chapter 8

1. The phrase is from Leviticus 25:10.

2. Far more pages are devoted to customer stories and core-value messaging than to financial results.

3. The formal title of this book is *Voices of Discover: The Stories and Culture of Our People*, published by Discover Financial Services in 2012.

4. "Leadership Principles," Amazon, https://www.amazon.jobs/en/principles.

5. The company doesn't break into Glassdoor's 2020 Top 100 "best places to work" list, for example. By way of comparison, Google comes in at number 11, Microsoft at number 21, and Apple at number 84. "2021 Best Places to Work," Glassdoor, https://www.glassdoor.com /Award/Best-Places-to-Work-LST_KQ0,19.htm.

6. CEO letter to shareholders, Amazon 2020 annual report.

7. Dana Mattioli, Patience Haggin, and Shane Shifflett, "Amazon Restricts How Rival Device Makers Buy Ads in Its Site," *Wall Street Journal*, September 22, 2020, https://www .wsj.com/articles/amazon-restricts-advertising-competitor-device-makers-roku-arlo -11600786638.

8. Brad Stone, *The Everything Store* (New York: Little, Brown, 2014), 317.

9. Enron 2000 annual report, 55.

10. Ken Brown and Ianthe Jeanne Dugan, "Arthur Andersen's Fall from Grace Is a Sad Tale of Greed and Miscues," *Wall Street Journal*, June 7, 2002.

11. Greg Ryan, "Tamar Dor-Ner Keeps a Keen Eye on Company Culture at Bain," *Boston Business Journal*, January 3, 2019, https://www.bizjournals.com/boston/news/2019/01/03 /tamar-dor-ner-keeps-a-keen-eye-on-company-culture.html.

Chapter 9

1. Matthew 5:5.

2. Jim Collins, *How the Mighty Fall: And Why Some Companies Never Give In* (New York: HarperCollins, 2009).

3. Tom Donahoe is the father of John Donahoe, who wrote the preface to this book.

4. I hope you are listening, Amazon, Apple, Facebook, Alphabet, et al.

5. A more comprehensive checklist of actions and requirements is presented in appendix A.

6. Isabelle Lee, "Can You Trust That Amazon Review? 42% May Be Fake, Independent Monitor Says," *Chicago Tribune*, October 20, 2020, https://www.chicagotribune.com/business /ct-biz-amazon-fake-reviews-unreliable-20201020-lfbjdq25azfdpa3iz6hn6zvtwq-story .html.

7. "Jay Hennick: From Pool Boy to Billionaire," *OPM Wars*, September 8, 2020. *OPM Wars* is a newsletter for Canadian money managers, investors, and moguls.

8. GE was the unfortunate poster child of this phenomenon, with its former CEO, Jeff Immelt, earning hundreds of millions during his tenure as CEO while the firm delivered negative TSR to shareholders.

9. Jay's compensation was almost entirely equity-based, which reinforced his inherent respect for investors.

10. Jay recently converted his supervoting shares into common shares but remains the largest shareholder of both FirstService and Colliers.

11. CertaPro closes on more than 80 percent of referred leads.

12. I didn't let them know I was a board member of the parent company.

13. I did give him a couple of $20 bills in thanks.

14. The word "humble" derives from the same Latin root as "humus" (a gardener's best friend). Both humble and humus have "from the earth" connotations. We all share the same humble journey—from ashes to ashes and dust to dust.

Appendix A

1. The NPS Loyalty Forum grew out of a predecessor group, the Loyalty Roundtable, referred to in chapter 9. A full list of NPS Loyalty Forum participants appears in my acknowledgments.

Index

Note: Figures are identified by *f* following the page number. Endnote information is identified by n and note number following the page number.

Acknowledgments

When I first began the journey of creating a book—now more than twenty-five years ago—I learned a valuable lesson: more than I could have imagined, it's a team sport.

I keep relearning that lesson. This is my fifth book, and all of my books have been published by Harvard Business Review Press. I want to thank the entire HBRP team for their support over the years—especially executive editor Jeff Kehoe, who has been a loyal supporter and thoughtful adviser from the beginning. Jeff also introduced me to Jeff Cruikshank, who provided incomparable editorial assistance and helped shape the book from its earliest stages.

There are many colleagues at Bain to thank, beginning with my co-authors Darci Darnell and Maureen Burns, joined by the rest of Bain's editorial review board: Fred Debruyne, Gerard du Toit, Eric Garton, Richard Hatherall, Paul Judge, Erika Serow, and Rob Markey.

Rob deserves special thanks for his leadership of the NPS Loyalty Forum from its inception fifteen years ago, and for his steadfast dedication to building out Bain's NPS solution set. He has worked tirelessly to spread the Net Promoter gospel to our offices and clients around the world. Stu Berman, director of the NPS Loyalty Forum; Lisa-Clarke Wilson; Phil Sager; Tevia Segovia; Olga Glazkova; and Alastair Cox all made important contributions. Andrew Schwedel, Mark Bower, and Simon Heap offered helpful feedback. Maggie Locher and Kirti Yadav handled the fact-checking with good grace. The data gathering and analysis that support all the exhibits in this book were expertly overseen by Joanna Zhou.

Senior Bain partners and alums who joined me in the struggle to turn around our firm were most helpful in refreshing and enriching my understanding of the experience. These include Vernon Altman, Orit Gadiesh, Mark Gottfredson, Russ Hagey, Greg Hutchinson, Darrell Rigby, Harry Strachan, and finally Tom Tierney, who also read through my manuscript and provided helpful feedback. Andy Noble and Chris Bierly provided updated perspectives on Chick-fil-A and generously provided the data supporting the analysis of the impact of NPS on same-store sales across restaurant competitors. Ron Kermisch and Herbert Blum provided the competitive NPS data for the US Mobile Telecom business. Aaron Cheris provided historical NPS data on retailers, along with his expert insights.

Bain's Dan Brenner shared lessons from his years at Amazon, as did Robinhood's Eugene Shapiro. Bain alum Kent Bennett—now a partner at Bessemer Ventures—provided valuable feedback on the Earned Growth Rate and its application to new ventures. Bill Wade introduced me to BILT and helped tease out that firm's Earned Growth Rate; he also provided the analysis behind the SaaS valuation multiples in figure 5-9. Finally, he is the author of the Earned Growth Calculator on our website, NetPromoter.System.com. Thanks, Bill.

The team at NPS Prism—including Jason Barro, Rahul Sethi, and Quinn Aldrich—provided the uniquely reliable NPS data that underpins much of this book's analysis. I expect NPS Prism will play an important role in helping the world understand the importance of trustworthy NPS data—and enable firms to know precisely how they stack up against the competition, in terms of customer love. I'm convinced that this business will play a vital role in advancing the Net Promoter Revolution.

The team at Medallia, especially Leslie Stretch, Elizabeth Carducci, and Akash Bose, provided invaluable support for my work. They helped recruit companies to participate as beta-participants in the development and execution of the Earned New Customer questionnaire, the Earned Growth Rate analysis, and our customer culture diagnostic.

Many thanks are due for the contributions and support from the following list of executives who spent valuable time with me in interviews and email exchanges:

BILT: Nate Henderson

Charles Schwab: Walt Bettinger

Chick-fil-A: Mark Moraitakis, Alan Daniel

Discover: David Nelms, Roger Hochschild, Julie Loeger, Kate Manfred, Dennis Michel, Steve Bayans, and Jon Drummond

FirstService: Jay Hennick, Scott Patterson, Charlie Chase, Chuck Fallon, Jeremy Rakusin, Mike Stone, Roger Thompson, Laurie Dietz, Bill Barton (formerly CEO of California Closets, now CEO of Bob's Discount Furniture), and director Steve Grimshaw.

First Republic Bank: Jason Bender and Shannon Houston

Intuit: Scott Cook

Marriott: Stephanie Linnartz

Peloton: Brad Olson and Brenna Healy

PURE: Ross Buchmueller, Matt Schrebeis, Mary Loyal Springs

Qantas: Rob Marcolina, Alison Webster

T-Mobile: Callie Field

Vanguard: Al Weikel

Warby Parker: Dave Gilboa, Kaki Read Mackey

Geoff Colvin of *Fortune* provided helpful feedback on an early draft of my manuscript and bolstered my confidence to focus on the moral challenges facing business leaders today.

Apple's Cate Harding has been a steadfast supporter of my work and organized many of my interactions with her firm, including my visit to the Boston flagship store featured in chapter 1.

Max and Caitlin Hoblitzell both shared useful perspectives on their work experiences as relatively new employees at Bain and Amazon, respectively.

Adam Grant—noted author, teacher, and organizational psychologist—shared his research on the portion of takers in today's world. Steve Kaplan, professor at the University of Chicago Booth School of Business, generously provided feedback about my ideas in chapter 5 and data about private equity investor returns.

In his development and teaching of the California Closet case, HBS Professor Boris Groysberg gave me important insights into the challenges of communicating the Net Promoter message. I am also indebted to Boris for introducing me to First Republic Bank. Professor Zeynep Ton connected me with Costco's Jim Sinegal, a truly remarkable (and loving) leader. The time I spent in Zeynep's classroom and touring the Waltham Costco with Jim would not have happened without Zeynep's generous support.

I've already thanked Rob Markey for his leadership of the NPS Loyalty Forum. Now I want to extend thanks to the members of that group. Our quarterly meetings and interim Zoom calls have done more to clarify my thinking about NPS than any other single resource. These pioneering companies are responsible for developing and sharing many of the best practices that comprise "Net Promoter 3.0." Many Loyalty Forum members read early chapters of my manuscript and provided important advice on improvements needed. I especially want to thank Matt Smith, managing director of Brookfield Asset Management's Property Group, for sharing thoughts and data quantifying referral flows. Barbara Higgins, chief customer officer at Duke Energy, was extremely generous with her time, reading chapter revisions and contributing many thoughtful editorial suggestions. Again, my heartfelt thanks to all the companies listed below who attended and/or hosted the NPS Loyalty Forum over the past fifteen years.

NPS Loyalty Forum Attendees/Hosts

24 Hour Fitness
Advance Auto Parts
Aggreko
Allianz
American Express
American Honda
   Motor Co.
Archstone
Aristocrat Digital
Ascension Health
Asurion
Atlas Copco
Avid Technology
BBVA Bancomer
Belron

BMO Financial
   Group
Brookfield Asset
   Management
Cancer Treatment
   Centers of
   America
CBRE
Charles Schwab
Chick-fil-A
Cintas
Cisco
Comcast
Cummins Inc.
Deliveroo

Desjardins
Deutsche Post
   (DHL)
Deutsche Telekom
Duke Energy
E.ON
eBay
Eli Lilly and
   Company
Ermenegildo Zegna
Experian Consumer
   Division
Facebook
FirstService
   Corporation

FranklinCovey
GE Healthcare
General Electric
   Company
Gilbane Building
   Company
Grocery Outlet
Honeywell
   Aerospace
Humana
ING Group
Intuit
JetBlue Airways
Joie de Vivre
LEGO
LexisNexis
Lloyds Banking
   Group
Logitech
LPL Financial
Macy's
Medtronic

Michelin
NatWest Group
Nike
Nokia
Oracle
Paul Davis
   Restoration
Peloton
Philips
PNC Bank
Pricewaterhouse-
   Coopers
Progressive
   Insurance
Prologis
Qantas
Rackspace
RSC Equipment
   Rental
Safelite
Schneider Electric
Sodexo

Stora Enso
SunTrust
Swiss Reinsurance
   Company
Symantec
   Corporation
TD Bank
TD Canada Trust
Teach For America
Tech Data
Teleperformance
Thermo Fisher
   Scientific
T-Mobile
TPG
University of
   Phoenix
Vanguard
Verizon
Volaris
Westpac Group
Zappos

I also want to thank my executive assistant, Maura McNamee Dudas, for organizing my schedule through this chaotic period when the pandemic frequently reshuffled all of our plans. Her unflappable optimism was deeply appreciated.

My four children—Chris, Jenny, Bill, and Jim—read the manuscript, offered helpful suggestions, and generously allowed me to include their stories in this book.

Finally, my wife, Karen, has played an enormously important role as sounding board and counselor for all of my book projects. But this time around, she also nursed me through my surgeries and cancer fight. Without her courage, judgment, patience, wisdom, love, and loyalty that sustained me throughout this most challenging experience of my life, this book would not exist.

About the Authors

FRED REICHHELD is the creator of the Net Promoter system of management, the founder of Bain & Company's Loyalty practice, and the author of five books including the *New York Times* bestseller *The Ultimate Question 2.0*. He is currently a fellow and senior advisory partner at Bain, where he has worked since 1977. Fred is a frequent speaker at major business forums, and his work on customer loyalty has been widely covered in the *Wall Street Journal*, *New York Times*, *Financial Times*, *Fortune*, *Businessweek*, and *The Economist*. He has made fifteen contributions to the *Harvard Business Review* and, in 2012, became one of the original LinkedIn Influencers, an invitation-only group of corporate leaders and public figures who are thought leaders in their respective fields. In 2003, *Consulting Magazine* named Fred as one of the world's "25 Most Influential Consultants." According to the *New York Times*, Fred "put loyalty economics on the map." *The Economist* refers to him as the "high priest" of loyalty. Reichheld graduated from Harvard College (BA, 1974) and Harvard Business School (MBA, 1978). He is based in Cape Cod and Miami.

DARCI DARNELL is the global head of Bain's Customer practice, responsible for the firm's client solutions in customer strategy, loyalty, commercial excellence, pricing, and marketing. Darci has served in multiple global leadership roles and today sits on the firm's top-elected governance committee. Darci earned an MBA from The Tuck School at Dartmouth College as well as a BS in accounting from Washington University in St. Louis. She is based in Chicago.

MAUREEN BURNS is a senior partner in Bain's Customer practice. She is one of Bain's foremost experts on the Net Promoter System and Customer

Loyalty. Maureen has led some of Bain's most notable digital transformations, helping her clients harness technology and data to earn Customer Loyalty. Maureen earned an MBA from Harvard Business School and graduated from Georgetown University's School of Foreign Service. She is based in Boston.

3 9082 14622 0309